Palgrave Studies in European Union Politics

Edited by: **Michelle Egan**, American University USA, **Neill Nugent**, Manchester Metropolitan University, UK, **William Paterson**, University of Birmingham, UK

Editorial Board: **Christopher Hill**, Cambridge, UK, **Simon Hix**, London School of Economics, UK, **Mark Pollack**, Temple University, USA, **Kalypso Nicolaïdis**, Oxford UK, **Morten Egeberg**, University of Oslo, Norway, **Amy Verdun**, University of Victoria, Canada, **Claudio M. Radaelli**, University of Exeter, UK, **Frank Schimmelfennig**, Swiss Federal Institute of Technology, Switzerland

Following on the sustained success of the acclaimed *European Union Series*, which essentially publishes research-based textbooks, *Palgrave Studies in European Union Politics* publishes cutting edge research-driven monographs.

The remit of the series is broadly defined, both in terms of subject and academic discipline. All topics of significance concerning the nature and operation of the European Union potentially fall within the scope of the series. The series is multidisciplinary to reflect the growing importance of the EU as a political, economic and social phenomenon. We will welcome submissions from the areas of political studies, international relations, political economy, public and social policy, economics, law and sociology.

Submissions should be sent to Amy Lankester-Owen, Politics Publisher, 'a.lankester-owen@palgrave.com'.

Titles include:

Ian Bache and Andrew Jordan (*editors*)
THE EUROPEANIZATION OF BRITISH POLITICS

Richard Balme and Brian Bridges (*editors*)
EUROPE-ASIA RELATIONS
Building Multilateralisms

Derek Beach and Colette Mazzucelli (*editors*)
LEADERSHIP IN THE BIG BANGS OF EUROPEAN INTEGRATION

Milena Büchs
NEW GOVERNANCE IN EUROPEAN SOCIAL POLICY
The Open Method of Coordination

Dario Castiglione, Justus Schönlau, Chris Longman, Emanuela Lombardo, Nieves Pérez-Solórzano Borragán and Mirim Aziz
CONSTITUTIONAL POLITICS IN THE EUROPEAN UNION
The Convention Moment and its Aftermath

Morten Egeberg (*editor*)
MULTILEVEL UNION ADMINISTRATION
The Transformation of Executive Politics in Europe

Kevin Featherstone and Dimitris Papadimitriou
THE LIMITS OF EUROPEANIZATION
Reform Capacity and Policy Conflict in Greece

Stefan Gänzle and Allen G. Sens (*editors*)
THE CHANGING POLITICS OF EUROPEAN SECURITY
Europe Alone?

Isabelle Garzon
REFORMING THE COMMON AGRICULTURAL POLICY
History of a Paradigm Change

Heather Grabbe
THE EU'S TRANSFORMATIVE POWER
Sebastian Krapohl

RISK REGULATION IN THE SINGLE MARKET
The Governance of Pharmaceuticals and Foodstuffs in the European Union

Katie Verlin Laatikainen and Karen E. Smith (*editors*)
THE EUROPEAN UNION AND THE UNITED NATIONS
Intersecting Multilateralisms

Esra LaGro and Knud Erik Jørgensen (*editors*)
TURKEY AND THE EUROPEAN UNION
Prospects for a Difficult Encounter

Paul G.Lewis and Zdenka Mansfeldovà (*editors*)
THE EUROPEAN UNION AND PARTY POLITICS IN CENTRAL AND EASTERN EUROPE

Ingo Linsenmann, Christoph O. Meyer and Wolfgang T. Wessels (*editors*)
ECONOMIC GOVERNMENT OF THE EU
A Balance Sheet of New Modes of Policy Coordination

Hartmut Mayer and Henri Vogt (*editors*)
A RESPONSIBLE EUROPE?
Ethical Foundations of EU External Affairs

Lauren M. McLaren
IDENTITY, INTERESTS AND ATTITUDES TO EUROPEAN INTEGRATION

Christoph O. Meyer, Ingo Linsenmann and Wolfgang Wessels (*editors*)
ECONOMIC GOVERNMENT OF THE EU
A Balance Sheet of New Modes of Policy Coordination

Philomena Murray (*editor*)
EUROPE AND ASIA
Regions in Flux

Daniel Naurin and Helen Wallace (*editors*)
UNVEILING THE COUNCIL OF THE EUROPEAN UNION
Games Governments Play in Brussels

Frank Schimmelfennig, Stefan Engert and Heiko Knobel
INTERNATIONAL SOCIALIZATION IN EUROPE
European Organizations, Political Conditionality and Democratic Change

Justus Schönlau
DRAFTING THE EU CHARTER

Angelos Sepos
THE EUROPEANIZATION OF CYPRUS
Polity, Policies and Politics

Marc Weller, Denika Blacklock and Katherine Nobbs (*editors*)
THE PROTECTION OF THE MINORITIES IN THE WIDER EUROPE

Palgrave Studies in European Union Politics
Series Standing Order ISBN 978–1–4039–9511–7 (hardback) and ISBN 978–1–4039–9512–4 (paperback)

You can receive future titles in this series as they are published by placing a standing order. Please contact your bookseller or, in case of difficulty, write to us at the address below with your name and address, the title of the series and one of the ISBNs quoted above.

Customer Services Department, Macmillan Distribution Ltd, Houndmills, Basingstoke, Hampshire RG21 6XS, England

Europe and Asia

Regions in Flux

Edited by

Philomena Murray
Associate Professor in Political Science
University of Melbourne, Australia

Editorial matter, selection, introduction and conclusion © Philomena Murray 2008
All remaining chapters © respective authors 2008

All rights reserved. No reproduction, copy or transmission of this publication may be made without written permission.

No portion of this publication may be reproduced, copied or transmitted save with written permission or in accordance with the provisions of the Copyright, Designs and Patents Act 1988, or under the terms of any licence permitting limited copying issued by the Copyright Licensing Agency, Saffron House, 6-10 Kirby Street, London EC1N 8TS.

Any person who does any unauthorized act in relation to this publication may be liable to criminal prosecution and civil claims for damages.

The authors have asserted their rights to be identified as the authors of this work in accordance with the Copyright, Designs and Patents Act 1988.

First published 2008 by
PALGRAVE MACMILLAN

Palgrave Macmillan in the UK is an imprint of Macmillan Publishers Limited, registered in England, company number 785998, of Houndmills, Basingstoke, Hampshire RG21 6XS.

Palgrave Macmillan in the US is a division of St Martin's Press LLC, 175 Fifth Avenue, New York, NY 10010.

Palgrave Macmillan is the global academic imprint of the above companies and has companies and representatives throughout the world.

Palgrave® and Macmillan® are registered trademarks in the United States, the United Kingdom, Europe and other countries.

ISBN-13: 978–0–230–54266–2   hardback
ISBN-10: 0–230–54266–2   hardback

This book is printed on paper suitable for recycling and made from fully managed and sustained forest sources. Logging, pulping and manufacturing processes are expected to conform to the environmental regulations of the country of origin.

A catalogue record for this book is available from the British Library.

Library of Congress Cataloging-in-Publication Data

Europe and Asia : regions in flux / edited by Philomena Murray.
    p. cm. — (Palgrave studies in European Union politics)
  Includes index.
  ISBN 978–0–230–54266–2
  1. Europe—Relations—Asia. 2. Asia—Relations—Europe. I. Murray, Philomena.
  JZ1570.A55E976 2009
  303.48'2405—dc22

2008030678

Printed and bound in Great Britain by
CPI Antony Rowe, Chippenham and Eastbourne

In memoriam.
I dedicate this book to my friend, Maria Pickering, with love.

Contents

Lists of Figures and Tables		ix
List of Abbreviations and Acronyms		x
Acknowledgements		xiii
Author Biographies		xiv

1. Europe and Asia: Two Regions in Flux
   Philomena Murray — 1

2. The EU, ASEAN and APEC in Comparative Perspective
   Alex Warleigh-Lack — 23

3. The East Asian Experience of Regionalism
   Derek McDougall — 42

4. Comparing and Contrasting Economic Integration in the Asia-Pacific Region and Europe
   Bernadette Andreosso-O'Callaghan — 61

5. Political Integration in the European Union: Any Lessons for ASEAN?
   Edward Moxon-Browne — 84

6. The Origins and Development of ASEM and EU–East Asia Relations
   Yeo Lay Hwee — 102

7. The Economic Geography of Regionalization in East Asia and Europe
   Christopher M. Dent — 122

8. European and Asian Security and the Role of Regional Organizations in the Post-9/11 Environment
   Nicholas Rees — 149

9 Asian (ASEAN Plus Three) Perspectives on European Integration
  Toshiro Tanaka 170

10 European Perspectives on Engaging with East Asia
  Philomena Murray 188

Index 210

Lists of Figures and Tables

List of Figures

Figure 4.1	Intra-regional trade: EU-25	68
Figure 4.2	Main trading countries in the Asia-Pacific region, 2005	68
Figure 7.1	Types of international production within a regional economic space	127
Figure 7.2	East Asia's pan-regional development corridor	143
Figure 7.3	Europe's vital axis	144
Figure 10.1	Assessment of the importance to the EU of its relationship with East Asia	194
Figure 10.2	Asia: What comes to mind? (analysts' responses)	196
Figure 10.3	Have the EU's New Strategies changed how the EU perceives Asia?	197
Figure 10.4	Is the EU promoting norms?	205
Figure 10.5	Assessment of East Asian economic and political integration	206

List of Tables

Table 4.1	Intra-regional trade — Asia-Pacific countries (2005)	69
Table 4.2	Intra-EU FDI position (flows and stocks, 2001–2005)	71
Table 4.3	Intra-regional FDI in the Asia-Pacific region — selected countries, various years	72
Table 4.4a	Revealed comparative advantage: EU-15 and EU-25 (vis-à-vis the world)	75
Table 4.4b	Revealed comparative advantages: Asia-Pacific region (vis-à-vis the world)	75
Table 4.5	Intra-industry trade of each region with the RoW (static and dynamic indices) (2000 and 2005)	77
Table 4.6	Trade complementarity between the EU-25 and the Asia-Pacific Countries	79
Table 7.1	Cross border regions (CBRs) in Europe: Selected projects	139

List of Abbreviations and Acronyms

9/11	Terrorist attacks of September 11, 2001
ACU	Asian Currency Unit
ADB	Asian Development Bank
AEBF	Asia Europe Business Forum
AEC	ASEAN Economic Community
AECF	Asia–Europe Cooperation Framework
AFTA	ASEAN Free Trade Area
AJCEP	ASEAN Japan Comprehensive Economic Partnership
AMF	Asian Monetary Fund
APEC	Asia-Pacific Economic Cooperation
APRIS	ASEAN–EC Project on Regional Integration Support
ARF	ASEAN Regional Forum
ASA	Association of Southeast Asia
ASEAN	Association of South-East Asian Nations
ASEF	Asia–Europe Foundation
ASEM	Asia Europe Meeting
CBR	Cross-border region
CEE	Central and Eastern Europe
CEPT	Common Effective Preferential Tariff
CFSP	Common Foreign and Security Policy
CMI	Chiang Mai Initiative
CMLV	States Cambodia, Myanmar, Laos and Vietnam.
DG	European Commission Directorate General
DGRELEX	European Commission Directorate General responsible for External Relations
EACU	East Asian Currency Unit
EAEC	East Asian Economic Caucus
EAEG	East Asian Economic Group
EAS	East Asian Summit
EC	European Commission
ECB	European Central Bank
ECJ	Court of Justice of the European Communities (European Court of Justice)
ECU	European Currency Unit

List of Abbreviations and Acronyms xi

EDC	European Defence Community
EEC	European Economic Community
EFTA	European Free Trade Association
EMS	European Monetary System
EMU	Economic and Monetary Union
EPG	Eminent Persons Group
ESDP	European Security and Defence Policy
EU	European Union
EU15	European Union of 15 member states
EU25	European Union of 25 member states
Euratom	European Atomic Energy Community, EAEC
euro	European single currency
Europol	European Police Office
FDI	Foreign Direct Investment
FTA	Free Trade Agreement
G7	Group of Seven. Meeting of finance ministers from seven major industrialized economies: United States, Japan, Germany, France, Britain, Italy and Canada.
GATT	General Agreement on Tariffs and Trade
GCC	Gulf Cooperation Council
GDP	Gross domestic product
GSP	Global systems of production
HDI	Human Development Index
ICT	Information and Communication Technology
IIT	Intra-industry trade
IMF	International Monetary Fund
IPN	International Production Network
IT	Information technology
JI	Jemaah Islamiah
MILF	Moro Islamic Liberation Front
MNE	Multinational enterprise
NATO	North Atlantic Treaty Organization
NEAT	Network of East Asian Think Tanks
NIE	Newly industrializing economies
NRA	New Regionalism Approach
NTB	Non-tariff barriers
OECD	Organization for Economic Cooperation and Development
OSCE	Organization for Security and Cooperation in Europe
RCA	Revealed Comparative Advantage
READI	Regional EU-ASEAN Dialogue Instrument
RTA	Regional Trade Agreements

SARS	Severe Acute Respiratory Syndrome
SEATO	South East Asia Treaty Organization
SME	Small to medium enterprise
SOM	ASEAN Senior Officials Meeting
TAC	ASEAN'S Treaty of Amity and Cooperation
TREATI	Trans-Regional EU-ASEAN Trade Initiative
UAE	United Arab Emirates
UK	United Kingdom
UN	United Nations
US	United States
WMD	Weapons of mass destruction {**1 app**}
WTO	World Trade Organization
ZOPFAN	Zone of Peace, Freedom and Neutrality

Acknowledgements

This book is the result of collaboration across three continents, involving scholars initially from the University of Melbourne, the University of Limerick, Keio University and the Katholieke Universiteit, Leuven. We extend our gratitude and appreciation to the European Commission for the Jean Monnet Transnational Research Grant for this project.

During the life of the project, processes of regionalism in Europe and Asia were explored, along with the extent to which the EU might be considered a model for Asia, as well as perceptions of Europe and Asia as international players. The growing dialogue and linkages, both formal and informal, between these two dynamic regions were given particular attention with regard to trade, human rights, civil society and democratic development. I would like to thank the contributors for their hard work.

The project participants would like to thank the project's research assistants Bronwyn Hinz, Belinda Cleeland, Dora Horvath, Tony Wilson, Niall Duggan, Ana Maria Dobre, Eijiro Fukui, Utai Uprasen and Deirdre Quinn. Geraldine East's sterling work for the conference is greatly appreciated. I am grateful to colleagues at the University of Melbourne and especially at the Contemporary Europe Research Centre and School of Social and Political Sciences. I would like to express my appreciation to the European Commission officials interviewed in Brussels. The staff of Palgrave have been very helpful. Finally, my special thanks go to John and Stephen and my family, who were always supportive throughout this project. Grazie and go raibh maith agaibh.

Author Biographies

Alex Warleigh-Lack is Professor of Politics and International Relations at Brunel University, where he is also Head of Politics and History. His most recent research monograph is *Democracy in the European Union* (Sage, 2003), and his principal research interests are reform of the European Union and comparative regionalization.

Derek McDougall is an Associate Professor in the School of Political Science, Criminology and Sociology, University of Melbourne. His area of interest is Asia-Pacific international politics with particular reference to Australian engagement. Recent books include *Asia Pacific in World Politics* (Lynne Rienner Publishers, 2007) and *Australian Security After 9/11: New and Old Agendas* (Ashgate, 2006), co-edited with Peter Shearman.

Bernadette Andreosso-O'Callaghan is Jean Monnet Professor of European Economic Integration and Director of the Euro-Asia Centre, University of Limerick, Ireland. Her research interests encompass economic integration in Asia and in Europe, and EU–Asian relations (trade, investment and technology). Some of her latest publications include: *The Changing Economic Environment in Asia* (Palgrave, 2001), co-edited with J.P. Bassino and J. Jaussaud; *The Economics of European Agriculture* (Palgrave, 2003); *Regional Integration — Europe and Asia Compared* (Ashgate, 2005), co-edited with Woosik Moon; *Industrial Economics and Organization. A European Perspective* (McGraw-Hill, 2005), co-authored with D. Jacobson; and *The Feasibility of an EU-ASEAN Free Trade Area* (Report for the EU Commission, 2006), with L. Low, F. Nicolas, A. Petschiri, S. Thompsen and U. Uprasen.

Edward Moxon-Browne is Jean Monnet Chair of European Integration and Director of the Centre for European Studies at the University of Limerick; and previously Lecturer, Senior Lecturer, and Reader in Politics at the Queens University, Belfast. He has held visiting appointments at Wesleyan University, Connecticut; Hollins University, Virginia; Harvard; and the UN Peace University at San Jose, Costa Rica. Among his research interests are: ethnic conflict, European integration, and post-conflict peacebuilding. Recent publications include *Who are the Europeans Now?* (Ashgate, 2005) and *A Future for Peacekeeping?* (Palgrave, 1997).

Yeo Lay Hwee is Senior Research Fellow at the Singapore Institute of International Affairs and Honorary Fellow at the Contemporary Europe Research Centre (CERC), University of Melbourne. An international relations expert, her research interests revolve around comparative regionalism; ASEAN and the EU; and the Asia–Europe Meeting (ASEM) process. She also teaches part-time at the National University of Singapore, and participates actively both in policy dialogue and in academic workshops and conferences.

Christopher M. Dent is Reader in East Asia's International Political Economy, Department of East Asian Studies, University of Leeds, UK. He is the author of seven books and around 50 academic articles and other papers. He has acted as a consultant advisor to the British and United States Governments, and the European Commission on trade issues, and as an invited speaker at conferences and other events in Asia, Europe, North America, Latin America, Africa and Oceania. Christopher Dent is also an Expert (Brains Trust) member of the Evian Group.

Nicholas Rees is Vice President for Research and Graduate Studies at the National College of Ireland. His research interests include European Union institutional and policy development, Ireland and the European Union, EU common foreign and security policy and UN peacekeeping. He has authored and edited three books, with a fourth co-authored book on Ireland and Europeanization underway and planned for publication in 2008, as well as having edited a number of conference proceedings and produced numerous book chapters and refereed journal articles. Recent publications include a co-authored book with on *UN Peacekeeping in the Post-Cold War Era* (Routledge, 2005) and the co-edited *EU Enlargement and Multi-Level Governance in Public Policy-Making* (Ashgate, May 2006). Much of his work is focused on the European Union and Ireland, with a particular emphasis on public policy.

Toshiro Tanaka is Professor of European Political Integration, Jean Monnet Chair ad personam, Faculty of Law, Keio University. He is a founding member of EUSA–Japan and was President (2002–04). He was also President of EUSA Asia-Pacific (2004–06). He has been co-editor of *The European Union and Citizens* (2005) and *The Historical Developments and Vectors of the European Union* (2006) both from Keio University Press.

Philomena Murray is Associate Professor in the School of Political and Social Sciences and Director of the Contemporary Europe Research

Centre at the University of Melbourne. She holds a personal Jean Monnet Chair. Her research interests are in European Integration analysis; EU–Australia relations; EU–Asia relations, EU governance and comparative regional integration. Her publications include *Australia and the European Superpower: Engaging with the European Union* (Melbourne University Press, 2005); *Citizenship and Identity in Europe* (Ashgate, 1999), co-edited with Leslie Holmes; *Europe — Rethinking the Boundaries* (Ashgate, 1998), co-edited with Leslie Holmes; *Visions of European Unity* (Westview, 1996), co-edited with Paul Rich; and numerous journal articles and chapters.

1
Europe and Asia: Two Regions in Flux

Philomena Murray

Setting the Context

This book aims to enhance our understanding of the engagement of the European Union with East Asia and to provide a comparative context in which the characteristics of the two regions can be identified and assessed. It is an edited collection that is distinctively multidisciplinary in approach, bringing together a set of contributions which, although they share common themes, are nonetheless diverse in their subject matter and disciplinary approaches.

In investigating the external impact of the EU on the East Asian region, *Europe and Asia: Regions in Flux* attempts to contribute to our understanding both of the EU as a political, economic and security actor with civil society dimensions and of its regional integration agenda and that agenda's influence on East Asia. In bringing together scholars from three continents, the book aims not simply to provide an examination of EU–East Asia relations, but also to explore the idea that the EU might constitute a paradigm for East Asian regionalism. It examines EU links with East Asia in the Asia Europe Meetings (ASEM), the role of formal and informal integration and networks within the East Asian region, the new wave of regionalism in Asia and the role of institutions and actors.

Coming as they do from varied academic backgrounds, in political science, economics, history and legal studies, the contributors draw on a large body of literature and original research dealing with the experience of regional integration in both Europe and East Asia. This book is therefore the result of a valuable interdisciplinary dialogue and exchange of views. It is hoped that it will challenge specialists on the European Union (as these constitute the majority of the contributors) to understand the impact of the EU on East Asia and East Asia's impact on the EU, whilst seeking to illustrate that there is a commonality of interests in both Europe and East Asia as well as in a global context. This book emerged from a transnational research grant from the Jean Monnet project, funded by the European Commission, which initially brought together specialists on the EU and on the EU's relationship with East Asia, and then broadened to include specialists on East Asia and the Asia-Pacific.

Europe and East Asia are two dynamic regions whose respective collective powers are growing in the international arena. As far as culture, values, development levels, economic and political systems are concerned, the two regions could not be more different. However, they do have one important factor in common that renders the Europe–East Asia relationship a fascinating and important subject of research — both continents are currently undergoing processes of economic and political integration (albeit at different stages and in different ways) and are increasingly interacting with each other, and the rest of the world, *as regions*. This new regionalism has increasingly become the focus of academic study, and although there have been numerous studies on regionalism in Europe and Asia, scholars could still benefit from a sound, and comprehensive, comparative perspective. As the Eurasian axis is far less developed than both the Transatlantic (EU–United States) and Transpacific (United States–Asia) axes, it has generally received less attention and is perceived to be of lesser value. As the studies in this book will demonstrate, this is certainly not the case — on the contrary, interregional relations between Europe and East Asia are particularly important as they could pave the way for a new region-based world order. While the EU continues the consolidation of its enlargement and greater political integration, the East Asian region, still a contested concept in itself, continues on its own trajectory, with the question frequently being raised as to how useful the European model of integration is to the East Asian context. This book explores the experiences of European and East Asian regionalism, looking at political, economic and security aspects as well as at the current interregional dimension of relations and both European and Asian perspectives on the relationship. In this exercise, there are no fixed conclusions to be reached, only future prospects to be imagined.

What Do We Mean by Europe and Asia in this Volume?

This volume brings together scholars who examine the EU and East Asia — that is, the Association of Southeast Asian Nations (ASEAN: Brunei Darussalam, Indonesia, Malaysia, the Philippines, Singapore, Thailand, Vietnam, Laos, Burma Myanmar and Cambodia) Plus Three (China,

Japan and South Korea). Yet it is clear that what Europe and Asia mean differs for the governments and organizations discussed in this volume. For East Asia, Europe can mean both the EU and its individual member states, as we see in Toshiro Tanaka's chapter. For Europe, Asia can mean ASEAN or ASEAN Plus Three or even the Asia-Pacific Economic Cooperation forum (APEC), as seen in the chapters by Alex Warleigh-Lack, Yeo Lay Hwee and Philomena Murray. What is meant by 'region' is also the subject of considerable debate in this volume, as Alex Warleigh-Lack explains. Further, the term 'flux' is utilized to illustrate that both the EU and Asia are in a process of considerable change, often at considerable speed. Both are regions that are moving targets in the sense that their ambitions and objectives may change over time, and that they are also altering their membership and the scope of their activities.

Asia encompasses almost every type of state apart from the postmodern (Garton Ash 2004, p. 156). It is the fastest growing region in the world, in terms of economic production and population. Many of its countries are Europe's greatest competitors. It is where all the world's major religions are. Some half of the world's population lives in Asia. Almost all of Asia has a relationship with the EU.

The countries of East Asia have experienced some difficulty in determining common goals and shared agendas, due to significant heterogeneity. There is a risk that Asia's more dominant states may dominate regional agendas with their preferred policy goals, to the detriment of their weaker, poorer neighbours. Katzenstein argues that the Asian region cannot be defined as, or confined to, East Asia alone. He argues that Asia exists as a geographic term, but is a construct without racial or cultural meaning. For Katzenstein (2000, p. 355), there is no such thing as an Asian identity or Asian values, whereas the contrary is the case with Europe or Western Europe. He suggests, for example, that the political leaders of Asian states define Asia to suit their own political purposes and the domestic and international needs of their states. Angresano (2004, p. 919) postulates that 'people in Southeast Asia identify almost exclusively with national interest and culture'. ASEAN, the only region-wide entity to date, was not established to work toward supranational objectives. From its inception, ASEAN 'has been quite decentralised so as not to interfere with member nation desire for political independence' (Angresano, 2004, p. 919). Yet the current discussions regarding the creation of an ASEAN Charter suggest that this may be changing, as the Charter attempts to develop ASEAN's institutional structure and create a legal personality for it. Institutionalized integration of the sort experienced in Europe is not, however, replicable, precisely because of the very distinctive historical experiences and governance structures in each region.

Bhattacharyay (2006, p. 9) groups Asia into four subregions: East and Southeast Asia, South Asia, Central Asia and the Pacific. The challenge of understanding 'Asia' in terms of regions and subregions is evident in the 2001 EU document on Asia (EC, 2001). One area of particular concern to this volume is that of a common community for ASEAN. For example, the 2005 East Asian Summit focused on an official theme entitled 'One Vision, One Identity, One Community' and committed ASEAN to the establishment of an 'ASEAN Charter' intended as a 'legal and institutional framework' for the Association, one that would 'codify all ASEAN norms, rules and values' (EAS, 2005). For Asians and Europeans alike, Europe can mean both the European Union and the individual countries of Europe. While the focus of this volume is the EU's relationship with East Asia, it would be erroneous to assume that engagement with any part of Asia or any region of Asia is carried out solely by the EU, for example, as represented by the European Commission. The individual member states of the EU actively promote their exports to East Asia in a state-to state bilateral manner, in what can be termed 'traditional bilateralism'.

Why Examine Europe and Asia in Comparative and Inter-Regional Contexts?

There are several reasons to carry out a comparative analysis of the EU and East Asia. Both continents have undergone, and are undergoing, processes of economic and political integration. Although the EU is by far the most advanced example of regional integration in the world, East Asia is likely to undergo processes that may have some resonance. As far as influence is concerned, it is important to note that, as East Asian states become more influential because of their growing economies and large populations, the rest of the world is looking to engage with East Asia. The collective influence of Asia and Europe is growing in the international arena. Asia accounts for more than 30 per cent (and the EU for some 25 per cent) of world Gross Domestic Product (GDP) and contributes half of global growth. It is in the process of rapid modernization and is regarded as a 'powerhouse in the global economy' (Bhattacharyay, 2006, pp. 2, 9).The study of regionalism and the international role of regions is burgeoning, precisely because there has been an emergence and resurgence of regional projects in the 1980s and 1990s (Breslin and Higgott, 2003, p. 168). There remains a great deal of research to be carried out in this area, and although there have been many studies of regionalism in

Europe and East Asia, there have been relatively few that have offered a comparative perspective. This comparative approach needs to be firmly embedded in an understanding of the past. Beeson is of the view that there are few studies of comparative regionalism, 'especially with a historical dimension' (2005, p. 989). There is also a need to complement case studies with interdisciplinary analysis.

These two regions are important and powerful in the context of the 21st century world order for a number of reasons. Both regions are part of what is known as the Triad — they constitute anchors for the world economic order and are also economic superpowers in their own right. As we shall see in this volume, there are distinctive differences in the political power of both regions, their influence in international organizations, and their military strength. How then do the two regions shape up? The EU is controversially perceived as both an international actor and as a normative power, and this book will explore those notions. The jury is still out as to whether East Asia has any similar roles, or aspires to have such roles. In this regard, demographics and growth are important, especially as they affect East Asia's influence on the world stage.

It is important to be aware of the problematic nature of comparisons in examining Europe and East Asia. The EU's defining characteristic is its apparent relative homogeneity, in terms of religion, race and historical experiences. It is characterized by adherence to democratic systems and the rule of law; a high level of economic and social development; a common economic ideology (capitalism) and, finally, in stark contrast with East Asian regional entities, by supranational institutions and a pooling of sovereignty among its 27 member states.

The defining characteristics of East Asia include the fact that it is highly heterogeneous, in terms of race, ethnicity, religion and the different historical experiences in different parts of East Asia, such as experiences of colonialism. It is certainly true that democracy exists in the region, but alongside authoritarianism and communism and with no common economic ideology. There are varying levels of development and, on the whole, lower standards of living. Finally, as we see in this volume, sovereignty is very important; there are no supranational institutions and state-building is still in progress.

Asia's heterogeneity certainly makes it difficult to make comparisons across the region, let alone with another region. This does not mean that comparison cannot be carried out, or that it is not useful, but it is necessary to understand some of the possible pitfalls. Adopting a comparative approach helps us to find patterns and rules across region and process. An expert on comparing the EU and East Asia highlights the advantages of a comparative analysis: it 'allows us to understand and rethink the incentives for, and constraints on, regional integrative processes', reveals the dynamics that underpin regional processes, and, importantly, highlights what he calls 'another crucial, but oddly neglected variable in regional phenomena: the role of the dominant or hegemonic power of the era' (Beeson, 2005, p. 969).

The Problematic Nature of Comparison: Two Regions a World Apart

It is important to be cognizant of the comparative context of the EU and East Asia. Yet it is equally important to keep these comparisons in rein as we examine the idea that the EU might constitute a form of paradigm or model for East Asia, since there are as many weaknesses and flaws in such an approach as strengths. We are, for example, aware that there are different defining characteristics of each 'region', relating to pluralism, multiculturalism, homogeneity, democracy, economic and social development, economic and political ideologies and also institutions and sovereignty.

Further, it is evident that integration or regionalism in each of these regions is based on different original goals and often dissimilar development of these goals over time. The EU is not necessarily a model in this regard, although Edward Moxon-Browne, in his chapter in this volume, is at pains to illustrate the limitations and possibilities of the EU as a putative political model.

In order to assess the possibility of the EU as a point of comparison and point of reference, it is important to call to mind the challenge of comparability among East Asian states, in ASEAN and ASEAN Plus Three. A further challenge for comparison and for those who seek to see the EU as a reference point is the existence of sociological, cultural and political norm differences, and their effect on general interactions between the EU and East Asian countries and regional bodies. This has been examined as the 'Consensual' Asian way versus the 'Contractual' European way (Dent, 2001, p. 40). While there are considerable cultural differences between the two regions, this book explores whether other factors, such as economic interaction and region-specific responses to global phenomena, may contribute to mutual understanding and intensification of interaction. Regions, after all, are not isolated and discrete entities, but rather are interdependent, involved in multilateral decision-making and confronting global challenges and often common concerns (Song, 2007, p. 68). The reasons for establishing or joining a regional entity may be based on a recognition of interdependence. Rather than a method of gaining independence from the global economy, regionalism is a recognition of the need to ensure continued participation in it, with increased access to investment and markets and the enhancement of a regional voice in wider global economic dialogue (Breslin and Higgott, 2003, p. 173).

There are different interpretations regarding the similarities between the two regions and any future trajectory of East Asian regional integration. Former commissioner Pascal Lamy (2003, p. 4), for example, points to the similarities between East Asia and the EU. He regards diversity as a characteristic that both Europeans and Asians accept and welcome as part of their daily lives and perceives a commonality in the way both regions regard the opportunities and challenges of globalization and reject the idea that 'unfettered market forces should dictate their way of life, culture and nature of their societies and core values'. Both, furthermore, are challenged to reconcile the management of their societies with the need to modernize and integrate into the global economy, in what he sees as a fine balance between market forces and the role of the state.

Shared goals and values remain a key theme that merits increased research. As is clear from the chapters by Edward Moxon-Browne, Derek McDougall and Yeo Lay Hwee, there are distinctive trajectories that have been characterized by often distinctive objectives and values. Levine has described the development in Asia of what he calls 'unifying views', based on increased awareness of globalization, and of broader perspectives, such as commitments to democracy, human rights and cooperation. He adds to this the existence of common values *against* war, exploitation, racism and injustice. These values, he argues, bring peoples and states closer together, making national borders increasingly irrelevant (2007, p. 127).

Jones and Plummer perceive a clear alignment of some objectives among EU and ASEAN leaders. They suggest that the use of the term 'economic community' is indicative of an openness among ASEAN leaders to the idea of learning from the largely successful European integration process. They go so far as to see this as a sea-change in ASEAN thinking, given that the EU's highly formal approach to integration, established supranational institutions and far-reaching regional economic policies was the antithesis of Asian cooperation in the past, (2004, p. 830).

The term economic community can be justified in part by the increase in trade integration in Asia in general and some increase in East Asian intraregional trade, although less than in Europe, an issue that is explored in Bernadette Andreosso-O'Callaghan's chapter in this volume.

As far as intraregional trade is concerned, the heavy market concentration of 27 member states of the EU differs markedly with the more global-market approach of East Asian countries. Ruffini suggests that deeper regional integration in East Asia would 'require a more regional pattern of trade' (2006, p. 22).

Solans (2004, p.13) points to the doubling of the share of trade within the region to more than 40 per cent of total trade and suggests that, as a share of production, regional trade in Asia is as important as in Europe, although there is no institutional integration. Such embedded integration of an institutional nature will not necessarily develop in East Asia, as Moxon-Browne illustrates in his chapter. He is part of a group of scholars who regard 'deep integration' as unlikely to develop in Asia. These scholars concur that the lack of a formal and binding institutional structure intended to bring about regional integration, along with the issues of lack of shared sovereignty; limited solidarity and sense of shared goals and few informal mechanisms for cooperation mean that an EU-style integration will not develop in East Asia. The strong economic imperatives of the EU were strongly supported by political will and a sense of 'regional solidarity' (Ruffini, 2006, p.20). Ruffini, like Jones and Plummer, acknowledges the specificity of the EU experience with its inward-looking regional approach, but suggests that it could prove useful to ASEAN leaders who seek to advance open regionalism. Yet the fact that the European experience has been so distinctive and is the most advanced form of integration in the world suggests that there is no EU model: '[t]he European experience cannot be set as a blueprint, and can only inspire limited practical solutions to policy makers in East Asia. The scope, depth and sequencing of the integration process of East Asian countries have to be their own' (Ruffini, 2006, p. 22)

Regionalism, Regionalization and New International Relationships

What are regions? The answer varies across time and groupings of countries and according to scholarly discipline and actor. There is some agreement that regions are international actors. There is also some consensus that what is taking place in in East Asia is regionalization, not regionalism (Tso Tse, 2005, p. 138). Brian Bridges (2004, p. 387) defines regionalism as the tendency to create institutions or at least mechanisms to assist in the interaction and regionalization as the process of interaction within a region. Beeson (2005, p. 971) draws on Breslin and Higgott (2003) in defining regionalism as 'the political process in which states drive co-operative initiatives', while 'regionalisation by contrast refers to the processes of economic integration which, while they may be influenced by state policies, are essentially uncoordinated consequences of private sector activities'.

Not only are there marked differences between EU and East Asian experiences, so too are there tensions between East Asian and Asia-Pacific conceptualizations of regionalism. Regionalism in the Asia-Pacific is often regarded as 'new regionalism' as opposed to the 'old regionalism' of Europe (Bridges, 2004, p. 390).

Pempel (2006, p. 240) regards regionalization as 'largely bottom-up, corporate or society driven, informal and predominantly independent of official governmental actions'. Regionalization occurs as the forces of globalization play out within a particular geographic context (Katzenstein, 2005, pp. 13–19), manifested in multinational production networks, foreign direct investment, export free zones, trade, enhanced communication and transportation links. In contrast to this, regionalism 'involves top-down, governmentally driven and formally institutionalized connections. ASEAN, Asian Development Bank, APEC, ASEAN Regional Forum (ARF), ASEAN Plus Three and the like are familiar examples. Part of the same process, but typically less comprehensive in membership and scope are minilateral, problem-specific arrangements among governments aimed at cooperation on specific problems ... in all such cases, problems are addressed by governments through formal, institutionalized agreements.'

Pascal Petit suggests that there are two ideal types of regional integration:

> in one mode of integration, countries enjoying similar levels of development, associated themselves by more and more binding trade agreements, while progressively expanding to include neighbouring countries, which then catch up with the average level of development ... in the other mode of integration, countries with highly differentiated levels of development set up a rather segmented and hierarchical division of labour and overall development of the zone, largely prompted by firms of the zone, manifests itself by the entry of new emerging members while other members upgrade their part in the regional division of labour (Petit, 2006, p. 123).

Finally, Jones and Plummer (2004, p. 829) place the two conceptualizations in context, suggesting that East Asia is the most important example of a region where 'economic integration has proceeded through regionalisation, rather than regionalism', as increases in intraregional trade and investment flows have been led by market actors, not government actors.

EU–East Asia Engagement

EU–East Asia engagement is based on calculations of national and regional interests. For example, the EU's primary objective is economic, as it seeks increased access to East Asian growing markets, (Katzenstein, 2000, p. 377) thereby also seeking to offset the considerable EU trade deficit with East Asia. The East Asians seek economic engagement too, as well as European influence to counterbalance the United States. Each region actively seeks increased market integration and interstate cooperation, although at different paces and with often differing processes and styles.

There has been a burgeoning body of scholarly literature in recent years relating to the EU and East Asia. For example, the EU's political and economic relations with East Asia have been the focus of a number of monographs and edited collections. The establishment of ASEM has led to analysis of its structure, objectives and outcomes. The rise of new regionalism studies, the comparative analysis of regional integration and the complexities of interregionalism have brought new perspectives to both comparative analysis and to our understanding of the EU's external relations, trade objectives and the projection of the EU experience as a putative paradigm. The EU's integration process has been proposed as a possible exemplar or comparative yardstick for the Association of South East Asian Nations (ASEAN) and the Asia-Pacific Economic Cooperation forum. There is also some interest in the feasibility of monetary union for ASEAN and ASEAN Plus Three, especially since the aftermath of the Asian financial crisis of 1996–97.

The EU and Asia are involved in a complex, multi-layered and multi-actor engagement. This is based in part on a long historical engagement, in part on extensive trading over several centuries, on colonialism, and on the new relationships forged by newly independent Asian states. The engagement has thus always been based in part on specific bilateral relations. Forster illustrates this:

> The history of initial trading contacts, the colonial relationship, and then a protracted period of withdrawal form the basis of current links. This has left a patchy, thought important, level of bilateral contacts between a number of member states. ... These links have co-existed alongside the group-to-group contact and in many ways have been distinct from it (Forster, 2000, pp. 790–1).

The engagement of the EU and East Asia has been elaborated in EU policy documents, yet there remains a perception that the two regions do not fully understand each other. A 2005 report suggested that the EU paid insufficient attention to the developments there (EIAS, 2005, p. 3). Yet the economic imperatives of the relationship are evident. These are certainly important but not central to their strategic considerations of economic and political relations. This is in part due to the key role played by the US in the region and it has been argued that it is precisely that role that led to a reconsideration of in-depth engagement between the EU and East Asia. Yeo (2004, p. 25) argues that since the 'war on terror', East Asia and Europe have become uneasy about the US's weight and its policies, giving rise to a new appreciation of the urgent need to strengthen multilateralism.

Asia has perhaps been misunderstood by Europeans for centuries, and if this misunderstanding has been perpetuated over the last few decades, this is partly because Asia has often been off the EU radar screen. But this situation has partly changed — for a number of reasons. East Asia simply cannot be ignored, due to its economic competitiveness. The EU is increasingly engaging economically with much of East Asia. There is the context of globalization — Asia often shares common agendas with the EU regarding globalization. Further, the EU is expanding its own international role to such an extent that it sees itself as some form of political actor in the region. This role is based on: a desire to expand its soft power capabilities there; sometimes on encouraging the countries of Asia to see things the European way; on increased dialogue on economic, political and socio-cultural issues; and, in part, on the EU's norms agenda. It is, moreover, largely based on the EU's changing understanding of actual developments in, and the potential of, Asia. A further, highly significant factor is the emergence of China as a powerful economic player in world trade and a potential competitor with the US for the position of hegemon in the region, as well as, more recently, of India as a serious industrial and technological actor. The increasing importance of World Trade Organization (WTO) membership and the commitment of the EU to multilateral trade talks have also contributed to more recent EU engagement with Asia.

European and East Asian relations have long been influenced, and impeded, by mutual stereotypes. Preston and Gilson (2001, p. 6) have suggested that the expansion of material linkages such as economic flows, growing tourism, political summits and 'real time' contact have not reduced the impact of mutual stereotypical perceptions of East Asia and Europe today. Rather, continuing stereotypes are frequently reinforced in trade disputes, political wrangles and cultural misunderstandings. Distance and the fact that Europe and East Asia, however defined, do not feature prominently on each other's radar screens have been recent recurrent challenges.

Regionalization in East Asia in recent years has received impetus in the aftermath of the Asian Financial Crisis, as the nations of ASEAN in particular seek to confront the challenges of economic globalization, the demands for trade and investment liberalization and the rise of China. These factors, according to one European analyst, may render the stakes increasingly political, resulting in 'a new pattern of cooperation and distribution of power in the region' (Boisseau du Rocher, 2006, p. 237).

Of course, it is clear that neither the EU not the countries of East Asia regard each other as completely united regional entities. Each is transforming in a number of ways and each is establishing relations with the other that are multi-layered and multifaceted. The engagement is in part influenced by the burden of history and of memory. Yet engagement is not as embedded as the economic, political and strategic importance of the East Asian region might suggest. Gilson suggests that the EU's commitment to Asia, in its many official documents, is not matched by action, owing to the EU's concern with its own internal integration processes, the relative lack of contentious issues and the existence of many, often complementary, fora for similar issues (2005, p. 381).

This is not to undermine the actual and tangible benefits of EU–East Asia engagement, such as access to markets (especially for Europe) and a reduction in economic and potentially strategic dependence on the US (for East Asia), as well as a potential counterbalance to the US hegemon in international affairs (Dent, 2001, pp. 34–5) and a strengthening of multilateralism. It has been argued that the EU appears to prefer interregional rather than international relations in trading with other countries and regions, as seen in the increase in Free Trade Agreements (FTAs) that the EU negotiates with other regions (Park and Kim, 2005, p. 5).

Yet the relationship is far more than free-trade-focused. There is an increased understanding of the political aspects of the relationship — including the divergence of stances — and this has been attributed to the transformation of the European Community into a more politically oriented EU, with Forster (2000) arguing that the EU's promotion and defence of 'European values', including human and fundamental rights, democracy and environmental issues, have become the cornerstones of a 'new agenda', as the old Community–ASEAN agenda based on regulating trade issues has been supplanted by an EU–ASEAN one of new political priorities. The EU's emphasis on conditionality and other soft power instruments firmly places values such as democracy, human rights, fair trade and environmental issues on the dialogue table, and has not always been perceived in a positive way by the ASEAN interlocutors (Forster, 2000, pp. 792–3).

The EU has often regarded itself as the 'leader' in regional integration, and as 'assisting' ASEAN. There has been little acknowledgment that Europe could perhaps learn from East Asia. 'Europe has led the way in exploring the possibilities and advantages of regional integration.... We will continue to do all we can to support ASEAN in this to help bring greater stability and prosperity to the region' (EC, 2007, p. 1).

Issues and Challenges

The first challenge to each of the two regions is the growing role of China and the question of how to respond to its new self-perception as an important regional player. While the ASEAN states have considerable concerns about China, there is a new EU focus on the development of relations with China, almost to the exclusion of the other East Asian states. ASEAN has attempted to capitalize on Sino–Japanese tension and differences. Certainly, stabler China–Japan relations would render it more difficult for ASEAN members to play one off against the other. Between 1995 and 2005, which coincided with the stalling of their relations, ASEAN effectively used the China card to extract concessions from Japan both in political and economic areas In addition, most ASEAN members gave little more than a lukewarm response to the Japanese attempt to procure a permanent UN seat in 2005, due to concern about the reaction of China (SIIA, 2007) as well as living memories of Japanese policies in the past, both before and after the Second World War. While there has been criticism of Japan's reaction to the Asian Financial Crisis of 1997–98, it has been argued that Japan can be regarded as having been more effective in augmenting its regional leadership role than previously understood (Hook et al., 2002). There is a view among some Asian analysts that, without a solid Sino–Japanese relationship, the region cannot make substantial progress to an East Asian economic community (Kawai, 2005, p. 51).

From the EU side, there has been a recent coming together of the EU and China with similar views on multilateralism and the importance of the UN (Tong, 2005). The focus on China can be seen as leading to less EU interest in other parts of East Asia. Gilson's critique of the EU's according insufficient priority attention to Asia could well be revised; insufficient attention to all but China is the current failing. It is argued by one European expert that China and the EU regard themselves as complementary global actors, due to 'shared vested interest in pursuing a stable world order and a commitment to effective multilateralism' (van der Geest, 2006, p. 129). What remains important for all interlocutors on both sides is certainly that long-term stability in the region will require that the US–China relationship become more predictable, a feat that will depend far more on the relationship with the external hegemon, the United States, than on the one with the EU, given the extensive hard power capabilities of the US.

The EU is China's most important trading partner and there have been significant increases in European investment in the Chinese economy, motivated by individual member states of the EU, especially the United Kingdom, France and Germany. It is not only investment that the EU is exporting to China — it is also exporting an EU model there, according to one think tank (Barysch et al., 2005). Furthermore, the EU's normative dimension is evident in its faith that Chinese progress towards market economics, the rule of law and greater democratic accountability will render it a more reliable and responsible world player and partner in multilateralism (ibid.). The relationship in increasingly multifaceted, encompassing energy and the environment, migration and human rights, for example. The EU sees China as its top priority and in 2005 a group of experts suggested that the EU risked squandering its potential unless it started thinking about China more strategically and moved beyond a 'shopping list of priorities' to a coherent strategy (ibid.). Clearer and more coherent messages are emanating from the European Commission but it is equally clear that the individual member states guard their own relationships with China closely. Finally, China may well determine the future direction of East Asian regionalism, and the projection of a form of eventual East Asian regional identity (van der Geest, 2006, p. 130).

The External Hegemon

Linked to China's role as the hegemonic power situated within the region is that of the external hegemon — the US. Pempel (2006, p. 244) encapsulates the issue well, asserting that Asian security is not ensured by multilateral treaties but by a series of bilateral relationships centring on Washington. The fact remains that the US is an influential and strong player in Asia. Currently, the EU's projection of 'soft' power cannot rival the considerable 'soft' and 'hard' power of the US in the region. It is useful to recall that US's hard power consists of some 80,000 active troops in the East Asian region and military bases in Japan, South Korea, the Philippines and Guam and that all this is backed up by troops afloat. In addition, the US's soft power is backed up by economic power, as the US is East Asia's largest export market, and by cultural influence. While some Asian countries view EU engagement as a means to reduce their dependency on the US in a counterbalancing context, there is little evidence as yet of the EU surpassing the US in either soft or hard power. Both the US and EU are working on bilateral relations with China and, to a lesser extent, with Japan. While the US has supported APEC, as seen in the 2007 APEC summit in Sydney, it has been less supportive of other regional initiatives in East Asia.

Normative Power: A Distinctive Characteristic of EU–Asia Relations

While scholarly discussion of soft power and normative power has focused on specific policies or stances rather than regions, and on issues relating to expectations and capabilities and the gap between the two, there is scope to examine the role of the EU as a norms exporter in East Asia. The 'normative power' debate, which has developed principally around the work of Ian Manners (2002; 2006), has raised a series of questions that are central to our understanding of the EU's identity as an international actor, including in the East Asian region. Few scholars to date have moved beyond debates that focus on specific issues (for example, the environment, human rights) and beyond the establishment of their own criteria for determining whether or not the EU can claim a normative status. Understanding the EU's relationship with East Asia, as this book attempts to do, will provide some background and context for these debates.

There are numerous questions that still require more fruitful research. These include: How coherent are the EU arguments surrounding the exportation of norms in Asia? How important is the US as a security provider — and norms exporter — in the region? Does the EU's lack of hard power undermine its role as a norms promoter in Asia? How might this contrast with the role of the United States in East Asia? The security dimensions are examined by Nicholas Rees in this volume. Yet it is clear that much remains to be learned regarding the projection of EU soft power and the role of the EU as a norms exporter in East Asia.

It has been argued that East Asia's shallow institutionalization could provide the EU with opportunities to actively project its soft power. The contrast with the role of the US features prominently in some discussions of how the EU could 'use its soft power to protect its vast interests in East Asia thereby contributing to the stability of the region', with an emphasis on what has been called the EU's comparative advantage and 'moral authority' over the US (EIAS, 2005, pp. 7–8).

The Future of EU–Asia Relations

An EU–ASEAN 'Vision Statement' of March 2007 attempts to build on 30 years of cooperation and calls for closer political relations at bilateral and multilateral level and lists areas for joint action, especially in security, energy, environmental and development matters (EC, 2007). It is to be expected that the EU will continue its development aid programmes, building on the commitment between 2000 and 2007 of €80 million in regional programmes in Southeast Asia (EC, 2007). The EU has expressed its commitment to accede to the ASEAN Treaty of Amity and Cooperation (EIAS, 2005). Trade between the EU and ASEAN continues to grow, reaching €116 million in June 2007. In addition, the EU has commenced free trade talks with ASEAN, Korea and India. In the case of ASEAN, it is to be expected that the Myanmar issue will result in separate agreements with the individual states. The expected result is that this EU–ASEAN agreement (or series of agreements) will lead to increases in two-way trade and investment between the two regions of up to 20 per cent (EurActiv, 2007). On the political level, the European Commission is clearly committed to stability, with Commissioner Ferrero-Waldner stating that the EU has a huge stake in the region's political stability and 'want[s] to play a bigger political role' (2007, p. 10). There will continue to be engagement between the two regions in discussions regarding global governance. There will continue to be interregional dialogue and agreements. ASEM will continue to provide a dialogue platform for cooperation on economic, political and socio-cultural and cultural issues, although its role will continue to be debated. So too will the role of ASEAN. As we see from this volume, Yeo argues that ASEAN is a successful diplomatic community, while Rees argues that it has not been a successful security community to date.

Regional integration in each of the regions is distinctive. There is scope to examine both the processes and consequence of European integration and the experience of East Asian regionalism, as seen in this book. In a sense, East Asia cannot really be described as a process, but as an experience, whilst the EU is both.

Overview of the Chapters

Alex Warleigh-Lack's chapter two on the EU, ASEAN and APEC in comparative perspective investigates the theoretical challenges involved in the comparative study of regionalization, with particular attention to a comparison of the EU, ASEAN and APEC. The regions are selected for comparison not only for their salience to the present volume, but because of their substantial differences, as demonstrated by their location at rather different positions on Hettne's spectrum of 'region-ness'. In recent work on the new regionalism, two issues are striking on this score. First is the explicit revision process being undergone by the principal body of conceptual work in the field, Hettne's 'new regionalist approach'. Second, but by no means unconnected, are the many recent calls by scholars such as Laursen and Söderbaum for further comparative study of contemporary regions in the global political economy in order to test and develop more robust theoretical perspectives. The chapter seeks to help meet these challenges, and sets out a conceptual framework for the comparative study of global regions and regionalization — that is, a linked set of research questions, hypotheses and variables which can respectively be asked and tested through empirical comparison. The chapter concludes by using the framework to compare the EU, ASEAN and APEC and drawing conclusions about the revision of the framework for use in future studies.

The third chapter, by Derek McDougall, looks at the East Asian experience of regionalism and assesses it in the light of the changing dynamics of international politics within the region. It takes the major manifestations of regionalism in East Asia and asks what have been the driving forces behind them and what regionalism has amounted to. Where regionalism has been weak or non-existent, it asks why this has been the case. The major manifestations of regionalism to be examined are the Association of Southeast Asian Nations (ASEAN), the Asia-Pacific Regional Cooperation (APEC), the ASEAN Regional Forum, ASEAN Plus Three and the East Asia Summit (EAS). Although ASEAN does not embody regional integration, it is the strongest of the groupings, reflecting some of the features of international politics in Southeast Asia. There is nothing comparable in Northeast Asia, which is dominated by the interactions of the US, China and Japan, with Taiwan and Korea as key zones of conflict. 'Asia Pacific' and 'East Asian' conceptions of regionalism have competed to some extent, with the latter receiving a fillip in the aftermath of the 1997–98 Asian financial crisis. Institutionalization is weak in both instances, reflecting the domination of the major powers in both the 'East Asian' and 'Asia Pacific' contexts.

Following on from this, the fourth chapter by Bernadette Andreosso-O'Callaghan compares and contrasts economic integration in the Asia-Pacific region and Europe. It examines the level of *de facto* and *de jure* economic integration in the two regions, and compares the regions along a number of statistical indicators. The milestones of government-led economic integration in both regions are presented. In the case of Asia, this is done with a focus on hubs of economic integration such as ASEAN, and ASEAN Plus Three. The degree of structural similarity within the two regions is assessed, the two tenets of economic integration, trade and investment, are examined and the role of China is highlighted. The chapter further examines other initiatives such as economic cooperation and development aid.

The fifth chapter, by Edward Moxon-Browne, asks whether and, if so, to what extent the experience of political integration in the European Union could be applicable to ASEAN. It analyses the features of European integration that are unique to that process and links these to contextual specificities in the West European political landscape. The chapter then evaluates the likelihood of ASEAN being receptive to the institutions, values and political assumptions that underlie the European integration process. It argues that ASEAN lacks a key background condition for political integration: a societal 'platform' on which a common set of values can be constructed. Moreover, many regimes in ASEAN are not willing to open themselves to the external scrutiny that institutions of the type intrinsic to the EU would require. Divergences in defining and protecting human rights within ASEAN are conspicuous, and emblematic of a wider debate about contrasting 'values'. A lack of cultural homogeneity at the regional level in ASEAN is matched by an autarchic approach to economic development. A key component of political integration, a viable civic society, is largely absent.

The sixth chapter, by Yeo Lay Hwee, on the Asia-Europe meeting (ASEM) and the origins, potential and reality of EU–East Asia relations illustrates that there are many strands of cooperation that make up the relationship such as the longstanding EU–ASEAN partnership, growing EU–China relations, relations between the EU and Japan, and between the EU and South Korea. It argues that ASEM is the latest and the most ambitious attempt to provide a framework of EU–East Asia relations. It examines what ASEM has achieved and whether the ASEM framework provided a significant boost to EU–East Asia relations.

The seventh chapter, by Christopher Dent, suggests that the density of regionalized economic activity is significantly high in both East Asia and Europe. This so-called 'regionalization' derives from various transnational business and infrastructural linkages that have deepened in both regions over time. These networks represent an important micro-level foundation to regional integration in East Asia and Europe on which state-led projects of regionalism, such as the Single European Market and the ASEAN Free Trade Area have been built. Conversely, these projects have further spurred the development of international production networks, thus suggesting a symbiotic relationship. International production networks are also inextricably linked with the economic zonal development of East Asia and Europe. Contrasts and comparisons between East Asia and Europe are made, as well as an assessment of how both regions are interconnected through certain global production network linkages.

Nicholas Rees's chapter, number eight, examines European and Asian security and the role of regional organizations in the post-9/11 environment. He argues that the post-9/11 security environment challenged many states in Europe and Asia to rethink their approaches to security and to consider whether regional security arrangements might provide one means of responding to such threats. He looks at the responses of the two regions, focusing specifically on the impact that heightened concern over security has had on the regional organizations in the respective regions. The chapter highlights the lack of understanding that still exists with regard to what is meant by regionalism and regional identity, and the very different perspectives that exist in 'Europe' and 'Asia' over security. It also points to the limitations of adopting regional security solutions to regional problems, given the different types of regional organizations that exist in Asia and Europe. The chapter concludes by arguing that while there are more differences than similarities on security matters, there is a need to develop intra- and inter-regional dialogue within and between Europe and East Asia as the regions have much to learn from each other in their respective approaches to security matters.

The ninth chapter, by Toshiro Tanaka, examines the perspectives of different elites in ASEAN Plus Three regarding Europe and European integration. It illustrates that East Asian governments, companies and academics still manifest a clear preference for dealing bilaterally with individual EU member states rather than with the EU as a 'bloc'. Overall, these elites regard the EU's achievements in both economic and political integration as positive developments and many perceive them as being worthy of emulation in East Asia — although with varying degrees of understanding of adaptability. The question of the EU as a model for East Asian regionalism is addressed from a number of perspectives that can be regarded as broadly East Asian, illustrating that no common perspective is evident and that it is important to understand the role of distinctive Asian and regional approaches and the need to understand the nuances of responses to the European experience from a number of national and sectoral perspectives.

The final chapter, by Philomena Murray, examines European perspectives on engagement with East Asia. Murray argues that little has been written about the EU's motives in engaging with Asia and its attitudes towards the region as a whole. She argues that EU policy towards East Asia has been essentially reactive and motivated by EU economic interests in the early years of its Asia Strategy and that its current engagement is characterized by a combination of bilateral and regional arrangements and, in particular, changing conceptions of what constitutes 'Asia'. While economic interests remain paramount, political and normative elements are also evident. She also explores why and how the EU is advancing normative values in Asia.

Concluding Remarks

As the EU becomes more distinctive as a region, there are questions as to the extent to which deep, embedded, regionalist integration may or may not be taking place in a similar manner in Asia. Is there a trend to increasing consolidation of regionalism in East Asia and in Asia more generally? What will be the roles of ASEAN and ASEAN Plus Three? Will China remain a key player within ASEAN Plus Three, or go it alone in international affairs, trade and geopolitics? To what extent might ASEAN be a motor of regionalism or a driving force to bring together the parts of East Asia? What of India — and its relationship with China? Finally, to what extent will there be a convergence of EU–East Asian views on China, on North Korea and on the WTO? These all require further research.

This book discusses the idea that the EU may constitute a paradigm for East Asian regionalism. This is an important issue in EU–East Asia relations and constitutes a unique dimension of this interregional relationship. The question of the EU as a model for regional integration has attracted much attention in the academic literature. Many Asianist scholars have become rather guarded about this approach because they correctly perceive that the Asian experience of regionalism or of regionalization is fundamentally an endogenous process. Equally, it has also become clear that there are many Asian and Asianist scholars who do not share this opinion. Being aware of this complexity this book endeavours to present a balanced view of the issues involved, including Asian difficulties with the idea of the EU as a model. It is clear that there are major problems with the idea of the EU as a paradigm but the debate will continue for some time among analysts and actors alike.

References

Angresano, J. (2004) 'European Union integration lessons for ASEAN + 3: the importance of contextual specificity', *Journal of Asian Economics*, 14, pp. 909–26.

Barysch, K., Grant, C. and Leonard, M. (2005) 'Embracing the Dragon: the EU's partnership with China', Centre for European Reform, May.

Beeson, M. (2005) 'Rethinking regionalism: Europe and East Asia in comparative historical perspective', *Journal of European Public Policy*, 12. 6, pp. 969–85.

Bhattacharyay, B. (2006) 'Understanding the Latest Wave and Future Shape of Regional Trade and Cooperation Agreements in Asia', CESIFO Working Paper no 1856.

Boisseau du Rocher, S. (2006) 'ASEAN and Northeast Asia: Stakes and Implications for the European Union-ASEAN Relationship', *Asia Europe Journal*, 4, pp. 229–49.

Breslin, S. and Higgott, R. (2003) 'New Regionalism in Historical Perspective', *Asia-Europe Journal*, 1. 2, pp. 167–82.

Bridges, B. (2004) 'Learning from Europe. Lessons for Asian Pacific Regionalism?' *Asia Europe Journal*, 2. 3, pp. 387–97.

Dent, C. (2001) 'ASEM and the "Cinderella Complex" of EU–East Asia Economic Relations', *Pacific Affairs*, 74. 1, Spring, pp. 25–52.

EAS (East Asia Summit) (2005) *Kuala Lumpur Declaration on the East Asia Summit, Kuala Lumpur 14 December 2005*, available at http://www.aseansec.org18098.htm, accessed 10 June 2008.

EurActiv (2007) 'EU Launches Free Trade Talks with ASEAN', EurActiv, 4 June, http://www.euractiv.com, accessed 5 June 2007.

European Commission (2001) Communication from the Commission. Europe and Asia: A Strategic Framework for Enhanced Partnerships. Brussels, 4 September 2001, COM(2001) 469 final. http://ec.europa.eu/comm/external_relations/asia/doc/com01_469_en.pdf, accessed 17 November 2006.

European Commission (2007) 'EU-ASEAN: increasing engagement with South East Asia', Brussels, 13 March 2007, European Commission RAPID Press Release, Reference: IP/07/319, http://europa.eu/rapid/pressReleasesAction.do?reference=IP/07/319&format=HTML&aged=0&language=EN&guiLanguage=en, accessed 8 June 2008.

EIAS (European Institute for Asian Studies) (2005) *The EU's strategic interests in East Asia*, Volume I: Main report and synthesis, 22 August, Brussels: Consortium of European Institute for Asian Studies and Nomisma.

Ferrero-Walder, B. (2007) 'Common experiences, common hopes and engagement in our common interests', *Asia Europe Journal*, 5. 1, pp. 9–11.

Forster, A. (2000) 'Evaluating the EU–ASEM relationship: a negotiated order approach', *Journal of European Public Policy*, 7. 5, pp. 787–805.

Garton-Ash, T. (2004) *Free World*, London: Allen Lane, Penguin.

Gilson, J. (2005) 'New Interregionalism? The EU and East Asia', *European Integration*, 27. 3, pp. 307–26.

Hook, G. D., Gilson, J., Christopher, W., Hughes, C.W. and Dobson, H., (2002) 'Japan and the East Asian Financial Crisis: Patterns, Motivations and Instrumentalisation of Japanese Regional Economic Diplomacy', *European Journal of East Asian Studies*, 1. 2, pp. 177–97.

Jones, E. and Plummer, M. G. (2004) 'Introduction: EU-Asia, links and lessons', *Journal of East Asian Economics*, 14, pp. 829–42.

Katzenstein, P. (2000) 'Regionalism and Asia' *New Political Economy*, 5. 3, pp. 353–68.

Katzenstein, P. (2005) 'Introduction: Asian Regionalism in Comparative Perspective' in P. Katzenstein and T. Shiraishi (eds), *Network Power: Japan and Asia*, Ithaca: Cornell University Press.

Kawai, M. (2005) 'East Asian Economic Regionalism: Progress and Challenges', *Journal of Asian Economics*, 16, pp. 29–55.

Lamy, P. (2003) 'Asia–Europe relations: a joint partnership' *Asia Europe Journal*, 1. 1 February, pp. 3–9.

Levine, S. (2007) 'Asian Values and the Asia Pacific Community: Shared Interests and Common Concerns', *Politics and Policy*, 35. 1, pp. 102–35.

Manners, I. (2002) 'Normative Power Europe: A Contradiction in Terms?' *Journal of Common Market Studies*. 40. 2, pp. 235–58.

Manners, I. (2006) 'Normative power Europe reconsidered: beyond the crossroads', *Journal of European Public Policy* 13. 2, pp. 182–99.

Park, S.-H. and Kim, H. (2005) 'Asia Strategy of the European Union and Asia–EU Economic Relations: Basic Concepts and New Developments', paper presented at the 3rd EUSA–AP conference, Tokyo, December 8–10.

Pempel, T. J., (2006) 'The Race to Connect East Asia: An Unending Steeplechase', *Asian Economic Policy Review*, 1, pp. 239–54.

Petit, P. (2006) 'Globalisation and Regional Integration: a Comparative Analysis of Europe and East Asia', *Competition and Change*, 10. 2, pp. 113–40.

Ruffini, P.-B. (2006) 'Regional Integration in East Asia: Which Lessons to Draw from the European Experience?' Paper presented at the Asia-Pacific Economic Association Conference, University of Washington, Seattle, USA, July 29–30.

Singapore Institute of International Affairs (SIIA) (2007) 'Neighbourly Ties and ASEAN developments', *SEAPS Net News*, 1 June.

Solans, E. D. (2004) 'The International Role of the Euro. Its Impact on Economic Relations between Asia and Europe', *Asia-Europe Journal*, 2. 1, pp. 7–14.

Song, W. (2007) 'Regionalisation, Interregional Cooperation and Global Governance', *Asia Europe Journal*, 5. 1, pp. 67–92.

Tong, S. C. (2005) 'The EU's policy towards China and the Arms Embargo', *Asia Europe Journal*, 3. 3, 313–21.

Tso Tse, E. (2005) 'Towards an Asian Union', *Asia Europe Journal*, 3. 2, 137–40.

van der Geest, W. (2006) 'The European Union's Strategic Interests in East Asia', *Asia Europe Journal*, 4. 2, pp. 129–30.

Yeo, L. H. (2004) 'Dimensions of Asia–Europe Cooperation', *Asia Europe Journal*, 2. 1, pp. 19–31.

2
The EU, ASEAN and APEC in Comparative Perspective[1]
Alex Warleigh-Lack

Introduction: Contemporary Regionalization and the Problem of Theory

This chapter investigates the challenges involved in the comparative study of regionalization, understood as 'an explicit, but not necessarily formally institutionalized, process of adapting participant state norms, policy-making processes, policy styles, policy content, political opportunity structures, economy and identity to both align with and shape a new collective set of priorities, norms and interests at regional level, which may itself then evolve, dissolve or reach stasis' (Warleigh-Lack, 2006, p. 758).[2] With both integration theory (Rosamond, 2000; Wiener and Diez, 2004) and the new regionalism approach, or NRA (Söderbaum and Shaw, 2003; Hettne, n.d.) undergoing re-evaluation, the opportunity for mutual learning and cross-fertilization presents itself. No matter when they began, all processes of regionalization in the contemporary global political economy can be understood as products of member state (or 'member economy') adaptations to globalization, with particular dynamics dictated by the interplay of national interests, culture, norms and geopolitical context, and scholars need more convincing comparative studies of them (Hettne, 2003; Laursen, 2003).

Achieving this goal requires an explicit process of dialogue and mutual learning. This chapter analyses three contemporary regionalization processes through the lens of a new, explicitly intradisciplinary conceptual framework.[3] The European Union (EU), Asia-Pacific Economic Cooperation (APEC) and the Association of Southeast Asian Nations (ASEAN) are selected not just because of their salience to the present volume, but also because of their differences. Hettne's non-hierarchical scale of 'regionness' shows that regionalization is dynamic, but also that various modes of regionalization can be discerned, and hence attempts to deepen our comprehension of contemporary regionalization must be grounded in an appreciation of diversity (Hettne, 2002). The EU has evolved into a transnational polity with common citizenship rights and a currency of its own. ASEAN, similarly a product of 'first wave' regionalism (that is, undertaken in the period roughly 1950–70), is much less densely institutionalized and embedded in a network of extra-regional bodies largely of its own creation. APEC is perhaps best understood as a case of 'transregionalism' (Hettne, 2005, p. 279), an attempt to create a regional association while bringing together states and economies from several different continents. Thus, by studying these entities comparatively one might discover what are common features and problems of 'new regionalism', and what are idiosyncrasies of a given region. This in turn will allow reformulation of theory.

The chapter begins with a brief discussion of the main legacies of both EU studies/integration theory and new regionalism studies/the NRA, and the potential this generates for the project of comparative theory-building in regionalization studies. It then addresses the barriers and problems in the process of constructing a conceptual framework for regionalization studies. Such a framework and four related hypotheses are then set out. These are then tested against the literature on the EU, APEC and ASEAN. The conclusion then recasts the framework after this testing.

Regionalism Studies Old and New — Legacies and Potential for Comparison

The comparative use of EU studies and new regionalism work requires confrontation of scholarly historiography (Warleigh, 2004, Warleigh, 2006, Warleigh-Lack, 2006), on which this section draws. First, the failure of neofunctionalism to develop as a theory of regional integration in light of both its own internal difficulties and the failure of many 'first wave' regional projects downgraded international relations (IR) scholars' views of the EU, EU studies and integration theory. It also made EU scholars dubious regarding the feasibility of comparative regionalist studies, and inclined many of them to emphasize the *sui generis* character of the EU and point out where orthodox IR simply failed to grasp the EU accurately.[4] However, this also encouraged parochialism and, by omission as much as by commission, reinforced the notion that if other regions were to be worthwhile they would have to follow the EU 'model' (Haas, 1961).[5] Consequently, and in keeping with the rejection of the EU as a template by several region-builders outside Europe, many scholars of new regionalism have argued that EU studies and integration theory have no utility for them. This problem of auto-definitions and exclusions restricts the number of scholars who are willing to collaborate across sub-field boundaries. Thus, to facilitate such endeavours, it is necessary to spell out what their key advantages might be.

Perhaps the main use of EU studies for scholars of new regionalism is its potential to act as a repository of scholarship from a variety of perspectives, including interdisciplinary work. Thus, EU studies should be understood as a broad church, with an enormous literature from which scholars of other regions can glean both cautionary tales and ideas for more rewarding research of their own. For example, EU studies show how a region can be both intergovernmental and supranational at the same time — different policy issues can have different decision rules, and 'intergovernmental' decisions can have 'supranational' consequences. It is therefore not contradictory to see a region as a polity while emphasizing that it exists because states have constructed it and remain in charge even if they are thereby transformed. Moreover, EU scholarship shows the potential for drawing on comparative politics as well as IR, meaning new questions about the nature and impact of the regional political systems can be asked, such as questions investigating their effectiveness, legitimacy, impact on national systems and policies. This will help chart the potential complexity of the various regions. These questions need to be asked in appropriate ways, but if they are pertinent to the nascent global polity[6] (Wæver, 2004), it makes no sense to rule them out in regional entities that are best understood as part of that very global transformation process (Hettne, 2005).

The utility of new regionalist work for EU studies scholars can also be demonstrated. New regionalist studies show the links between the region and the global, emphasizing their coexistence and partial co-constitution in a manner often overlooked in EU studies. As a result, new regionalist scholars demonstrate the utility of drawing on a wider range of literatures, particularly international/global political economy. New regionalism studies also, and consequently, help to understand the differences between first and second wave regionalism — an issue often ignored in EU studies, which tends to treat the last two decades of change in the EU polity as if they were without parallel elsewhere and almost entirely shaped by member state domestic politics and the manipulations of EU-level institutions and business groups. Such insights could have a major impact in understanding why and how EU governance styles or norms change. From the perspective of theory-building, new regional studies increases the range of cases available, liberating EU scholars from the 'N = 1' problem and adding a fresh range of comparators — other regions in the global political economy, not the federal nation-states chosen for comparison in the immediate post-Maastricht era.[7] Consequently, new regionalism studies demonstrate the need for awareness of context: just as EU studies can help IR scholars think about how to study decision-making in the global polity, new regional scholars can help EU studies scholars differentiate between the general and the EU-specific in terms of the regionalization process.

In sum, the legacy of previous scholarship in regionalization studies is the need to emphasize contingency and reflexive approaches to theory-making, coupled with an injunction to avoid unnecessary barriers to comparative study. It will always be useful to have work which focuses on particular regions in depth: after all comparative politics builds on work by country specialists and cannot by definition replace them. The next section discusses how such a comparative study of regionalization might unfold.

Comparative Regionalization Studies — Towards Intradisciplinarity

When seeking synthesis, scholars must address a range of issues regarding the viability and need for such endeavours (Warleigh, 2004, pp. 301–9). Some scholars can be fundamentally opposed to the suggestion. Others prefer other means of addressing the problem: why not just try running different perspectives on the same issue in parallel, as part of an emphasis on problem-centred research? This can certainly alert scholars to different methods, evidence and ways of interpreting it. It may also be more practical given the difficulties of establishing new research agendas and mastering new literatures. However, such an approach may fail to harness any insights that are generated in particular cases or projects for use in the study of the wider research problem.

As it now seems clear that there are few theoretically salient differences between regionalisms 'old' and 'new' (Hettne, 2003), this may be a time for boldness and methodological pluralism in order to ensure maximum insight (Best, 2006; Van Langenhove, 2006). The elaboration of an intra-disciplinary conceptual framework would aid the intellectual coherence of investigations of regionalization, and also help ensure the comparability of research by paying serious attention to multiple cases, methodological and epistemological clarity, and contingency. There is no reason why different conceptual frameworks could not be generated and tested in parallel; what follows is an offering to the debate. Moreover, establishing a viable comparative framework must be a medium-term goal, to be achieved through a process of elaboration, critique and refinement.

A Framework for Comparative Regionalization Studies: Variables and Hypotheses[8]

Building on the definition of 'regionalization' set out above, there are four main independent variables to explore. Each has a range of research questions which, when answered, will help generate a robust understanding of the independent variable to which they relate. In turn, analysis of the four independent variables should generate useful insights about the dependent equivalent — regionalization.

The four principal independent variables are:

- *Genesis* (why and how the regionalization process began)
- *Functionality* (how the process works)
- *Socialization* (affective factors)
- *Impact* (the effect on component states and third countries)

The first independent variable, genesis, asks why states join, and continue participating in, a regionalization process. What are the stated objectives of the latter? How are inclusion and exclusion determined and defined? Investigating these issues will allow scholars to identify similarity or otherwise in the teleology of regionalization processes, and establish the links between this and the region's membership and identity. It also allows scholars to study whether and, if so, why the stated objectives of a region may change (a key question in the shift from 'old' to 'new' regionalism for both the EU and ASEAN).

Hypothesis One: States take part in regionalization because they perceive a specific common interest in managing the economic and/or security consequences of globalization (or post-World War Two recovery, depending upon the date of establishment) that is not shared with states outside the region.

The second independent variable, functionality, investigates how a region functions once it is established. Who is involved in decision-making, and what is their relative influence? Does this vary according to issue area or type? What range of issues does the region address, and does this change over time? If so, why? What are the decision rules? Is the region designed to eradicate, or coexist with, bilateral relations between its members? What implementation capacity does the region have, and how favourably do members consider its performance? This set of questions elucidates the internal workings and power distribution of a region, whether internal or external pressures have greater catalysing powers on its activities, and whether the system is responsive to members' desires for reform (if such desires exist).

Hypothesis Two: Regionalization is a stop-go process dominated by member governments and dictated by their interests, with a tendency towards informal decision-making.

The third independent variable, socialization, investigates whether the region has any impact on the ideational and normative contexts of its component parts, at both elite and mass levels. Does popular support grow or decrease over time? Do senses of cross-border trust and solidarity develop? If so, why? Is there any regionalization of political identity, and, if so, does this impact upon political behaviour? Studying this set of questions allows scholars to establish the links between political identity and legitimacy, and also to establish whether and how regions shape or are shaped by affective factors.[9]

Hypothesis Three: Policy-learning and joint problem-solving are more apparent than regionalized identities at either mass or elite level.

The fourth independent variable, impact, investigates the products and outputs of the regionalization process. To separate it from variable three, the focus here is on material rather than ideational outcomes, such as the region's impact on the domestic political economy, policies and structures of its members or on the global political economy. Has the region impacted on third countries, and if so, how? Has the region impacted on how its component states relate to each other and their external influence?

Hypothesis Four: Regionalization empowers the member states collectively *vis-à-vis* third countries and has significant structural impacts on its component states.

The EU, ASEAN and APEC Compared

The following paragraphs draw on my own previous work in EU studies and on published literature by ASEAN and APEC scholars. The contents of this section should be considered my synthesis of these literatures.[10]

Genesis

The EU owes its origins to the need for post-1945 economic and political reconstruction. Although ideals of cooperation or federalism were present, there were more influential drivers behind the creation of a community of nations in Europe. First, the need of the West European states to re-establish themselves peacefully. Second, United States policy, which favoured innovative forms of European cooperation as part of its strategy to revise the world economic order and 'contain' communism. Thus, both 'hard' and 'soft' security concerns were crucial, with the US as the capitalist superpower providing encouragement, financial aid (the Marshall Plan), and the necessary security guarantee (North Atlantic Treaty Organization, NATO). Although it still remains difficult to integrate foreign and defence policies — despite recent developments such as EU missions to Bosnia-Herzegovina and Rwanda — it was inherent in the design of the joint European venture that its initial range of competences would expand (Coombes, 1970, p. 25). Participation in the integration process was theoretically available to any European state which chose to sign up, but has actually always been a matter of high politics: the Cold War prevented accession by states in Central and Eastern Europe, and the absence of liberal democracy prevented early accession by Greece, Spain and Portugal.

ASEAN's creation results from a remarkably similar rationale to that of the EU, despite the different historical and political context (emerging from colonialism rather than the devastation of the 1939–45 war). Also, the US played a less economically generous role. Setting up ASEAN was seen by its member states as a means to cement and ensure their independence. It also helped legitimize their various domestic regimes in the face of political unrest, and, notably, communist forces both domestic and foreign. Although the new regional entity was aimed at creating a social community rather than a military alliance or economic bloc, it had several clear security functions. These were to preserve both new states and particular regimes, reduce dependence on both the US and former colonial masters, and contain any aggression by Indonesia, while also allowing that state a peaceful leadership role. Providing a bulwark against China was a further intended security benefit. The Association's identity and mechanisms of inclusion and exclusion have always been norm-driven rather than drawing on historically-rooted senses of mutuality, centring on adhesion to the so-called 'ASEAN Way',[11] with geopolitics determining the scope of membership. As with the EU, security concerns have played a key role in ASEAN's recent institutional enlargement and creativity, as expressed in the ASEAN Regional Forum (ARF) and ASEAN Plus Three initiatives.

APEC's origins emanate from a drive for economic security. Bringing together member economies over a vast geographical range, APEC was established as a result of different but complementary concerns regarding the possible economic consequences of globalization and regionalism elsewhere, particularly the EU's single-market programme. The US considered APEC a useful means to wield soft power for security purposes in the emerging 'post-1989' world. It also considered that APEC would provide both bargaining chips in World Trade Organization (WTO) negotiations with the EU and further opportunities for economic growth in expanding markets. China and Indonesia considered APEC a useful way to 'commit themselves to internationally-oriented development strategies' (Garnaut, 2000, p. 1). The smaller economies of the region sought an insurance policy regarding access to the US and global markets. Although various states claim leadership of the process, Australia played a key 'frontman' role, with Japanese and US diplomacy active behind the scenes. The necessary policy focus was provided by acceptance of the neoliberal economic agenda, prepared in advance by the Eminent Persons Group of (often only apparently) non-state actors — who often had close connections to their respective governments, worked to a mandate provided by governments, and evinced a handy acceptance of the Washington Consensus (Aggarwal, 1993; Ravenhill, 2001).

Thus, hypothesis one appears largely valid, but in need of refinement. Regionalization projects both 'old' and 'new' are begun and adapted primarily for security reasons, and the particular understanding of the initial participant states regarding what security constitutes and requires has a significant impact on the remit of the regionalization process and organization. However, it is necessary to acknowledge more fully the role of the US in launching, shaping or constraining regionalization projects even as a silent partner. Moreover, economic security concerns (as well as methods) are much more apparent in the cases of the EU and APEC than in ASEAN. In the EU and ASEAN, the viability of member states is more apparent as a motivating factor than in APEC, perhaps as a function of their earlier establishment. Shared identity does not appear as a strong driver of regionalization: such processes may be initiated with the hope of deepening such awareness, but the regions studied here do not result from a drive to harness already-existing shared identities. This has an impact on mechanisms of inclusion and exclusion, with initial sets of member states in each case decided as functions of utility, willingness to participate, and the bounds of the geopolitically possible.

Functionality

The EU operates a complex array of decision-making procedures, with a sharing of powers between the EU institutions, and between the EU and national institutions, that differs according to both the policy issue and the EU's evolutionary stage. The basic trend is towards greater supranationalization of policy-making, with increasing numbers of policy issues decided upon at EU level, and with the EU institutions — particularly the European Parliament — given increasing powers. In some policy areas, the member states have agreed a system of qualified majority voting. The European Central Bank has sole charge of monetary policy in the euro-zone. The European Court of Justice (ECJ) has done much to make the EU a rule-based polity in which national law is often inferior to its European equivalent. Everyday decision-making results from processes of network-creation and contestation which can empower civil society and other interest groups, and also ensures that the de facto balance of power between the institutions is often less clear-cut than the Treaty rules indicate (Richardson, 2006). However, three important caveats apply. First, the member states set the EU's overall agenda and agree on new treaties. Second, the member states are the most powerful decision-makers in the day-to-day running of the EU, with certain areas of policy, such as tax, kept firmly at national level, while other policy areas such as defence policy are decided at EU level, but intergovernmentally. Third, the EU increasingly uses 'soft law' as a means of making decisions, so in many cases the shift away from national sovereignty is less than appears at first.[12]

The EU can expand both its policy scope and its membership, taking on new competences as a result of both recalculated cost-benefit analyses by the member states and supranational policy entrepreneurship. EU reforms and competence change are largely reactive, responses to external challenges such as enhanced economic competition or changed geopolitical circumstances such as '1989'. The EU's main competences are in economic, environmental and agricultural policies, not hard security. There is also a redistributive 'cohesion policy', which compensates from the EU budget areas of member states that are disadvantaged by the formation of the internal market. Strategic leadership (when it exists) has tended to come from the Franco-German axis, although the Commission has played a key role at certain moments, notably during the early and mid-1980s, and the European Court of Justice has also sporadically shaped the integration process. The EU coexists with both opt-outs and rival policy regimes. For example, the common travel area between the UK and Ireland rivals the EU's 'Schengen programme' of personal freedom of movement, from which both Dublin and London opt out. The EU seeks to replicate its norms through processes of enlargement to neighbouring third countries and development aid, and this 'Europeanization' strategy has been very successful.

ASEAN functioning is based on the 'ASEAN Way', with primacy given to norms of informality and non-interference. It has managed to create a successful external policy, notably via the establishment of the ASEAN Regional Forum and ASEAN Plus Three projects, in which ASEAN has managed to export not just its influence but also its norms. However, quiet reformulation of the ASEAN Way has been ongoing for some time; core norms are being revised to meet the challenges of increased interdependence between member states, and also their increased diversity in the wake of enlargement to Cambodia, Myanmar, Laos and Vietnam. This diversity has been values-based (the 'CMLV states' are all in transition from communism), and also economic, with talk of a multi-tier ASEAN as commonplace as calls for a more active sense of regional solidarity (Acharya, 2001; Pangestu, 2005). Institution-making has occurred, thanks to the institutionalization of the ASEAN summit, and the upgrading of the ASEAN secretariat and General Secretary, even if member states retain the lion's share of administrative power. The 1997 financial crisis ultimately broadened the range of issues with which ASEAN engages. That said, decision-making remains almost entirely in the hands of the member states, and is by consensus. Non-state actors have a small emerging role as co-shapers of the agenda in certain new policy issues addressed by ASEAN, via Track Two measures which blur the governmental/non-governmental distinction somewhat.

Both the deepening and the widening of the ASEAN agenda are best understood as crisis-response measures, part of the Association's quest for continued relevance after the Cold War. This has been particularly evident in 'new' security issues such as the environment and migration, but has also taken place in economic cooperation, with the agreement to form an ASEAN Free Trade Area and, in Vision 2020, an ambitious programme of cooperation across a wide range of issue areas.[13] However, doubts about ASEAN's ability to deliver Vision 2020 persist, not least because of a leadership vacuum. Moreover, a plethora of bilateral arrangements between ASEAN member states exists; this state of affairs has been considered a key part of what distinguishes the 'ASEAN Way' from 'Western' forms of multilateralism.

APEC, in contrast, has an almost purely economic agenda based on trade liberalization. However, APEC *can* address other issues. Asian, and particularly Japanese, opposition to liberalization has seen APEC develop a concern with economic cooperation, and it has also reached into issues such as gender equality. Moreover, APEC is capable of enlargement — albeit with a rationale that has been criticized for lacking clarity and logic. APEC has pledged itself to deepening its economic cooperation programme, with the 1994 Bogor Declaration constituting a commitment to develop a trade-barrier-free zone by 2020 (although developed countries in APEC are due to complete this by 2010, and do not appear to be on schedule). APEC also has at least some concern with internal development policy. This is not redistributive, but does entail both technical assistance measures and giving temporary derogations to member governments unable to keep pace with those in the vanguard. Opt-outs for objecting states are sometimes necessary in order for the majority to make progress on that issue (such as Japan's opt-outs over the liberalization of forestry and fisheries), and APEC has long accepted the idea of multi-speed cooperation as a model (for example the Early Voluntary Sectoral Liberalization programme, or EVSL).[14]

The smooth working of APEC depends on bilateral relations between its key states, with the functioning of the grouping dependent on the value attached to it by its most important members at any given time, particularly the US. The decision rule is consensus, with Asian member governments resisting the attempts for further institutionalization (beyond the agreement to formalize meetings between heads of member governments as summits) made by the US and Australia. APEC's relationship with the WTO has also been key. At times, the latter has been a useful device for the resolution of problems incapable of solution within APEC, but this very success has had negative impacts on the calculations of key member governments regarding APEC's utility. Member governments retain all formal power, and there is no independent APEC secretariat. However, the initial APEC agenda was set to a great extent by actors who were, if not completely non-governmental, at least at one remove from the national governments (the Eminent Persons Group), and non-state actors can still have an impact indirectly, for example via their access to domestic decision-making. With the US reluctant to make sacrifices for, or pay regular attention to, APEC, leadership is provided by Japan and Australia. This can be a source of tension in the bloc, as Canberra and Tokyo are often considered to be proxies for Washington. The 1997 financial crisis has had a major impact on APEC, but not a transformative one; instead, it has fostered a flurry of new bilateral relations, and a shift by its Asian members towards cooperation in ASEAN and APT networks, as a function of new calculations about the desirability of neoliberalism and the dependability of the US.

Thus, hypothesis two appears water-tight. In all three regions, development has been uneven, and although their policy scope can be both broadened and deepened, this tends to take considerable time and require a significant external shock to catalyse extensive reform. Member governments retain core decision-making powers, even if civil society and other non-state actors can be more influential than appears at first sight. Moreover, in each of the regions studied, there is a tendency to rely on multi-speed approaches to common policy, and even opt-outs; informal decision-making is used as much as possible. Even in the EU, the complex sharing of powers between the legislative institutions leads to a reliance upon informal politics, and most of the EU's key new ventures have been decided intergovernmentally or by soft policy.

Socialization

The EU has had a clear socialization impact on its member states. The EU is, *inter alia*, a security community and has fundamentally altered the ways in which its member states conceive of dealing with each other in terms of defence and security. The interlocking of the EU and national levels of governance means that the EU has had two further important socialization effects: on actor behaviour and world views. Thus, the ways in which elite actors consider it legitimate or useful to approach 'everyday' policy have also become increasingly 'Europeanized'. The Copenhagen Criteria and conditionality measures set out values and norms to which aspirant member states and those seeking aid from the EU must conform, essentially requiring liberal democracy, as discussed in chapter three of this volume. The EU has a Charter of Fundamental Rights that may become binding law, and has also had an important impact on interest group use of political and legal opportunity structures.

However, the socialization effect of the EU also has clear limits, particularly regarding the growth of shared values on a wider range of issues. After 50 years, there is only limited convergence around an EU norm on, say, abortion, and the EU suffers from a notorious, if often misunderstood, legitimacy crisis (Warleigh, 2003). *Juste retour*, or fair return on contributions, dominates EU budget politics, not solidarity. Member state nationals enjoy a unique legal status as both EU and national citizens, but neither this nor freedom of movement have eroded the primacy of national identity.[15] Enlargement to Central and Eastern European states has proved very controversial, and has produced more questions about the viability of a European identity than positive answers — although previous enlargements indicate this may not be a permanent problem.

ASEAN's socialization impact is rather impressive. Its coherence and durability reflect member state socialization into a new identity and set of norms which were previously latent at best. This is beginning to bite more deeply into the domestic structures and norms of member states, with, for example, conditionality placed on Cambodia's membership and shifts towards a more active policy to aid less developed member states since the CLMV enlargement. Since its inception, new states have joined ASEAN and adopted its norms, often as part of the transition from communism. Moreover, ASEAN has succeeded in norm exportation to other networks of which it is the core, giving it some ability to socialize third countries. On the minus side, however, ASEAN has not succeeded in establishing a common Southeast Asian political culture, and member states remain clearly divided on certain key issues, such as human rights (Thailand and the Philippines are at one [liberal] extreme, while Burma/Myanmar is at the other). The CLMV enlargement has diluted member states' sense of 'we-ness' even though it has prompted calls for a more active development policy. Moreover, on the back of the 1997 crisis, ASEAN identity may be losing out to a rising sense of 'East Asian-ness' which extends beyond the Association to China, Japan and South Korea.

APEC's initial socialization effect was strong at elite level, as the bloc partially owes its existence to an explicit subordination of 'Asian values' to neoliberalism. Moreover, the institutionalization of APEC summits and the perceived utility of their conclusions socialized actors into a new forum, and a somewhat artificial region began to embed itself. However, later socialization processes are not good auguries for APEC success. Since the financial crisis of 1997, instead of an Asia-Pacific identity, a sense of *Asian* identity and shared interests between Asian members has been more discernible. The role of Australia and New Zealand in the bloc is very controversial, with many Asians considering these states to be culturally beyond the bounds of meaningful cooperation. The initial acceptance of neoliberalism has also been seriously questioned, not least by Japan. APEC has enlarged on six occasions, but has not had an impact on the fundamental calculations, norms and interests of its member economies — particularly the US. The attempt to devise an 'Asia-Pacific Way' has not yet been successful, revealing more differences than commonalities, and there is little if any popular sense of APEC identity.

Thus, hypothesis three appears rightly to imply that regionalized identities are difficult to generate and sustain. Even the EU finds this problematic. APEC identity has fallen foul of geo-economics, although its initial success implies that suitable future geopolitical trends might reverse this. ASEAN identity initially proved strong, but, as in the EU case, has been strained by enlargement. It also seems that regions are fundamentally about joint problem-solving rather than giving expression to pre-existing senses of identity. However, the hypothesis appears weaker in suggesting that policy-learning will be more common than new regional identities. Arguably each of the regions began, in part, as an attempt to engineer a new identity, even if this was not intended to replace national equivalents. In APEC, this original act of creation has had a greater impact than policy-learning, because it established the frame for the bloc and, in its failure to resonate post-1997, restricted the scope for policy-learning between members. In ASEAN, policy learning as opposed to socialization of general norms is a recent development, facilitated by often less than overt adaptations of the ASEAN Way. Atypically, the EU is replete with examples of policy-learning at both macro (or normative) and meso (or day-to-day politics) levels — this is the essence of Europeanization and much EU 'soft policy'.

Impact

Through various means — EC law, de facto constitutionalization of the Treaties, explicit agreement by the member governments — the EU has transformed the meaning of national sovereignty within its borders. Major structural and policy adjustments to conform with EU policy or systemic needs have been undertaken, and in some issue areas member states have effectively abandoned their sovereignty, for example competition policy. As a security community, the EU has had a significant impact on the relations between its member states, and has coupled this with major successes in economic integration such as the internal market. Through its economic power, the EU is a major player in world trade politics, and is also, increasingly, a major actor in non-trade aspects of diplomacy. Thus, although it is easy to point to failures and incompleteness in some of the EU's achievements — for instance, the limited progress in defence policy — there is no doubt regarding the structural and material impact of the Union both domestically and abroad.

ASEAN has had limited impact on the structures of its member states, mostly centred on its progress towards constituting a security community, with little impact on trade patterns between its member states. However, it has begun to deepen its capacity for such impact in recent years, with the revisions to the 'ASEAN Way' and the shift towards addressing a broader range of issues such as tariff reduction. ASEAN has gained institutional depth, lending some credibility to the Vision 2020 strategy. ASEAN's primary impact to date, however, may be its capacity to reinforce its member states as a collective in other forums, such as APEC or the ARF. It has also had an impact on the foreign policies of the regional powers beyond its membership, Japan and China.

APEC has had a marginal impact on the economic development of its members, given the 1997 crisis and its aftermath. Indeed, the direction of influence is more the reverse, with member economy domestic politics impacting negatively on APEC's development capacity and state decisions to join or use APEC largely a function of other, higher-priority goals: China's accession can be seen as part of its bid to balance Japan and gain credibility for its WTO membership case. APEC has acquired competence in a greater range of policy areas than it initially enjoyed, but has not generated meaningful obligations on its members in these areas of policy either, not least because of its norm of voluntarism. That said, APEC decisions have sometimes been used discursively to justify national policy content, and by providing a forum for elite idea exchange that can then shape national policy-making, APEC's influence may sometimes have been greater than appears obvious.[16]

Thus, hypothesis four appears to hold valid in its first part. In all cases studied here, the region is a means of strengthening its members against third countries, even if in APEC this capacity can be used only sporadically. The second part of the hypothesis is more problematic. The EU's domestic material impact is incontestable. ASEAN's domestic impact is less obvious, but growing, particularly via its insertion into the APT process. However, the APEC case asks searching questions about the domestic impact of regional associations or blocs, and in particular the role of shared norms, identities and non-voluntary approaches to policy delivery as necessary background conditions. In this case, ASEAN may provide interesting lessons.

Conclusions: Assessing the Framework

This chapter discussed some of the principal epistemological issues for scholars trying to undertake theoretically informed comparative study of contemporary regionalization. It argued that the most suitable way to do this was via the elaboration of a conceptual framework, to be treated as work in progress, which could be tested and refined. The chapter then sought to do just this by comparing the EU, ASEAN and APEC. Clearly, a full testing of the framework requires application to a wider range of cases — not least to regions in North, Latin and South America, and Africa. It would also benefit from drawing on original empirical work rather than solely upon secondary literature. This points to the limits of the 'lone scholar' model of research, and also to the need for a long-term programme of study.

Nonetheless, the framework has provided a useful means to marshal information regarding each of the regions under the microscope, and thereby to compare them. Although readers will judge for themselves whether this has altered their perceptions of any of the regions concerned, from the perspective of theory building and designing future research it has proved beneficial in demonstrating the utility of the independent variables that were selected, and also in refining the hypotheses. It has also shown that the EU can usefully be chosen as a comparator in such studies, and that there are more similarities between the regions studied here than first meets the eye.

By way of conclusion, it seems appropriate to re-state the four hypotheses of the framework as they now stand.

Hypothesis One: States take part in regionalization projects because they perceive a common interest in managing the security consequences of globalization and see this as a means to address the priorities of the US.

Hypothesis Two: Regionalization is a stop-go process (one that is prone to fits and starts) dominated by member governments and dictated by their interests, with a tendency towards informal decision-making.

Hypothesis Three: Joint problem-solving by member governments is a more frequent outcome of regionalization than regionalized identity.

Hypothesis Four: Regionalization empowers member governments vis-à-vis third countries, with norms of non-voluntarism required for a significant structural impact on member states/economies.

Hypothesis Two is substantively unchanged, but all the others have been modified. Hypothesis One upgrades the importance of the US in the establishment of regionalization processes, but whether this role is positive (providing support) or negative (providing impetus for regionalization in opposition to Washington) is likely to vary.[17] Hypothesis Three no longer focuses on policy-learning, which instead will be added to the list of issues to investigate under the 'socialization' independent variable. Hypothesis Four refines its predecessor by suggesting that the key catalyst for domestic impact is non-voluntarism as a governance norm. This should not be mistaken for a focus on deep institutionalism; ASEAN shows potential for both conditionality and limited institutional depth to coexist, and the EU shows how deep institutionalism often belies implementation deficiencies. The Sisyphean task continues!

Notes

1. I am grateful to Richard Stubbs for comments on a previous draft. All remaining weaknesses are, of course, my responsibility.

2. See Hettne's distinction between regionalization, which includes bottom-up, informal and non-state actor elements, and regionalism, which is state-driven and focused on the construction of regional organizations (Hettne, n.d.). This chapter focuses on three regional organizations, but understands them to be situated in broader regional contexts, as indicated by the range of variables.
3. 'Intradisciplinarity' expresses 'the need of scholars of a given discipline to ensure they engage with work undertaken in all pertinent subfields of their subject ... a conscious effort by scholars to learn what they can from — and teach what they can to — other scholars in their own discipline' (Warleigh 2004: 303). It is intended to complement interdisciplinarity.
4. A good example is the failure to grasp the nature of European Community law and the implications of various landmark rulings by the European Court of Justice.
5. To deal effectively with complex contemporary political issues, regions may have to develop stronger formal institutions than originally envisaged (Tay et al., 2004). However, this is an argument about the required structures of a regional entity, and not necessarily one about how such phenomena should be studied.
6. This can be understood as 'that totality of political structures, agents and processes, with transnational properties, that ... have developed a high level of *thick* interconnectedness and an element of *thin* community that transcends the territorial state' (Higgott and Ougaard, 2002: p. 12, emphasis in original).
7. The '$N = 1$ problem' refers to a basic problem of social science theory-building: how can we make theory, which is by definition supposed to be generalizable, if we consider we have a unique phenomenon under the microscope? See Rosamond, 2000 for an overview of how this has applied to EU studies/European integration theory.
8. For a broader discussion of these variables and hypotheses than space allows here and a typology of regionalization, see Warleigh-Lack 2006.
9. This overlaps with the evaluation element of the second variable. Indeed the four variables set out here are distinguished for analytical purposes only: feedback loops and inter-linkages are likely findings of empirical work.
10. For excellent overviews of the state of the art in EU studies, see Bourne and Cini, 2006 and Jørgensen, Pollack and Rosamond, 2007. The ASEAN and APEC studies works consulted are listed in the reference section.
11. This is considered a unique process relying on consensus, discretion, informality, non-confrontation and expediency — a deliberate contrast with 'Western' emphasis on bargaining and formal institutions (Acharya, 1997).
12. See Wallace, 2005 for a discussion of EU 'policy modes', and its trend towards soft policy.
13. Vision 2020 was agreed at the 2003 Bali summit. It pledges ASEAN to a deeper form of integration using similar terminology to that of the EU — ASEAN would become based on its own 'three pillars', and would upgrade its competence in political, security, economic and social policy areas. See Weatherbee, 2005.
14. The EVSL programme is often considered substantively unsuccessful, but shows the flexibility of APEC's working methods.

15. See Standard Eurobaramoter 54.1 (2000) for particularly interesting data regarding how EU citizens consider national and European elements of their identities.
16. See Garnaut, 2000.
17. US involvement in regionalization processes is a function of its strategy to create an imperium (Katzenstein, 2005).

References

Acharya, A. (1997) 'Ideas, Identity and Institution-Building: From the "ASEAN Way" to the "Asia-Pacific Way"?', *The Pacific Review* 10. 3, pp. 319–46.

Acharya, A. (2001) *Constructing a Security Community in Southeast Asia: ASEAN and the Problem of Regional Order*, London: Routledge.

Aggarwal, V. (1993) 'Building International Institutions in Asia-Pacific', *Asian Survey* 23. 11, pp. 1029–42.

Best, E. (2006) 'Regional Integration and (Good) Regional Governance: Are Common Standards and Indicators Possible?', in P. De Lombaerde (ed.) *Assessment and Measurement of Regional Integration*, London: Routledge, pp.183–214.

Bourne, A. and Cini, M. (eds) (2006) *Advances in European Union Studies*, Basingstoke: Palgrave.

Coombes, D. (1970) *Politics and Bureaucracy in the European Community*, London: George Allen and Unwin.

Garnaut, R. (2000) 'Introduction: APEC Ideas and Reality: History and Prospects', in I. Yamazawa (ed.) *Asia-Pacific Economic Cooperation: Challenges and Tasks for the Twenty-First Century*, London: Routledge, 2000, pp. 1–18.

Haas, E. (1961) 'International Integration: The European and the Universal Process', *International Organization* 15, pp. 366–92.

Hettne, B. (n.d.) 'Beyond the "New" Regionalism', available at [http://www.eki/liu.se/content/1/c4/36/46/autumn20%- %20NPE_Hettne_3.pdf], accessed 28 November 2005.

Hettne, B. (2002) 'The Europeanisation of Europe: Endogenous and Exogenous Dimensions', *Journal of European Integration* 24. 4, pp. 325–40.

Hettne, B. (2003) 'The New Regionalism Revisited', in F. Söderbaum and T. Shaw (eds) *Theories of New Regionalism: A Palgrave Reader*, Basingstoke: Palgrave, pp. 22–42.

Hettne, B. (2005) 'Regionalism and World Order', in M. Farrell, B. Hettne and L. Van Langenhove (eds) *Global Politics of Regionalism: Theory and Practice*, London: Pluto Press, pp. 269–86.

Higgott, R. and Ougaard, M. (2002) 'Introduction: Beyond System and Society — Towards a Global Polity?', in M. Ougaard and R. Higgott (eds) *Towards a Global Polity* London: Routledge, pp. 1–19.

Jørgensen, K.E., Pollack, M. and Rosamond, B. (eds) (2007) *Handbook of European Union Politics*, London: Sage.

Katzenstein, P (2005) *A World of Regions: Asia and Europe in the American Imperium*, Ithaca: Cornell University Press.

Laursen, F. (2003) 'International Regimes or Would-be Polities? Some Concluding Questions and Remarks', in F. Laursen (ed.) *Comparative Regional Integration: Theoretical Perspectives*, Aldershot: Ashgate, pp. 283–93.

Pangestu, M. (2005): 'Southeast Asian Regional and International Economic Cooperation', in D. Weatherbee (ed.) *International Relations in Southeast Asia: The Struggle for Autonomy*, Oxford: Rowman and Littlefield.

Ravenhill, M. (2001) *APEC and the Construction of Pacific Rim Regionalism*, Cambridge: Cambridge University Press.

Richardson, J. (2006) 'Policy-making in the EU: Interests, Ideas and Garbage Cans of Primeval Soup', in J. Richardson (ed.) *European Union Power and Policy-making*, 3rd edition, London: Routledge, pp. 3–30.

Rosamond, B. (2000) *Theories of European Integration*, Basingstoke: Macmillan.

Söderbaum, F. and Shaw, T. (eds) (2003) *Theories of New Regionalism: A Palgrave Reader*, Basingstoke: Palgrave.

Tay, S. (2004) 'ASEAN and East Asia: A New Regionalism?', in S. Tay, J. Estanislao and H. Soesastro (eds) *Reinventing ASEAN*, 2nd edition, Singapore: Institute of Southeast Asian Studies, pp. 206–25.

Tay, S., Estanislao, J. and Soesastro, H. (eds) (2004) *Reinventing ASEAN*, 2nd edition, Singapore: Institute of Southeast Asian Studies.

Van Langenhove, L. (2006) 'Towards a Qualitative Monitoring of Regional Integration', in P. De Lombaerde (ed.) *Assessment and Measurement of Regional Integration*, London: Routledge, pp. 42–51.

Wæver, O. (2004) 'Discursive Approaches', in A. Wiener and T. Diez (eds) *European Integration Theory*, Oxford: Oxford University Press, pp. 197–215.

Wallace, H. (2005) 'An Institutional Anatomy and Five Policy Modes', in H. Wallace, W. Wallace and M. Pollack (eds) *Policy-Making in the European Union*, 5th edition, Oxford: Oxford University Press, pp. 49–90.

Warleigh, A. (2003) *Democracy in the European Union: Theory, Practice and Reform*, London: Sage.

Warleigh, A. (2004) 'In Defence of Intra-disciplinarity: "European Studies", the "New Regionalism" and the Issue of Democratisation', *Cambridge Review of International Affairs* 17. 2, pp. 301–18.

Warleigh, A. (2006) 'Learning from Europe? EU Studies and the Re-thinking of "International Relations"', *European Journal of International Relations* 12. 1, pp. 31–51.

Warleigh-Lack, A. (2006) 'Towards a Conceptual Framework for Regionalisation: Bridging "New Regionalism" and "Integration Theory"', *Review of International Political Economy* 13(5), pp. 750–71.

Weatherbee, D. (ed.) (2005) *International Relations in Southeast Asia: The Struggle for Autonomy* Oxford: Rowman and Littlefield.

Wiener, A. and Diez, T. (eds) (2004) *European Integration Theory*, Oxford: Oxford University Press.

3
The East Asian Experience of Regionalism
Derek McDougall

Introduction

The focus for this chapter is the East Asian experience of regionalism. It examines the shape of regionalism in East Asia, and attempts to explain the origins and development of this phenomenon. For the purposes of this chapter East Asia comprises Northeast Asia (China, together with Taiwan and Hong Kong, Japan, and the two Koreas) and Southeast Asia (the ten members of the Association of Southeast Asian Nations (ASEAN) and East Timor). Other countries are involved in East Asian affairs, including Russia (particularly through the Russian Far East), the United States, Canada, Australia, New Zealand and India. The US and a number of these countries have promoted the Asia-Pacific concept as a means of legitimizing their involvement in East Asia.

In the history of regionalism in East Asia it is only relatively recently that there have been organizations or groupings relating to this region as such. Among the current organizations the earliest to be formed was ASEAN, dating from 1967. It originally focused on non-communist Southeast Asia, rather than the whole of Southeast Asia. Asia-Pacific Economic Cooperation (APEC) and the ASEAN Regional Forum (ARF), founded in 1989 and 1994 respectively, were Asia-Pacific in focus. It was only after the Asian financial crisis of 1997 that groupings with a specifically East Asian focus emerged: ASEAN Plus Three and then, in 2005, the East Asian Summit (EAS).

If it is these various groupings that constitute regionalism as it affects East Asia, what does this phenomenon amount to? It would be a gross exaggeration to label this situation as 'regional integration'. It would be more accurate to describe it as one where various states have come together to pursue objectives that they believe are best promoted on a regional level rather than on the basis of action by just one or a few states. In most cases the goals set are limited in scope and the level of organizational development is low. ASEAN would be the most organizationally developed of the various groupings, but most members uphold a traditional view of sovereignty and its secretariat does not amount to a large bureaucracy. At the other end of the spectrum the EAS so far amounts to brief annual summit meetings, beginning in December 2005. Comparisons with the European Union are not very helpful. As Marchand and her colleagues argue, one serious problem with studies in this area is 'a tendency to use highly institutionalized forms of regionalization, in particular the EU and NAFTA, as the norm for understanding contemporary practices and processes of regionalization' (Marchand et al., 1999, p. 903). Although there might be some overlap in terms of the impetus for regionalism, the EU has moved more in the direction of a superstate or at the very least a highly integrated regional association, whereas East Asian regionalism has been much more circumscribed in the way it has developed.

It follows then that the task of this chapter is to explain why regionalism in East Asia has developed as it has. The argument presented here is that the development of regionalism in East Asia has been the outcome of the interaction of various factors. Priority is given to the role of the major powers in influencing this process, but middle and small powers have also had an impact in some situations. Some distinction needs to be drawn between Northeast Asia and Southeast Asia, with the major powers being more influential in the former. Alongside the role of states, developments in the international political economy have also been an important factor affecting regionalism in East Asia. The way in which the different factors have related to each other has varied also in relation to the particular historical phase. Issues concerning the Cold War and decolonization were important in the 1960s, whereas in the post-Cold War era the configuration of political and economic circumstances has been different.

The theoretical perspectives upon which this chapter draws are varied. At one level the argument is realist, given the emphasis on the role of the key states and the way in which their interaction has affected the development of regionalism in East Asia. The US has been a leading actor in this process (see Katzenstein, 2005), but the emphasis here is on the interaction of the relevant powers rather than the dominant role of the hegemon. Constructivist and liberal institutionalist approaches are also relevant. The development of regionalism in East Asia has been influenced by the perceptions of the various players. Insofar as the vision of how regionalism should develop has been a limited one or based on particular assumptions, this has been an influence in its own right. From a liberal institutionalist perspective there is an argument that the way the regional institutions themselves have developed has also been an influence. The process is not only determined by the interaction of the states involved (or not involved as the case may be) but is also affected by the institutional momentum set in train by the organizations, and by the configuration of organizations within the region; ASEAN's leading role in relation to a number of developments is a case in point.[1] While priority is given to political factors as an explanation for the direction taken by regionalism in East Asia, the impact of developments affecting the world economy also needs to be considered. In the post-Cold War era in particular the countries of East Asia, along with countries in other 'regions' of the world have looked to regionalism as one way of enhancing their position in relation to economic globalization.

In the body of the chapter the argument will be developed in relation to three main aspects of regionalism in East Asia: Southeast Asian regionalism, mainly manifested in ASEAN; Asia-Pacific regionalism (APEC, ARF); and East Asian regionalism as such (APT, EAS). Although these manifestations of regionalism now overlap, in terms of origins these groupings represent different phases in the history of regionalism in East Asia, with ASEAN dating from the 1960s, the Asia-Pacific groupings from the late 1980s and early 1990s, and the East Asian groupings from the late 1990s and early 21st century. The dynamics have varied in each instance, but a closer study of each dimension does give some substance to the argument about the way in which the various manifestations of regionalism derive from the character of interstate interactions at particular times and in particular contexts.

Southeast Asian Regionalism: ASEAN

Southeast Asian regionalism, focusing mainly on ASEAN, emerged in particular political circumstances in the 1960s. Earlier versions of regionalism had been very much influenced by the Cold War situation as it affected Southeast Asia, and this dimension was not absent in relation to ASEAN. The Southeast Asia Treaty Organization (SEATO) had been formed in 1954, mainly at the instigation of the US. The US had found it difficult to accept the outcome of the First Indochina War as embodied in the Geneva Agreement of July 1954. The US therefore looked to SEATO as an anti-communist organization to contain any further communist advance in Southeast Asia. As a manifestation of Southeast Asian regionalism SEATO was very limited, with Thailand and the Philippines as the only Southeast Asian members; Cambodia, Laos and South Vietnam were designated as 'protocol states' to whom the provisions of the Manila Treaty would apply should they come under communist threat. Most of the members of SEATO were from outside Southeast Asia: the US, the UK, France, Australia, New Zealand and Pakistan. Although SEATO was invoked from time to time for largely 'window dressing' purposes during the Vietnam War in the 1960s, it did not play any substantive role and was wound up in 1977.

The Association of Southeast Asia (ASA), formed in 1961, included not just Thailand and the Philippines but also Malaya. However, like SEATO, it was perceived primarily as an anti-communist grouping, which impeded its ability to become a more comprehensive organization. In any event, ASA became redundant with the formation of ASEAN in 1967.

While ASEAN's foundation was influenced by the broader Cold War setting, the main impetus came from within the region itself. The impact of the Cold War was most obvious in the US intervention in Vietnam and in the confrontation between the US and China. ASEAN was essentially an arrangement to bring the non-communist countries of maritime Southeast Asia together with a view to ensuring that any differences between them were resolved peacefully. The background to this development was Indonesia's campaign of confrontation or 'Konfrontasi' that had been launched in September 1963 against the newly proclaimed federation of Malaysia (uniting previously independent Malaya with newly decolonized Singapore, Sarawak and Sabah). From Indonesia's perspective Malaysia was a manifestation of British neo-colonialism, and therefore to be opposed. The differences between Malaysia and the Philippines over the latter's claim to Sabah (Gordon, 1966, chapter 1) should also be noted. President Macapagal of the Philippines promoted Maphilindo as an association or confederation for linking Malaysia, the Philippines and Indonesia; it was established in August 1963 but did not survive the formation of Malaysia in the following month.

With Sukarno's fall from power following the attempted coup of 30 September 1965, there was scope for new directions in the international politics of non-communist Southeast Asia. ASEAN was essentially an initiative among the founding members, rather than arising from pressures from external powers such as the US. This is not to say that ASEAN was not viewed favourably by the Western powers in particular. ASEAN was a sign of strengthened political resolve among the non-communist Southeast Asian countries. In the long term it made it easier for the US to look beyond the Vietnam War in terms of its engagement with the region;

it also made it easier for British withdrawal from 'east of Suez' to occur (announced in 1968). In the Southeast Asian context the underlying rationale for ASEAN was that it would provide a means for Indonesia to relate peacefully to its neighbours; situations such as 'Konfrontasi' could be avoided (see Acharya, 2001, pp. 48–9). At the same time the explicit objectives of ASEAN (as set out in the Bangkok Declaration of August 1967) emphasized political, social, economic and cultural cooperation. Clearly ASEAN was not intended to be another SEATO.

An interesting development in the early history of ASEAN was the Declaration of Southeast Asia as a Zone of Peace, Freedom and Neutrality (ZOPFAN) in November 1971. The Declaration emphasized the vision the ASEAN countries had for their region, while at the same time demonstrating their ability to compromise among contending outlooks. The aspiration was that Southeast Asia should be 'free from any form or manner of interference by outside Powers' (Sandhu et al., 1992, p. 539). While Malaysia had been most committed to establishing ZOPFAN, it was Indonesia that argued in favour of the declaration coming from the Southeast Asian countries alone; Thailand and the Philippines wished to retain their existing security links with the US, but believed the wording of the Declaration was compatible with that goal. Although clearly the external powers remained involved in Southeast Asia in various ways, ZOPFAN was indicative of the developing norms within ASEAN and also demonstrated both the possibilities and the limitations in terms of ASEAN countries shaping their own environment.

This determination to be a major factor in shaping the international situation in Southeast Asia was most strongly evidenced at the time of the Bali summit in February 1976. Previously ASEAN meetings had been attended by the foreign ministers of member countries; the Bali summit was the first meeting attended by heads of government. A permanent secretariat was established in Jakarta to provide ASEAN with a stronger organizational focus. Two major statements signalled the new direction being taken by ASEAN. The Declaration of ASEAN Concord was a statement of underlying principles and objectives; the Treaty of Amity and Cooperation (TAC) referred, among other things, to the promotion of 'common ideals and aspirations of international peace and stability in the region and all other matters of common interest' (McDougall, 2002, p. 179, Article 4). The background to ASEAN's renewal was the collapse of the Saigon government and US withdrawal from Vietnam; at the same time the Sino-American rapprochement of 1972 had brought about greater fluidity in the international politics of East Asia as a whole, and indeed of the entire Asia-Pacific. Through the developments set in train at the Bali summit ASEAN was asserting that it would be a major factor in the international politics of Southeast Asia and beyond.

A clear test of what this would amount to was the Third Indochina War that arose after Vietnam intervened in late 1978 to depose the Khmer Rouge government in Cambodia, mainly in response to that government's anti-Vietnamese stance rather than to end the 'killing fields' as such. The traditional rivalry between Thailand and Vietnam meant that this move was perceived as threatening by Thailand. Thailand accordingly called on its fellow ASEAN members for support. In terms of involvement by the major powers the Soviet Union was the main backer for Vietnam, whereas support for the Cambodian resistance (dominated by the Khmer Rouge) came primarily from China. The US and ASEAN, in opposing Vietnam, also gave support to the anti-Vietnamese Cambodian coalition. An external settlement of the Cambodian war was effectively achieved with the Sino-Soviet rapprochement of 1989. Agreement among the internal parties, leading to a period of transition under United Nations auspices in 1992–93, came about with the Paris agreement of 1991. ASEAN was a factor in the way the Third Indochina War developed, but perhaps not a major factor. The conflict strengthened the norm of solidarity among member countries when a member felt threatened. At the same time there were differences of emphasis within ASEAN, with Thailand and Singapore being most resolutely anti-Vietnamese over the issue, whereas Malaysia and Indonesia were more inclined to believe that accommodation with Vietnam could be achieved.

During the Third Indochina War, ASEAN had remained an organization of non-communist Southeast Asian countries; with the end of that conflict the way was open for ASEAN to move towards comprehensive Southeast Asian membership. While this development might have been viewed positively by external powers such as the US, Japan and perhaps China, again the impetus came primarily from within ASEAN itself. The underlying assumption motivating expansion was that the incorporation of the Indochinese countries and Burma into ASEAN would facilitate economic development and contribute to political stability. More progressive members also saw expansion as encouraging democracy and the protection of human rights. On this basis Vietnam became a member in 1995, followed by Burma and Laos in 1997, and Cambodia in 1999.

As a virtually comprehensive organization the character of ASEAN has been largely shaped by developments within the membership. This is not to say that international politics in Southeast Asia has been determined only by ASEAN as the involvement of external powers and organizations has been important on a number of occasions. Scholars such as Amitav

Acharya have argued that ASEAN has acquired the characteristics of a 'security community', meaning that the member states invariably resolve their disputes through peaceful means (see, for example, Acharya, 2001). Disputes among members are resolved peacefully, and there is some commonality in how the ASEAN countries view the outside world. This does not mean that there are no major differences of emphasis within ASEAN, as this can sometimes be the case. However there is a political process within ASEAN, and members normally abide by the outcome of that process.

One important debate in ASEAN in the late 1990s was over the issue of 'flexible engagement' (see Henderson, 1999, pp. 48–55). Thailand and the Philippines pushed for some modification in ASEAN's more traditional approach to sovereignty. They argued that there were many 'domestic' issues occurring in ASEAN countries that had implications for other members. These included human rights issues and environmental issues (the notorious 'haze' arising from illegal forest fires in Indonesia), as well as a range of political, economic and social issues. One argument in favour of Burma's admission to ASEAN was that 'engagement' would provide a better means of furthering human rights and democracy in that country than would ostracism. ASEAN's decision, however, strongly supported by its new members, was against 'flexible engagement'. 'Enhanced interaction' was the preferred term, upholding the principle of sovereignty while also allowing for the reality of interaction occurring over many issues.

While ASEAN was engaged with its internal debates at this time, one should note that the organization was largely ineffective in dealing with a number of major issues affecting Southeast Asia. ASEAN did not play a significant role in responding to the Asian financial crisis in 1997. Member countries were circumspect towards Indonesia during the East Timor crisis in 1999, and hence did not take the lead in responding to that situation (although Thailand, the Philippines, Malaysia and Singapore did subsequently contribute). At the time of the Boxing Day tsunami in 2004, ASEAN's limited resources meant that it was not in a position to assume leadership of the international response. In all these situations major roles were played by external powers, particularly the US, with Australia also particularly prominent in East Timor and the tsunami.

While the emphasis so far has been on the political circumstances affecting ASEAN's development, increased economic globalization has also drawn attention to the way in which ASEAN has been affected by the international political economy. Promoting economic cooperation was ostensibly one of the original reasons for establishing ASEAN. This aspect of the organization was limited by the fact that most ASEAN countries have competing rather than complementary economies. Nevertheless ASEAN countries looked to the organization to develop a common position in relation to external economic issues. This was the impetus for the establishment of relationships with the major external economic partners as 'dialogue partners' from the 1970s. Attempts to promote economic cooperation within ASEAN were highlighted with the conclusion of an agreement to establish an ASEAN Free Trade Area (AFTA) in January 1992 (taking effect in 1993). Tariffs on goods manufactured within ASEAN were to be gradually reduced and eventually eliminated.

In attempting to improve the economic lot of its members ASEAN has looked beyond the promotion of regionalism to play a significant role in both the Asia-Pacific and East Asian versions of regionalism. The argument here is that ASEAN can act as a caucus within broader bodies, thus having a strong impact on the direction of those bodies. Broader groupings in turn are likely to have a greater influence at the global level. This point will be taken up in the subsequent discussions of Asia-Pacific and East Asian regionalism.

Asia-Pacific Regionalism

The Asia-Pacific approach is an aspect of regionalism that affects East Asia as a whole, not simply Southeast Asia. In assessing the Asia-Pacific approach a starting point is the way in which this approach has frequently been at odds with one focused on East Asia alone. While a definition of East Asia has been given previously, definitions of the Asia-Pacific include not just East Asia but also the US and Canada to the extent of their Pacific involvement, and Australia and New Zealand; the broadest definitions include also India and the western seaboard of Latin America. The strongest support for the Asia-Pacific approach has come from the US, based on the argument that this approach legitimizes the involvement of the US in East Asian affairs in a way that a solely East Asian approach would not (Buzan, 1998). This is not to say that the US alone has determined the way in which Asia-Pacific regionalism has developed, but that it has been a major factor. Even before specifically Asia-Pacific groupings emerged, the US attempted to shape the affairs of this region in such a way as to maximize its own influence. In this section of the chapter the focus will initially be on the underlying dynamics that have encouraged the emergence of the Asia-Pacific concept. This will be followed by specific attention to the factors underlying the establishment of APEC and the ASEAN Regional Forum (ARF).

The emergence of the Asia-Pacific approach recalls Peter Katzenstein's argument that the shape of regionalism in both Europe and Asia is related to the demands of the 'American imperium' (Katzenstein, 2005; see also Hemmer and Katzenstein, 2002). In the Asia-Pacific the emphasis during the Cold War period was not on regionalism of a multilateral kind, but rather on the development of a 'hub and spokes' security arrangement centred on the US (this approach is also referred to as the San Francisco system — see Tow et al., 1997). Japan, through the 1951 security treaty (renewed in 1960) was the linchpin in this system, particularly in relation to Northeast Asia. Security treaties with South Korea (1953) and the Republic of China (Taiwan) (1954–78) were also important. The US was linked to the Philippines and Thailand through the Manila Treaty in 1954, of which SEATO was the organizational embodiment. The ANZUS Treaty of 1951 established formal security links between the US, Australia and New Zealand, although the US–New Zealand aspect became inoperative from 1986. Much of this Cold War security structure was directed towards the containment of both China and the Union of Soviet Socialist Republics (USSR). The structure was modified in various ways from the 1970s but the underlying shape remained relatively constant. The increasing significance of East Asia in economic terms was not directly reflected in this structure. However, one rationale for the structure was that it provided positive evidence that the US was directly committed to East Asian security, thus enabling countries such as Japan and South Korea to devote more resources to productive economic development. Clearly, in terms of the development of this US-centred 'regionalism', China was for some decades the pariah; from the 1970s it was at best a 'partner' and at worst an 'adversary'.

The shape of this Asia-Pacific 'system' changed significantly from the late 1980s, with the emergence of first APEC and then ARF. However the establishment of these new groupings needs to be related to the underlying power dynamics and, in the case of APEC, changing global and regional economic circumstances. These dynamics are also important in assessing the overall significance of these Asia-Pacific bodies.

APEC's inauguration in 1989 can be most directly related to the changing dynamics within the Asia-Pacific as the 'region' had evolved to that point. The strongest impetus for the establishment of the new grouping came from Japan. While Japan might have been the linchpin among the US allies in the San Francisco system, there was also an issue for Japan about how to deal with various economic issues in its relationship with the US. Multilateralizing these issues would improve Japan's bargaining position as compared with a situation where the issues were dealt with primarily on a bilateral basis. Because Japan did not wish to become involved in conflict with the US over the proposed grouping, the leadership it provided was often low-key. Australia was often more forthright in claiming credit for its contribution, but this did not necessarily mean that it was the main instigator. The US was averse to the emergence of a new Asia-Pacific grouping that did not accord it a prominent role. Both Japan and Australia were willing to accommodate the US's wish to be part of the forum, but this is different from saying that the US was a driving force in the new development. Clearly the US wanted to exert an influence in APEC, but was not an instigator as such.[2] (On APEC's origins, see Ravenhill, 2001, chapter 2; and also Terada, 1999; Krauss, 2000).

APEC's focus in its early phase related not so much to US–Japan relations as to the broader regional and global economic context. At one level, APEC saw itself as promoting economic liberalization among its own membership but on the basis of 'open regionalism'; the reduction of economic barriers would be done in such a way as not to discriminate against non-members. At another level APEC provided a caucus that could have a liberalizing influence in relation to the Uruguay Round of the General Agreement on Tariffs and Trade (GATT). Including the US as it did, APEC could put pressure on the US to maintain a liberalizing position. It could also be a source of influence on other individual members to adhere to that position, as well as exerting pressure on the EU much more strongly than any individual member could. In relation to the North American Free Trade Agreement (NAFTA) (1994), the existence of APEC meant that the three NAFTA members who were concurrently members of APEC would be under pressure to ensure that intra-NAFTA harmonization was not at the expense of other APEC countries.

US leadership within APEC became more evident with the inauguration of the Clinton administration in 1993. The Seattle summit in November of that year was the beginning of annual meetings of heads of government. This new development meant that there were more possibilities for APEC to play a more explicitly political role in the region. At the same time, the end of the Uruguay Round in 1994 signified a reduced role for APEC in the context of global trade negotiations. APEC's limitations as a means of facilitating regional trade liberalization also became evident, particularly in 1998 when various members baulked at going ahead with tariff reductions under the scheme for early voluntary sectoral liberalization (Wesley, 2001). It is interesting to note that APEC did not feature prominently in the Doha Round from 2001 to 2006. The scope for making use of APEC for dealing with emerging political situations was evident in both 1999 and 2001. For example, in September 1999 the APEC summit in Auckland occurred at the time of the crisis in East Timor following the pro-independence result in the referendum of 30 August. The high level diplomacy that was possible in the context of the APEC meeting facilitated Indonesian consent for a UN-authorized and Australian-led operation to deal with the situation. In October 2001 the APEC summit in Shanghai provided a platform for President George W. Bush to win support from Asia-Pacific countries for his planned 'war on terrorism'. The attention given to North Korea at the November 2006 APEC meeting in Hanoi provides a more recent example.[3]

Apart from APEC, the major manifestation of Asia-Pacific regionalism particularly focused on East Asia, has been the ASEAN Regional Forum (ARF).[4] Again the impetus for this grouping came from Japan rather than from the US (Leifer, 1996, p. 23), with Australia and Canada also being strongly supportive. ARF provides a good example of how ASEAN, as the most highly developed regional organization in East Asia and indeed the Asia-Pacific, is able to influence the format of broader regional groupings. When ARF was established in 1994 it was on the basis of ASEAN providing organizational support, and with the venue to be rotated among ASEAN countries; the foreign minister of the host country would act as chair.

Having described the context in which the ARF emerged it is important to keep in mind that it is only a forum, with meetings held annually. While there might be aspirations for the ARF to contribute more effectively to conflict resolution in various situations, these aspirations have not amounted to much. Optimistically one might argue that the ARF has contributed to the extension of the 'ASEAN Way' beyond Southeast Asia, thus playing a role in the development of regional norms. More realistically one might observe that neither China nor the US has assigned much significance to the ARF as a way of dealing with major conflicts involving themselves. China is adamantly opposed to any involvement of the ARF in the Taiwan issue. Although North Korea became a member of the ARF in 2000, the ARF has had no significant involvement in the Korean issue.

As far as the Asia-Pacific dimension is concerned, it might be concluded that the development of regional institutions has been weak and is indeed faltering. While the US might have promoted the Asia-Pacific concept during the Cold War and been involved in the initiatives of the post-Cold War era, it has not been in a position to establish the primacy of this approach to regionalism. The US continues to promote an Asia-Pacific approach, but the institutionalization of this concept has been weak. Since the late 1990s the East Asian approach to regionalism has gained ground, and it is to this dimension that this chapter now turns.

East Asian Regionalism

In explaining the increasing emphasis on East Asian regionalism in more recent times this chapter again returns to the question of the underlying dynamics.[5] There had long been a focus on an East Asian or indeed more broadly Asian approach to regionalism as reflected in such movements as pan-Asianism and the prominent role of countries such as Indonesia and India in the development of the nonaligned movement from the late 1940s (on pan-Asianism, see He, 2004). The East Asian approach had to contend with the strong influence of the US and its promotion of the Asia-Pacific approach (Higgott and Stubbs, 1995). In 1989 the US was able to overcome objections to its becoming a founding member of APEC. The main advocate of an East Asian approach at this time was Dr Mahathir of Malaysia. In December 1990 he proposed an East Asian Economic Grouping to promote economic cooperation among the East Asian countries, but this was stymied by the opposition of the US, supported in this instance by Japan. Mahathir did not receive strong support from East Asian countries more generally. However, the proposal survived as the East Asian Economic Caucus, enabling East Asian countries to come together on occasions in other contexts where there might be advantages in developing a joint position.

The Asian economic crisis of 1997 provided a fillip to East Asian regionalism. South Korea, Thailand and Indonesia were the countries most directly affected, but the implications were region-wide. While there were clear views within the region about what should be done in response to the crisis, the ability of those countries to provide the lead was limited. Rescue packages for the affected countries came primarily through the International Monetary Fund (IMF), within which the US played the leading role. The IMF's approach was essentially neoliberal, requiring the governments receiving assistance to implement policies based on 'free market' assumptions. Some critics charge that the policies were in fact pro-cyclical, and in fact deepened the crisis through recommendations for increased taxes, reduced spending and higher interest rates. However the policies are characterized, they sometimes ran counter to schemes designed to assist particular groups for political reasons (for example, petrol subsidies in Indonesia) and restricting such schemes could exacerbate political and social tensions. The US blocked a proposal for an Asian Monetary Fund (AMF), emanating primarily from Japan. The AMF would have allowed for a stronger emphasis on political criteria in the provision of assistance, but this ran counter to the neoliberal approach preferred by the IMF.

In the aftermath of the Asian economic crisis there were moves towards establishing a stronger East Asian regionalism. With ASEAN taking the initiative, ASEAN Plus Three began as an informal meeting at the time of the ASEAN summit meeting in Kuala Lumpur in 1997.[6] Apart from the ASEAN members, the countries involved were China, Japan and South Korea. While the Northeast Asian countries had not taken the lead with this initiative, it was in their interests to take part in this grouping as a means of enhancing their relationships with ASEAN. ASEAN was able to take advantage of the competitive relationship between China and Japan as a way of expanding its own influence in the region. In response to the failure of the AMF proposal, a currency swap agreement was concluded by ASEAN Plus Three finance ministers in May 2000. Known as the Chiang Mai Initiative (CMI), this agreement provided for APT members to assist each other with currency transfers should the currency of a member country come under threat. As with the earlier AMF proposal, Japan would be the country best placed to assist in the event of such a contingency (see further Lincoln, 2004, chapter 8).

Apart from the CMI as a specific achievement, the APT was significant as a forum facilitating the further development of East Asian regionalism, leading to the establishment of the East Asian Summit (EAS) at Kuala Lumpur in December 2005. This process began with the appointment of an East Asian Vision Group at the second ASEAN Plus Three summit in Hanoi in 1998. Being in the driver's seat, ASEAN was in a strong position to determine the direction that East Asian regionalism would take. At the same time the views of the major regional powers, China and Japan, had to be accommodated. The US was outside the process but not without influence. One issue in the process leading to the EAS concerned the extent to which the proposed regionalism would be open or restricted. Would membership be confined to the countries normally regarded as part of Northeast or Southeast Asia, or would there be some flexibility in this matter? ASEAN succeeded in its insistence that proposed members would have to subscribe to ASEAN's Treaty of Amity and Cooperation (TAC), with its commitment to the peaceful resolution of disputes. However, countries outside the normal definition of East Asia could become members once they made this commitment. This cleared the way for India, New Zealand and Australia (initially reluctant about the TAC) to take part in the summit. The US did not sign the TAC, but nor did it seriously consider entering the process. Its interest was in ensuring that the East Asian regionalism that developed would be relatively open. It could rely on allies such as Japan and Australia to argue for a more open approach. However it should be noted that while China preferred the APT to be the driving force for East Asian regionalism believing that this situation would maximize its own influence (Malik, 2006), in the end it opted for openness as the basis for the EAS (Wen Jiaobao, 2005). This might be seen as a strategy for ensuring that the EAS did not become too strong, but, more positively, Wen Jiaobao has argued that openness could maximize the value of the summit as a forum for dialogue on regional issues. In any event the EAS's role as agreed to at the Kuala Lumpur meeting entailed it becoming essentially an annual summit of heads of governments, with an East Asian focus that was broadly defined.

A complicating factor in the development of East Asian regionalism has been the trend towards bilateralism and 'minilateralism', mainly in the form of free trade agreements (essentially agreements to liberalize the terms of trade among the signatories). This process, affecting East Asia along with other regions of the world, has been influenced by the failure of global trade negotiations (specifically the Doha Round) to make much progress. There has also been a perception that the gains available through existing regional arrangements have been limited. Many countries have taken the view that in this situation they can strengthen their position through bilateral agreements and more limited regional agreements (see further Ravenhill, 2003 and Aggarwal and Urata, 2006, especially chapters 1, 2 and 13). Some advocates of bilateralism also see this process as providing 'building blocks' both for stronger regional arrangements and as a means of encouraging progress on a multilateral front at the global level (Aggarwal and Koo, 2006, p. 295).

If we consider the development of bilateral and minilateral FTAs involving East Asian countries, these are by no means confined to East Asia. Singapore has been one of the most active countries in negotiating FTAs. As of 2004, however, Japan was the only East Asian country with which it had concluded an agreement (out of six concluded) and South Korea was the only East Asian country with which it was negotiating one (out of eight under negotiation) (Ravenhill, 2006, p. 28, Table 2.1). Of the two major East Asian powers, China has been active in pursuing an FTA with ASEAN. Under a framework agreement concluded in November 2002, the proposed FTA would take effect in 2010 for the ASEAN-6, with the four newer members following in 2015 (Kwei, 2006, p. 131). Japan has been less committed to concluding an FTA with ASEAN, although negotiations were announced in 2005. Japan's preference is for 'open regionalism', but it needs to remain competitive with China on the issue of relations with ASEAN.

Given that most FTAs involving East Asian countries have been with countries outside East Asia, one might argue that this process has not significantly contributed to the development of East Asian regionalism (the 'building block' argument). Some of the FTAs have been with the US (for example, Singapore–US concluded in 2003; Thailand–US negotiations commenced in 2004, and Malaysia–US and South Korea–US negotiations in 2006), arguably contributing to the Asia-Pacific rather than the East Asian perception of region. On the other hand should the China–ASEAN FTA acquire real substance this would be a very significant manifestation of minilateralism within the East Asian context. The same could be said for a Japan–ASEAN FTA, even though Japan's approach is rather different from China's. Both processes involving the two major East Asian powers have contributed to the emergence of the EAS, seen by many as a context for constraining Sino-Japanese rivalry. In terms of the underlying dynamics this situation highlights the significance of the Sino-Japanese relationship as a factor contributing to contemporary developments in East Asian regionalism.

Conclusion

In concluding this chapter it is useful to highlight the extent to which the general argument needs to be modified, depending on whether one is referring to the Southeast Asian, Asia-Pacific or East Asian versions of regionalism. It is also worth commenting on the overall shape of regionalism in East Asia, and its significance for the international politics of the region.

In Southeast Asia the origins and development of ASEAN draw attention to the way in which the interaction of local powers has been the main factor shaping regionalism, even though the major powers have also played a significant role. This is also the subregion where regionalism has developed most strongly, even though it remains interstate in nature and organizationally low-key. However, because regionalism is most developed in Southeast Asia this is also the subregion where one can see regionalist norms acquiring some influence, manifested most obviously in the status accorded the 'ASEAN Way' and the emergence of the elements of a 'security community'.

When we turn to the Asia-Pacific approach to regionalism, focusing particularly on its impact in East Asia, the starting point is the way in which the US has promoted this approach. During the Cold War the 'hub and spokes' approach promoted by the US was Asia-Pacific in orientation. With the post-Cold War development of a more genuinely multilateral Asia-Pacific regionalism, the US wished to play a leading role to ensure a strong influence over the process. While Japan supported US involvement, it also had its own agenda in promoting APEC as one means of multilateralizing contentious aspects of its economic relationship with the US. With weak norms and low levels of institutionalization, liberal institutionalism and constructivism appeared less relevant than in the case of ASEAN. However APEC's emergence was also influenced by the way in which economic globalization was occurring and being dealt with politically in the late 1980s and early 1990s. The significance of the ASEAN Regional Forum as an Asia-Pacific security forum should not be exaggerated. Its emergence coincided with a high point in Asia-Pacific regional sentiment, while also providing a good example of ASEAN's ability as a relatively well organized grouping to influence wider regional agendas.

With East Asian regionalism as the latest phase of regionalism affecting East Asia, we see a relative weakening in US influence. Initially encouraged by the way in which the Asian economic crisis was handled, China and Japan have been major influences shaping this phase, and ASEAN has played a pivotal role (initially through the APT). Institutionalization has been weak, and emergent norms are not yet clear. The growth of bilateralism and minilateralism has been a factor at this stage, encouraging the development of the East Asian Summit as a possible grouping within which Sino-Japanese rivalry can be managed; ASEAN again occupies an important position in this process. With the slowing of global multilateralism as a way of managing the international economy, bilateralism and minilateralism have affected East Asia as they have other regions of the world, but the impact on East Asian regionalism has been ambivalent.

Given these qualifications that might be made in relation to the general argument, how might one characterize the overall shape or architecture of regionalism in East Asia? Clearly, it is a patchwork with the significance of groupings varying depending on the part of the region one is considering. Southeast Asia is unique in the region in having ASEAN as a relatively well-developed regional organization, although the level of institutionalization is weak in global terms. The Asia-Pacific groupings, APEC and ARF, are relevant to the whole of East Asia and beyond, but are of limited political significance, and probably declining in the case of APEC. The newer East Asian regionalism is nascent, representing a change of emphasis in the international politics of the region.

The groupings that have emerged so far (APT, EAS) are weak, and are perhaps most relevant as a dimension of China–Japan–ASEAN relations; they do represent some weakening in US influence.

Having characterized the different dimensions of regionalism in East Asia, it remains to emphasize the point that regionalism is but one aspect of international politics in the region, and not a particularly dominant aspect. Although one has to make distinctions between Northeast Asia and Southeast Asia, and the characterization can vary depending on the issue area, the key factor driving international politics in the region is the triangular relationship among China, Japan and the US. Local factors are also important, manifested most obviously in the role of the middle and small powers, but extending also to the range of non-state actors affecting international politics. In Northeast Asia the role of the two Koreas and Taiwan clearly has a big impact on international politics. In Southeast Asia the major powers are relatively speaking less significant than in Northeast Asia, and the impact of local factors (including non-state aspects) more marked. Nevertheless the policies pursued by the major powers in Southeast Asia can often be a decisive influence. If one is to understand the way in which regionalism in East Asia has developed, then this broader international context needs to be kept constantly in mind.

Notes

1. Realist and constructivist arguments in relation to understanding ASEAN are discussed in *Pacific Review* 18. 1, 2005.
2. APEC's founding members in 1989 were Japan, the United States, Australia, New Zealand, Canada, South Korea and the ASEAN-6. China joined in 1991, along with Taiwan and Hong Kong (the latter two as 'economies'). Later entrants were Mexico and Papua New Guinea in 1993, Chile in 1994, and Russia, Peru and Vietnam in 1997.
3. For a critique of APEC's securitizing agenda, see Taylor (2004). For an assessment of APEC's situation as of late 2006, see the essays in Elliott et al. (2006).
4. See Leifer (1996) for an early assessment. ARF is discussed more recently in Garofano (2002), Heller (2005), Emmers (2003, chapters 1 and 5) and Caballero-Anthony (2005, chapter 4).
5. See Ravenhill (2002) and Terada (2003), for overviews and analysis. Recent book-length assessments of East Asian regionalism include Lincoln (2004) and Pempel (2005).
6. Among the useful assessments of ASEAN Plus Three are Stubbs (2002), Webber (2001), Beeson (2003) and Hund (2003).

References

Acharya, A. (2001) *Constructing a Security Community in Southeast Asia: ASEAN and the problem of regional order*, London: Routledge.
Aggarwal, V. K. and Koo, M. G. (2006) 'The evolution and implications of bilateral trade agreements in the Asia-Pacific', in V. K. Aggarwal and S. Urate (eds), *Bilateral Trade Agreements in the Asia-Pacific: Origins, Evolution, and Implications*, New York: Routledge, pp. 279–99.
Aggarwal, V. K., and Urate, S. (eds) (2006) *Bilateral Trade Agreements in the Asia-Pacific: Origins, Evolution, and Implication*, New York: Routledge.
Beeson, M. (2003) 'ASEAN Plus Three and the Rise of Reactionary Regionalism', *Contemporary Southeast Asia*, 25. 2, pp. 251–68.
Buzan, B. (1998) 'The Asia-Pacific: what sort of region in what sort of world?', in A. McGrew and C. Brook (eds), *Asia-Pacific in the New World Order*, London: Routledge, in association with the Open University, pp. 68–87.
Caballero-Anthony, M. (2005) *Regional Security in Southeast Asia: Beyond the ASEAN Way*, Singapore: Institute of Southeast Asian Studies.
Elliott, L., Ravenhill, J., Nesadurai, H. E. S., and Bisley, N. (2006) *APEC and the search for relevance: 2007 and beyond*, Keynotes 07, Canberra: Department of International Relations, Research School of Pacific and Asian Studies, Australian National University.
Emmers, R. (2003) *Cooperative Security and the Balance of Power in ASEAN and the ARF*, London: Routledge Curzon.
Garofano, J. (2002) 'Power, Institutions, and the ASEAN Regional Forum', *Asian Survey* 42. 3, pp. 502–21.
Gordon, B. K. (1966) *The Dimensions of Conflict in Southeast Asia*, Englewood Cliffs, NJ: Prentice-Hall.
He, B. (2004) 'East Asian Ideas of Regionalism: A Normative Critique', *Australian Journal of International Affairs*, 58. 1, pp. 104–25.
Heller, D. (2005) 'The Relevance of the ASEAN Regional Forum (ARF) for Regional Security in the Asia-Pacific', *Contemporary Southeast Asia*, 27. 1, pp. 123–45.
Hemmer, C., and Katzenstein, P. J. (2002) 'Why Is There No NATO in Asia? Collective Identity, Regionalism, and the Origins of Multilateralism', *International Organization* 56. 3, pp. 575–607.
Henderson, J. (1999) *Reassessing ASEAN*, Adelphi Paper 328.
Higgott, R. and Stubbs, R. (1995) 'Competing Conceptions of Economic Regionalism: APEC Versus EAEC', *Review of International Political Economy*, 2. 3 pp. 516–35.
Hund, M. (2003) 'ASEAN Plus Three: Towards a New Age of Pan-East Asian Regionalism? A Skeptic's Appraisal', *Pacific Review*, 16. 3, pp. 383–417.
Katzenstein, P. J. (2005) *A World of Regions: Asia and Europe in the American Imperium*, Ithaca: Cornell University Press.
Krauss, E. S. (2000) 'Japan, the US, and the emergence of multilateralism in Asia', *Pacific Review*, 13. 3, pp. 473–94.
Kwei, E. S. (2006) 'Chinese Trade Bilateralism: Politics Still in Command', in V. K. Aggarwal and S. Urate (eds.) *Bilateral Trade Agreements in the Asia-Pacific: Origins, Evolution, and Implications*, New York: Routledge, pp. 117–39.
Leifer, M. (1996) *The ASEAN Regional Forum*, Adelphi Paper, 302.

Lincoln, E. J. (2004) *East Asian Economic Regionalism*, New York: Council on Foreign Relations; Washington, D.C.: Brookings Institution Press.

Malik, M. (2006) 'The East Asia Summit', *Australian Journal of International Affairs*, 60. 2, pp. 207–11.

Marchand, M. H., Bøas, M. and Shaw, T. M. (1999) 'The Political Economy of New Regionalisms', *Third World Quarterly*, 20. 5, pp. 897–910.

McDougall, D. (2002) *Historical Dictionary of International Organizations in Asia and the Pacific*, Lanham, MD: Scarecrow Press.

Pempel, T. J. (ed.) (2005) *Remapping East Asia: The Construction of a Region*, Ithaca: Cornell University Press.

Ravenhill, J. (2001) *APEC and the Construction of Pacific Rim Regionalism*, Cambridge: Cambridge University Press.

Ravenhill, J. (2002) 'A Three Bloc World? The New East Asian Regionalism', *International Relations of the Asia-Pacific*, 2, pp. 167–95.

Ravenhill, J. (2003) 'The New Bilateralism in the Asia Pacific', *Third World Quarterly*, 24. 2, pp. 299–317.

Ravenhill, J. (2006) 'The Political Economy of the New Asia-Pacific Bilateralism: Benign, Banal, or simply Bad?', in V. K. Aggarwal and S. Urate (eds), *Bilateral Trade Agreements in the Asia-Pacific: Origins, Evolution, and Implications*, New York: Routledge, pp. 27–49.

Sandhu, K. S., Siddique, S., Jeshurun, C., Rajah, A., Tan, J. L. H., and Thambipillai, P., (comps) (1992) *The ASEAN Reader*, Singapore: Institute of Southeast Asian Studies.

Stubbs, R. (2002) 'ASEAN Plus Three?', *Asian Survey*, 42. 3, pp. 440–55.

Taylor, I. (2004) 'APEC, Globalization, and 9/11: The Debate on What Constitutes Asian Regionalism', *Critical Asian Studies*, 36. 3, pp. 463–78.

Terada, T. (1999) *The Genesis of APEC: Australia–Japan Political Initiatives*, Pacific Economic Papers 298, Canberra: Australia–Japan Research Centre, Australian National University.

Terada, T. (2003) 'Constructing an "East Asian" concept and growing regional identity: from EAEC to ASEAN + 3', *Pacific Review*, 16. 2, pp. 251–77.

Tow, W., Trood, R., and Hoshina, T., (eds) (1997) *Bilateralism in a Multilateral Era: The Future of the San Francisco Alliance System in the Asia-Pacific*, Tokyo: The Japan Institute of International Affairs; Centre for the Study of Australia–Asia Relations, Faculty of Asian and International Studies, Griffith University.

Webber, D. (2001) 'Two Funerals and a Wedding? The Ups and Downs of Regionalism in East Asia and Asia-Pacific after the Asian Crisis', *Pacific Review*, 14. 3, pp. 339–72.

Wen Jiabao (2005) 'Wen Jiaobao Delivers a Speech at the East Asia Summit', 14 December, Ministry of Foreign Affairs of the People's Republic of China, http://www.fmprc.gov.cn/eng/wjdt/zyjh/t226715.htm#, accessed 22 November 2006.

Wesley, M. (2001) 'APEC's Mid-Life Crisis? The Rise and Fall of Early Voluntary Sectoral Liberalization', *Pacific Affairs*, 74. 2, pp. 185–204.

4
Comparing and Contrasting Economic Integration in the Asia-Pacific Region and Europe

Bernadette Andreosso-O'Callaghan[1]

Introduction

The main objective of this chapter is to assess, using a number of statistical tools, the intensity of economic integration in a comparative framework by focusing on the European Union and the Asia-Pacific region, which, for the purposes of this chapter, comprises the Association of Southeast Asian Nations (ASEAN) Plus Three (China, Japan, South Korea), and, in addition, Australia and New Zealand. The rationale for integrating Australia and New Zealand in the analysis stems from the fact that, from an economic viewpoint, these two countries are embedded in their own region. For example, according to figures released by the Australia Bureau of Statistics, more than two-fifths of Australia's merchandise trade is with North Asian countries (in particular Japan, China and South Korea). This pattern of trade is in line with the predictions of gravity models, that highlight the significance of proximity in explaining economic flows (such as trade flows) between any two countries.[2]

The first section of this chapter will very briefly analyse the process of economic integration in both regions. It will highlight the striking differences between these processes at the outset, with EU integration in the early years being fundamentally politically and institutionally driven, in contrast with the market-led approach chosen in the Asia-Pacific region. It will be argued that the process of economic integration in Europe increasingly resembles that of the Asia-Pacific; it is increasingly a *de facto* or a business-led approach, with only a few specific characteristics left. This section will also analyse the implications of the proliferation of free trade area agreements (FTAs) involving both regions. Following on from this, the second section of this chapter will propose a statistical analysis of the intensity of economic integration within each region.

A comparison of economic integration as a state of affairs across the two regions will rely solely on trade and investment data. Because of the increasing incidence of interdependence between the various regions of the world, the third section will suggest a concise examination of the linkages between the two regions, by starting with the issue of structural similarity between them. Structural similarity will be appraised using indicators such as the revealed comparative advantage index and intra-industry trade indices (static and dynamic). In this section, the interesting question of trade complementarity will also be posed; this entails, for example, looking at whether an excess supply from the Asia-Pacific region in a specific [trade] area corresponds to an excess demand in the EU in the same area. Trade complementarity is possible if the two regions are structurally dissimilar, and this is why structural similarity and complementarity are dealt with together. The analysis of trade complementarity will ultimately shed some light on the possibility of further linkages between the two regions in an increasingly interdependent world. Finally, avenues for further development will be suggested in a final section.

The Processes of Economic Integration in the Asia-Pacific Region and Europe — A Synoptic Comparison

The Process of Economic Integration in the Asia-Pacific Region

The Asia-Pacific region is characterized by a series of hubs and nodes of economic integration such as ASEAN, ASEAN Plus Three and Asia-Pacific Economic Cooperation (APEC), as well as numerous trade agreements signed on a bilateral basis. This chapter will look at these three different levels in turn.

On the whole, ASEAN is the most integrated regional grouping in Asia. Even from a purely economic viewpoint, ASEAN is difficult to compare directly to the EU, for at the outset it was not meant, in contrast with the then Common Market in Europe, to have supranational institutions representing the region as a whole and facilitating economic policy-making. Some forty years after its inception, ASEAN member countries are still very attached to (and sensitive about) the issue of sovereignty (Fong, 2005). In the eyes of some European analysts, ASEAN is a 'regional tool to maximize sovereignty and national interests' (Boisseau du Rocher, 2006, p. 233). In other instances, this unwillingness to transfer sovereignty, even on a partial basis, to supranational organizations is seen as proof of a 'low level of ambition' (Vandoren, 2005, p. 517). As will be discussed below, this is in sharp contrast with the EU where sovereignty has been gradually giving way to a number of common policies, substantiating the idea that its 'ambitions', in terms of regional integration, have been and are higher than ASEAN's.

Events such as the 1997 Asian crisis and the surge of China as an economic power have nevertheless fostered deeper economic integration among ASEAN countries. The word 'integration' now features quite prominently in official ASEAN documents, whereas before the 1992 ASEAN summit, this concept was avoided in favour of 'cooperation' (Severino, 2003). Since the November 2002 summit, ASEAN countries have committed themselves to the concept of an ASEAN Economic Community. More recently, the July 2006 Report of the Eminent Persons Group (EPG), a group entrusted by ASEAN Governments with providing recommendations on the directions and nature of the ASEAN Charter, called for a number of milestones to boost economic integration among these countries. Some of the most forward-looking recommendations include the 'creation of a Single Market with free movement of goods, ideas and skilled talent' (EPG, 2006, p. 2), the establishment of both a 'special fund for narrowing the development gap [...] with voluntary contributions from Member States' (ibid. p. 3), as well as dispute settlement mechanisms.[3]

ASEAN Plus Three, a constituent part of the Asia–Europe Meeting (ASEM), is a pure example of market-driven integration. Born as an extension of the *kûdôka* phenomenon (appreciating yen, higher labour costs in Japan, loss of Japan's comparative and competitive advantage in labour-intensive industries, and de-industrialization, including in electrical equipment), economic integration in this region has been stimulated by the relocation of Japanese plants across Asia, and by the constitution of Japanese pan-Asian systems of production.[4] Institutionally coordinated integration, through the signing of regional trade agreements (RTAs), has actually succeeded *de facto* (or business-led) integration in this case.

APEC, a scheme extending to North America, Australia and New Zealand and established in 1989, played a major role in promoting trade liberalization, investment facilitation and development cooperation in the region, at least up until the 1997 Asian crisis. As Hyun-Seok (2005) argues, many Asian countries have been disillusioned by the 'Washington consensus' and by the inability of APEC to assist crisis-hit countries in the region after 1997. The aim of this scheme has been to contribute to liberalization in the region, and to foster liberalization elsewhere, in line with World Trade Organization principles.[5] Important achievements of APEC include an increasing awareness of potential economic relations among businesses and officials, as well as a substantial decrease in transaction costs thanks to trade facilitation measures. In particular, the first 8 years of APEC led to a considerable acceleration of liberalization in many economies of the region (Yamazawa, 2000). Being again a perfect case of market-driven integration, this scheme has necessitated a minimal institutional involvement: the setting up of a secretariat in 1992 fell far short of US ambitions.

European Union Economic Integration: Distinctive Features

In contrast with all the other forms of integration outlined above, the EU is the most integrated of all subregional groupings and the most accomplished from an institutional viewpoint. From the outset, the process of integration in Europe has been politically driven and institutionally led. Its relative success, in particular in the monetary area, has led many commentators to see the EU as a 'model' to follow, or as an example that may inspire Asia (Murray, 2005).[6] The coordination of certain policies, harmonization in certain areas (such as in fiscal matters) and the implementation of common policies (such as in the fields of trade, competition and money) have meant a gradual surrendering of sovereignty amongst EU countries. The perceived incompatibility between 'deepening' and 'enlarging' became an issue after the fall of the Berlin Wall, and this heated debate was seemingly resolved by opting for both strategies at the same time. Inevitably, and from a purely economic policy perspective, the EU can be seen today as a rather incompletely integrated area. One striking omission from the policy area (and perhaps one contradiction) is the absence of common economic policies in the budgetary, fiscal and industrial spheres to complement economic and monetary union (EMU).[7] Nevertheless, in order to restore EU competitiveness in an increasingly globalized world, different regulations aimed at nurturing the creation of a favourable business environment have been adopted. These regulations (such as those related to the completion of the single market), dispense with the need to design and implement fully fledged economic policies. In short, with the successive enlargements and the increasing phenomenon of globalization, there has been a gradual shift from the political and policy agenda of the early decades to a pragmatic market-led approach or a business-elite-driven process. Therefore, economic integration in the EU is increasingly of the 'business-inspired' type, which increasingly resembles other forms of integration in the rest of the world, in particular in the Asia-Pacific region.

In spite of this, the European Union retains its distinctive feature of speaking with one voice at international fora. Therefore, concluding free trade area agreements involves the EU as a whole; this is in perfect contrast to the case of ASEAN and other economic groupings in Asia, where bilateral trade agreements have mushroomed since the Asian crisis, a point to which this chapter now turns.

Free Trade Agreement Mania

This section deals briefly with a selected number of free trade agreements, namely, those involving ASEAN, the EU and ASEAN countries separately.

Agreements Involving ASEAN *in Toto*

Since the early 2000s, ASEAN has engaged in a number of FTA negotiations with neighbouring economies, namely China, Japan, Korea, Australia and New Zealand and India. In parallel to these negotiations, some individual ASEAN countries have also engaged in bilateral negotiations.[8]

The China–ASEAN FTA was the first such agreement to be signed by ASEAN as a group. In 2002 — only one year after the negotiations started — a framework agreement laying out the FTA plan was signed, with a target of reducing tariffs, for products in the normal track list,[9] to zero by 2010 for the six original ASEAN members and by 2015 for the other four. The FTA is only one element of a 'Comprehensive Economic Partnership' which is planned to go beyond free trade. Negotiations on a dispute settlement mechanism were finalized in 2004 for implementation in 2005, while negotiations on trade in services as well as on investment are ongoing.

In 2004, Korea and ASEAN agreed to establish a 'Comprehensive Cooperation Partnership', which, among other things, contains measures to enhance economic relations, expand two-way trade and investment and further economic cooperation, especially capacity building in various fields such as tourism, agriculture, fisheries and forestry, energy, information technology, and science and technology. In early 2005, negotiations started on a Korea–ASEAN FTA and an agreement on the liberalization of trade in goods was reached at the end of the same year, with a target date for the full elimination of tariffs set for 2009.

The 'Framework for Comprehensive Economic Partnership between the Association of Southeast Asian Nations and Japan' was signed in October 2003.[10] Negotiations started in early 2005 toward the establishment of such a partnership (hereafter AJCEP).[11] Interestingly, Japan follows a dual strategy, negotiations with ASEAN being held in parallel to bilateral negotiations between Japan and each individual ASEAN member country. While an agreement was signed with Singapore in 2001 and Malaysia in December 2005, negotiations are still ongoing with Indonesia, Thailand and the Philippines, and initial contacts have been made with Vietnam and Brunei. This suggests that the AJCEP will essentially be an umbrella agreement for separate FTAs.

Agreements Involving the EU and Developing Countries

Free Trade Agreements involving the EU include the agreement establishing an association between the European Community and its member states, on the one part, and the Republic of Chile on the other. Signed in November 2002, this comprehensive agreement has been in force since March 2005 and it goes beyond the commitments of the signatories under WTO. It encompasses (i) a Free Trade Area in manufacturing products, fisheries and agriculture, as well as services; (ii) a political dialogue and (iii) a cooperation dimension including an investment agreement, the opening up of procurement markets, rules on competition, and intellectual property rights. The EU and the Gulf Cooperation Council (GCC) comprising Bahrain, Kuwait, Saudi Arabia, Oman, Qatar and the United Arab Emirates (UAE) signed a mutual cooperation agreement in 1988 that came into force in 1990. FTA negotiations started in 1988, and serious steps towards the agreement have recommenced since 2003 when the GCC formed a customs union. In the latest round of the FTA negotiations in November 2005, the EU proposed almost 100 per cent liberalization of trade in goods. The EU Commission now has draft mandates for negotiating FTAs with ASEAN and India, as well as South Korea. Preparatory work for the planned EU-ASEAN FTA has been concluded and final negotiations are expected to be completed in 2009.

Agreements Involving ASEAN Countries Separately

As a general rule, the smaller an economy, the more specialized it is, in terms of both production and trade. The industrial specialization of a country at the production level is the extent to which its industrial structure is dominated by a few industries, when measured with the help of output, employment, or value added figures.[12] In Asia, Singapore is one of the most specialized countries, with more than 10 per cent of its manufacturing labour force in radio, television and communication equipment.[13] Furthermore, the smaller an economy, the more open it is, and the more FTAs it tends to conclude. Not surprisingly, Singapore has signed or is in the process of signing more than 25 FTA agreements since 1999. Other ASEAN member countries and Asian countries such as Thailand, Malaysia and South Korea have followed suit.[14] For example, Singapore has concluded an Economic Partnership Agreement with Japan, which goes beyond the traditional reduction of tariff and non-tariff barriers (NTBs) on goods, and an FTA agreement with the United States.

While bilateral agreements increase bilateral trade (say between Singapore and a third country), it might be to the detriment of trade with other members of the regional grouping. These bilateral agreements may weaken or indeed retard economic cohesion within the ASEAN countries and risk undermining multilateral efforts. The issue of whether bilateral FTAs hinder or promote regionalism and multilateral trade liberalization has been explored in many empirical and less empirical economic articles. Baharumshah et al. (2007) summarized the arguments for concluding FTAs and show that studies on the issue are equally split between those who argue that discriminatory policies such as those enshrined in FTAs prevent wider trade liberalization and those who take the opposite view.[15]

An interesting question to ask at this juncture is whether economic integration in the two regions (as measured by trade and investment) is in line with the institutional and policy efforts that have been made over the years. The next section briefly analyses the degree of economic integration intensity in both the EU and Asia-Pacific region, defined as encompassing ASEAN Plus Three, Australia and New Zealand.

Measuring the Intensity of Economic Integration — Trade and Investment Data

The intensity of trade and investment flows (and stocks) within each region is a reliable measure of the depth of economic integration therein.[16] There are a number of indicators available for the measurement of intra-regional trade and investment intensity, as indicated below.

Intra-Regional Trade in the EU and the Asia-Pacific Region

As shown in Figure 4.1, the intensity of intra-EU-25 trade flows has stabilized over the last decade at around the two-thirds mark. In 2005, some 65.3 per cent of all EU-25 trade was intra-EU trade, a figure slightly below that for 1995.

In the case of the Asia-Pacific region (ASEAN Plus Three, Australia and New Zealand), it is first of all important to highlight the major trading countries in relative terms. Figure 4.2 shows unambiguously that there are two major players in the region (China and Japan), whose leadership positions are only slightly contested by South Korea and Singapore. The relative importance of the latter country is explained by its traditional role as export platform and warehouse for the region. As can be seen in Figure 4.2, China has now slightly surpassed Japan as the main trading nation in the Asia-Pacific region. Seen as a manufacturing powerhouse in

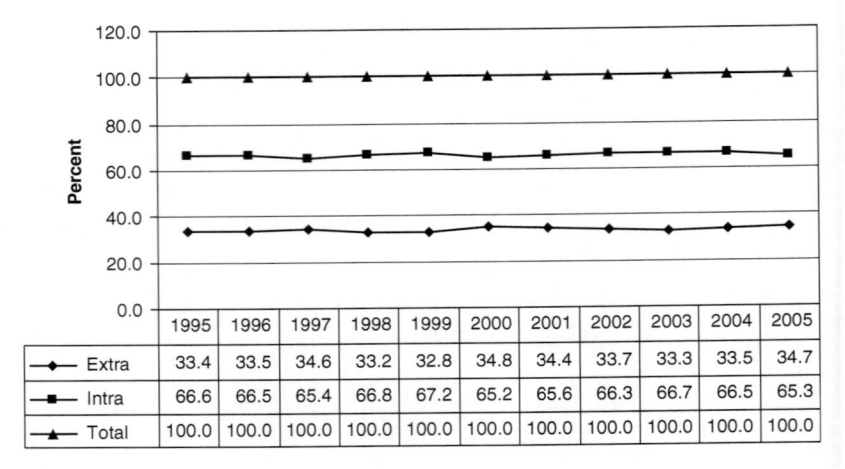

Figure 4.1 Intra-regional trade: EU-25.
Sources: EUROSTAT, COMEXT

	1995	1996	1997	1998	1999	2000	2001	2002	2003	2004	2005
Extra	33.4	33.5	34.6	33.2	32.8	34.8	34.4	33.7	33.3	33.5	34.7
Intra	66.6	66.5	65.4	66.8	67.2	65.2	65.6	66.3	66.7	66.5	65.3
Total	100.0	100.0	100.0	100.0	100.0	100.0	100.0	100.0	100.0	100.0	100.0

KOR	JAP	CHI	IND	MAL	PHI	SIN	THA	AUS	NZ
12.8	23.7	24.1	4.5	7.2	2.3	11.8	6.1	6.3	1.3

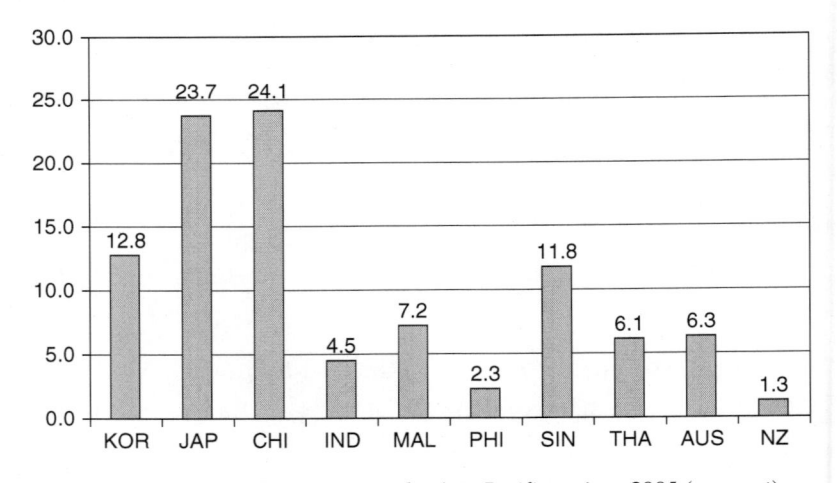

Figure 4.2 Main trading countries in the Asia-Pacific region, 2005 (per cent).
Sources: UN Comtrade. Recent data for Brunei, Cambodia, Lao PDR, Myanmar and Vietnam are not available

the region, China also serves as the manufacturing base for the western world, in particular for the US.

As can be seen in Table 4.1, the total intra-regional trade ratio for the Asia-Pacific region as a whole (41.1 per cent in 2005) is substantially lower than that of the EU. Also, all countries that show an intra-Pacific

Table 4.1 Intra-regional trade — Asia-Pacific countries (2005)

Percent		KOR	JAP	CHI	IND	MAL	PHI	SIN	THA	AUS	NZ	Asia-Pacific
Export to	Asia-Pacific	40.1	35.8	23.6	57.5	47.8	48.4	50.5	44.7	57.2	47.7	37.0
	Rest of World	59.9	64.2	76.4	42.5	52.2	51.6	49.5	55.3	42.8	52.3	63.0
Import from	Asia-Pacific	46.8	43.7	40.4	58.6	56.8	47.2	50.7	53.4	46.9	55.4	45.8
	Rest of World	53.2	56.3	59.6	41.4	43.2	52.8	49.3	46.6	53.1	44.6	54.2
Total trade with	Asia-Pacific	43.3	39.5	31.4	57.9	51.8	47.7	50.6	49.2	51.7	51.9	41.1
	Rest of World	56.7	60.5	68.6	42.1	48.2	52.3	49.4	50.8	48.3	48.1	58.9

Source: UN Comtrade (Recent data for Brunei, Cambodia, Lao PDR, Myanmar and Vietnam are not available)

trade ratio above 50 per cent are ASEAN member countries (Indonesia, Malaysia, Singapore), apart from the Pacific countries of Australia and New Zealand. The results for the ASEAN countries mentioned above denote the relative integration of this economic grouping in the Asia-Pacific region as a whole. By contrast, the intra-ASEAN trade ratio was barely above 20 per cent in 2004, in spite of major milestones to boost economic integration. One such major initiative was the 1992 agreement on establishing an ASEAN Free Trade Area (AFTA) aimed at reducing intra-regional tariffs and non-tariff barriers. Tariff reduction is formulated in a Common Effective Preferential Tariff (CEPT) scheme which is based on a negative list approach including four lists of goods (inclusion list, temporary exclusion list, sensitive list and general exclusion list). Undoubtedly, the number of products covered by the CEPT has grown steadily over time, while the level of applied tariff rates has fallen; for example, by September 2005, more than 98 per cent of the products in the CEPT Inclusion List of ASEAN-6 (Brunei, Indonesia, Singapore, Philippines, Thailand and Malaysia) had been brought down to the 0–5 per cent tariff range, with 64.2 per cent facing no tariff at all.[17] Again in the early 2000s and as seen in the previous section, ASEAN members agreed, *inter alia*, to establish a single market and an integrated production base within an ASEAN Economic Community (AEC). Despite these milestones, a number of obstacles to intra-ASEAN trade and investment still remain: technical and other barriers have not been lowered as required by the AFTA agreement; customs procedures in ASEAN still discourage firms from pursuing cross-border business activities; there is no dispute settlement mechanism; and the standardization of products traded within ASEAN is progressing only very slowly. Also, a major impediment to intra-ASEAN trade is the complexity of implementing the ASEAN rules of origin that set the criteria for eligibility to the CEPT.

It should nevertheless be noted that intra-ASEAN trade is higher in the case of some manufacturing products, such as electronics and office machinery. This, in turn, proves the existence of global systems of production (GSPs) in the ASEAN region (or again *de facto* economic integration).[18] Interestingly, the intra-Asia-Pacific trade ratio is higher than that of ASEAN, in spite of there being a more formalized integration process in the ASEAN region. This again suggests that what matters most in Asia-Pacific is a *de facto* type of integration, largely stimulated by (essentially Japanese) multinational firms. Because of the large inflows of FDI in the region and in particular in China, it might be that intra-Asia-Pacific trade will increase in the future.

Table 4.2 Intra-EU FDI position (flows and stocks, 2001–2005)

	Intra-EU25		
	Stocks	Flows	Income
Million euros			
2001	2745843	327828	127915
2002	2850118	362199	111904
2003	3139259	270688	116712
2004	3379707	217714	148189
2005	3878733	427424	180041
Percent			
2001	57.6	51.7	59.7
2002	59.9	73.0	56.6
2003	61.0	66.6	53.0
2004	62.3	61.5	49.6
2005	62.0	69.7	50.3

Source: EUROSTAT, Brussels

Sectoral differentiation between the two regions, the EU and the Asia-Pacific will be appraised in the next section with reference to an analysis of trade complementarity. Before that, this chapter completes the analysis of intra-group economic integration by turning to investment data.

Intra-Regional Foreign Direct Investment Flows

As shown in Table 4.2, between half and two thirds of all EU-25 foreign direct investment (FDI) flows and stocks abroad in the early 2000s were intra-EU. These figures include manufacturing and services industries, with services representing the largest share of all intra-EU FDI stocks and flows.[19] The shares of all EU FDI flows in 2002, 2003 and 2005 consigned to other EU countries were particularly high (73 per cent, 66.6 per cent and 69.7 per cent respectively) in the run–up to the fifth enlargement of the Union.

In the case of the Asia-Pacific Region, five countries account for 77.57 per cent and 93.62 per cent of total inward and outward FDI stocks in the region: Australia, China, Japan, Singapore and Malaysia. In contrast to the case of the EU, and as shown in Table 4.3, the degree of integration is generally low, with intra-regional FDI ratios ranging from 7.1 per cent (in the case of Japan) to 33.7 per cent (for Malaysia). Only 14 per cent of Australian FDI stock in 2003 had a regional origin.

Table 4.3 Intra-regional FDI in the Asia-Pacific region — selected countries, various years

AUS mill. AU$	%	CHI 100 mill. US$	%	SIN mill. US$	%	JAP mill. US$	%	MAL mill. US$	%
Origin:									
Asia-Pacific, Of which:	14.0	Asia-Pacific, of which:	46.4	Asia-Pacific, of which:	17.9	Asia-Pacific, of which:	7.1	Asia-Pacific, of which:	33.7
Japan (18404)	7.4	Hong Kong (197)	27.3	Japan (9142)	8.5	Asia (6636)	6.6	ASEAN (7009)	19.4
South, East and Southeast Asia (9535)	3.8	Japan (65)	9.0	ASEAN (6575)	6.1			Japan (4761)	13.2
New Zealand (7069)	2.8	Korea (51)	7.1	Asia-NIEs (3555)	3.3	Australia & New Zealand (473)	0.5	Australasia (413)	1.1
								Asia-NIEs (1973)	5.5
Others	86	Others	53.6	Others	82.1	Others	92.9	Others	60.8
Total (249858)	100	Total (724)	100	Total (107416)	100	Total (100300)	100	Total (36062)	100

Sources: Derived from a number of databases: (1) Australia: UNCTAD World Investment Directory Database. The data represent FDI stocks 2003. (2) China: MOFCOM FDI Statistics. The data for inward FDI represent realized FDI value, 2005. (3) Japan: JETRO. The data represent FDI stocks 2005. (4) Singapore: inward FDI data come from the ASEAN Secretariat-ASEAN FDI Database 2004. The data represent cumulative FDI flows for 1995–2003. (5) Malaysia: inward FDI data are from the ASEAN Secretariat-ASEAN FDI Database 2004. The data represent cumulative FDI flows 1995–2003

With a ratio as high as 46.4 per cent in 2005, China seems to be more integrated in the region than the other countries under review. However, great care should be exercised when interpreting data on FDI inflows in China, for, as argued by Chen (1997) and Hou (2002), a 'non trivial' share of FDI into China from Hong Kong may in fact be money-laundering through re-routing. Typically, funds that belong to China's state-owned enterprises or to Chinese transnational corporations are diverted to Hong Kong, and 're-invested' subsequently as 'Hong Kong' capital into China, for the sole purpose of benefiting from fiscal advantages accorded to foreign investors. This type of re-routed investment was estimated by Huang (1998) as representing nearly a third of all Hong Kong FDI to China in 1992.

With regard to ASEAN, the role of Singapore as a gateway for foreign investors into ASEAN should be noted. For different reasons than in the case of China, most of the intra-ASEAN FDI flows originate in Singapore. This country represents the managerial and research hub of a regional division of labour orchestrated in large part by multinational enterprises (MNEs) who, through their affiliates in Singapore, allocate labour-intensive production throughout the region. Owing to its geographical location, Singapore's role was, in the early years of ASEAN, confined to that of an export platform to other neighbouring countries, and most foreign direct investment was consigned to the larger or resource-rich countries in the region. The role of Singapore as a regional hub for foreign investors has grown in tandem with slightly greater integration in the ASEAN region. Again it can be inferred that MNEs have fostered regional integration within ASEAN, Asia and the Asia-Pacific region. In particular, Japanese firms have historically been the major actors in this instance (JETRO, 1995; Kobayashi, 1997; Dicken, 1998; Andreosso-O'Callaghan and Bassino, 2001).[20] As far back as 1995, a JETRO study noted the increasing visibility of the electric appliance GSP in Asia, and more particularly in Southeast Asia. Kobayashi (1997) noted that these coherent networks of affiliates involve several large companies (Nissan's sub-suppliers selling parts to Mitsubishi in Southeast Asia). The building-up of these Japanese GSPs in Asia has led some authors to note the *catalytic role* of Japanese FDI in the Asia-Pacific Region (Andreosso-O'Callaghan and Bassino, 2001). With the advent of China as a manufacturing platform and of FDI from emerging economies in Southeast Asia, the building up of these GSPs has become more common (Sachwald, 2004). Given that these GSPs tend nowadays to transcend regional boundaries, it might be worthwhile casting an eye on the linkages between the two regions.

Regional Linkages: Structural Similarity and Complementarity between the Two Regions

Theoretical Inputs

The concept of structural similarity, when applied in a context of international economics, brings us to Helpman's hypothesis, according to which intra-industry trade is more likely to occur between structurally similar countries, understood in this chapter as countries that present a number of similar characteristics: similar size, similar factor composition (that is, K/L ratios), similar productive structures and living standards (Helpman, 1987). In contrast, structurally dissimilar countries such as Germany and Burma Myanmar tend to exchange products that belong to different industries. Therefore, one would theoretically expect intra-industry trade to be low in this case, implying that these countries would present radically different comparative advantages.[21] One way to analyse structural similarity (conversely dissimilarity) is, therefore, by computing RCA (revealed comparative advantage) indices. In conducting this statistical analysis, this chapter bears in mind the fact that Helpman's hypothesis has been thrown into question by recent work highlighting the existence of high intra-industry trade ratios between highly dissimilar countries, at least at the two-digit level of analysis. In a pioneering work on the issue, Wakasugi (1997) argued that the rising share of Japanese intra-industry trade with Asian countries is due to intra-firm network transactions through FDI (the GSP phenomenon). This recent evidence implies that intra-industry trade and structural similarity do not always go hand in hand.

Measuring Structural Similarity: EU-15, EU-25 and Asia-Pacific

We use the following formula for the RCA index: $\text{RCA} = \left(\frac{x_i}{X}\right) - \left(\frac{m_i}{M}\right)$, where x_i and m_i are exports and imports in product i from source to destination country, and where X and M are total exports and imports of the country. The higher the index, the higher the revealed comparative advantage of the country. Negative figures denote a revealed comparative *dis*advantage in the product or industry in question. As can be seen from Table 4.4a, the EU-15 has consolidated and even improved its RCA over the five years examined in a number of industries, including machines and transport equipment, chemicals and basic manufactures. These are three industries, defined at the two-digit level, where the EU-15 has a revealed comparative advantage on world markets. Interestingly, the addition of ten new member states to the European Union in 2005

Table 4.4a Revealed comparative advantage: EU-15 and EU-25 (vis-à-vis the world)

	RCA in 2000		RCA in 2005	
	EU-15	EU-25	EU-15	EU-25
Food and live animals	−0.003	−0.003	−0.006	−0.004
Beverage and tobacco	0.004	0.004	0.004	0.003
Crude materials excludes fuels	−0.013	−0.012	−0.010	−0.009
Mineral fuels etc.	−0.046	−0.047	−0.070	−0.069
Animal, vegetable oil, fat	0.000	0.000	−0.001	−0.001
Chemicals	0.024	0.021	0.027	0.021
Basic manufactures	0.013	0.012	0.015	0.014
Machines, transport equipment	0.038	0.037	0.049	0.050
Misc manufactured goods	−0.009	−0.006	−0.010	−0.007
Goods not classed by kind	−0.008	−0.007	0.001	0.001

Source: EUROSTAT, COMEXT

Table 4.4b Revealed comparative advantages: Asia-Pacific region (vis-à-vis the world)

	2000	2005
Food and live animals	−0.021	−0.010
Beverage and tobacco	−0.004	−0.002
Crude materials excludes fuels	−0.031	−0.037
Mineral fuels etc.	−0.098	−0.115
Animal, vegetable oil, fat	0.002	0.003
Chemicals	−0.029	−0.024
Basic manufactures	−0.001	0.012
Machines, transport equipment	0.136	0.122
Misc manufactured goods	0.039	0.039
Goods not classed by kind	0.005	0.012

Source: UN Comtrade (Recent data for Brunei, Cambodia, Lao PDR, Myanmar and Vietnam are not available)

did not fundamentally change these results. All it does is slightly weaken the RCA index for chemicals.

The results for the Asia-Pacific economies show that apart from machines and transport equipment — the pillar of industrialization in any economy — RCAs differ when compared with those of the EU. Revealed comparative advantages for the Asia-Pacific are confined to miscellaneous manufactured products and to other products not classified elsewhere (Table 4.4b). These preliminary results suggest different specialization patterns between these two broad regions and therefore some degree of structural *dissimilarity*. In the case of machines and transport equipment, the RCA for the EU is much less pronounced than in the case of the Asia-Pacific countries, denoting the relative weakness of the EU in this area.

Another way to appraise structural similarity is to measure the intra-industry trade (IIT) patterns of the two regions vis-à-vis a reference group of countries. If these IIT patterns are similar, then structural similarity between the two regions may be inferred. Grubel and Lloyd indices, as well as dynamic IIT indices, are used here for the analysis of intra-industry trade within each region. In broad terms, these indices give an indication of net trade (that is, exports minus imports) in the total trade (exports plus imports) of a country. Standard Grubel and Lloyd indices have been criticized for being static, in the sense that they refer to trade data at one particular point in time. This is why this chapter's analysis will also use dynamic indices. The Grubel and Lloyd index, calculated for each regional grouping, is given as follows: $GL_i = 1 - \frac{|X_i - M_i|}{(X_i + M_i)}$, with ($0 \leq GL_j \leq 1$), where, X_i are the exports in product i by any of the two regions to the rest of the world, and where M_i refer to the imports of product i by the same region from the rest of the world. An index close to one denotes a large incidence of IIT, and therefore some degree of similarity between the region and the rest of the world. If two or more regions have similar levels of IIT with the rest of the world, then it can be concluded that there is structural similarity between these regions. This index has been calculated for the three regions (EU-15, EU-25 and Asia-Pacific) and for a number of industries defined at the two-digit level (Table 4.5).

Of even greater relevance is the way intra-industry trade evolves over time. By decomposing total trade (TT) between any of the three regions and the rest of the world into IIT and net trade (NT), and by using a dynamic analysis which assesses the contribution of IIT and net trade (NT) changes to the growth of total trade (TT) over time, we obtain the results presented in Table 4.5.[22] We look here at the contribution of IIT to the growth in TT between each of the three regions and the rest of the world (as a reference region) over the years 2000 and 2005 and at an industry level.

These results show on the whole that the EU-15 has generally higher IIT ratios with the rest of the world than the Asia-Pacific region.[23] Adding the other ten new member countries of the EU narrows the gap between the EU and the Asia-Pacific region only slightly. In particular, crude materials

Table 4.5 Intra-industry trade of each region with the RoW (static and dynamic indices) (2000 and 2005)

	GL		Growth Contribution		
	2000	2005	Cnt	$Ciit$	tt
EU-15 Products					
Food and live animals	0.968	0.955	2.2	17.0	19.2
Beverage and tobacco	0.839	0.856	0.8	16.4	17.2
Crude materials excludes fuels	0.785	0.834	−2.4	17.3	14.8
Mineral fuels etc.	0.626	0.604	29.7	39.8	69.5
Animal, vegetable oil, fat	0.997	0.925	10.7	35.3	45.9
Chemicals	0.902	0.908	3.3	39.4	42.8
Basic manufactures	0.962	0.949	2.1	12.1	14.2
Machines, transport equipment	0.959	0.936	2.8	4.6	7.5
Misc manufactured goods	0.957	0.956	0.8	14.0	14.7
Goods not classed by kind	0.835	0.972	−13.9	6.3	−7.5
EU-25 Products					
Food and live animals	0.966	0.960	1.6	21.0	22.6
Beverage and tobacco	0.848	0.869	0.4	18.8	19.1
Crude materials excludes fuels	0.795	0.843	−2.1	19.4	17.2
Mineral fuels etc.	0.615	0.604	29.1	41.6	70.7
Animal, vegetable oil, fat	0.979	0.913	10.7	36.2	46.9
Chemicals	0.922	0.929	2.5	41.6	44.1
Basic manufactures	0.970	0.957	2.0	16.2	18.2
Machines, transport equipment	0.966	0.939	3.4	8.1	11.5
Misc manufactured goods	0.965	0.966	0.5	16.9	17.3
Goods not classed by kind	0.835	0.989	−15.4	10.0	−5.4
Asia-Pacific Countries Products					
Food and live animals	0.851	0.916	−3.3	41.3	38.0
Beverage and tobacco	0.688	0.824	−6.8	45.5	38.7
Crude materials excludes fuels	0.683	0.636	37.7	53.1	90.8
Mineral fuels etc.	0.578	0.552	47.7	53.0	100.7
Animal, vegetable oil, fat	0.585	0.658	33.4	85.7	119.2
Chemicals	0.880	0.915	4.4	86.7	91.1
Basic manufactures	0.934	0.895	12.0	65.6	77.6
Machines, transport equipment	0.786	0.811	10.4	57.3	67.7
Misc. manufactured goods	0.764	0.778	15.4	60.3	75.7
Goods not classed by kind	0.800	0.609	45.4	21.6	67.0

Sources: For the EU, data are from EUROSTAT, COMEXT. Data for the Asia-Pacific countries are from UN Comtrade (Note: The data exclude Brunei, Cambodia, Lao PDR, Myanmar and Vietnam)

excluding fuels, mineral fuels, animal and vegetable oil, basic manufacturing and machinery are all industries with substantially higher IIT ratios in the case of the EU, compared with Asia-Pacific countries. These primary results confirm that there is a substantial degree of structural manufacturing *dissimilarity* between the EU and the Asia-Pacific region. Dynamic indices substantiate these results further, for they suggest that these trends have been reinforced over time. In particular, the industries showing increasingly high IIT ratios in the case of the EU (beverages and tobacco, crude materials and chemicals) are also those to which IIT (as opposed to net trade) has made a substantially higher contribution to the growth of total trade over the five years under review.

Trade Complementarity between the EU-25 and Asia-Pacific

The relatively important degree of structural and trade dissimilarity between the two regions can mask a certain complementarity in some specific industries. This chapter uses a trade complementarity index as defined in Vaillant and Ons (2002). The trade complementarity of country A in relation to country B and in industry s is computed as follows:

$$TCI_{Aj}^s = \frac{x_A^s}{t_{wA}^s} \cdot \frac{m_B^s}{t_{wA}^s}$$

where x_A^s is the share of industry s in region A's exports, and t_{wA}^s is the share of industry s in world imports. This index, which is in fact the product of the export specialization index of region A and the import specialization index of region B, measures the level of similarity between the export supply of a region and the import demand of one of its partners. A value substantially greater than one implies the existence of a strong complementarity between the export specialization of region A and the import specialization of its partner B. A value close to one implies that export and import specialization patterns are similar. Computing TCI indices between the Asia-Pacific countries and the EU-25 at the two-digit level gives the results shown in Table 4.6.

Taking first the case of the Asia-Pacific region as the consigning region (and the EU as the importing region) the table shows that there are two broad industries for which trade complementarity is strong. Asia-Pacific's excess supply of machines and transport equipment, and animal and vegetable oils is matched by a corresponding demand from the EU-25. Conversely, when the EU is taken as the exporting region, a strong complementarity exists in a greater number of areas such as food and live

Table 4.6 Trade complementarity between the EU-25 and the Asia-Pacific Countries

Industry	EU-25 as importer Asia-Pacific as exporter		EU-25 as exporter Asia-Pacific as importer	
	2000	2005	2000	2005
Food and live animals	0.61	0.53	0.72	0.53
Beverage and tobacco	0.23	0.18	1.40	0.99
Crude materials excludes fuels	1.30	1.27	0.89	0.98
Mineral fuels etc.	0.99	0.82	0.56	0.48
Animal, vegetable oil, fat	1.06	1.42	0.58	0.54
Chemicals	0.48	0.45	1.30	1.13
Basic manufactures	0.66	0.71	0.85	0.85
Machines, transport equipment	1.23	1.22	1.12	1.20
Misc manufactured goods	1.11	1.29	0.78	0.86
Goods not classed by kind	0.59	0.50	0.41	0.40

Source: UN Comtrade (Note: The data for Asia-Pacific countries exclude Brunei, Cambodia, Lao PDR, Burma Myanmar and Vietnam)

animals, beverages and tobacco, and chemicals. There is, in particular, complementarity in chemicals, given that the EU's excess supply in this industry (value well above 1 in 2003) can be met by a demand emanating from Asia-Pacific economies. Machinery and basic manufactures are two industries where EU export and Asia-Pacific import specialization patterns are rather similar, given that the value is close to one, although in the machinery industry, as we have noted above, the Asia-Pacific region is stronger than the EU on international markets.

Conclusion

Inherent characteristics of EU integration, compared with that of the Asia-Pacific region, are that it has been politically driven (in the early years at least), that it has been deeper (culminating in the euro), and that it allows the EU to be seen as one single actor on the world negotiating stage. Statistical analysis has also shown that the intensity of economic integration, measured by intra-regional trade and FDI ratios, is higher in the EU than in Asia-Pacific, a positive outcome of the chosen process of integration in Europe. The intensity of economic integration is also higher for the Asia-Pacific region as a whole compared with the ASEAN, which implies that economic integration in ASEAN is not in line with the policy effort that has been expended over the years. Much of the integration taking place in the Asia-Pacific region is *de facto* integration, for it has been largely orchestrated by MNEs and the constitution of their global system of production, in particular on the part of Japanese firms. Nevertheless, *de facto* integration also increasingly characterizes integration in the case of the EU.

In terms of the linkages between the two regions, the analysis in this chapter has shown that the EU and the Asia-Pacific region are two structurally dissimilar regions. Revealed comparative advantages differ between the two regions, with the EU having a number of relative strengths at the world level in chemicals and basic manufactures, in contrast with the Asia-Pacific region. Machinery and transport equipment is the only industry where both regions display a relative comparative advantage. These preliminary results imply, therefore, that there is scope for greater linkages or more exchange between the two regions in the future. The analysis has been made more complete by an examination of intra-industry trade, and trade complementarity between the two regions. IIT results confirm that there is a substantial degree of dissimilarity between the two regions. Finally, trade complementarity indices help to highlight a number of industries (such as food, beverages and machinery) where the excess of supply in one region can be matched by an excess of demand from the other. These further results substantiate the viability and desirability of economic linkages between the two regions in the future.

The analysis of economic linkages between the two regions either with the help of comparative advantage indices, intra-industry trade indices or trade complementarity indices all imply that there is scope for more economic exchange between the EU and the Asia-Pacific region in the future. This strengthens the need for government-led policies that foster the Asia–Europe relationship.

One way obviously in which the analysis can be taken one step further is by disintegrating the broad industries into their specific components (that is, by taking a more refined level of analysis in terms of industry categories).

Notes

1. The author wishes to acknowledge the help of Mr Utai Uprasen, Research Assistant (EAC), for sourcing the statistical material used in this study.

2. By applying Newton's law of gravitation to the field of international economics, the Dutch economist Jan Tinbergen developed the first gravity model in 1962 (see Tinbergen, 1962).
3. The interested reader can refer to *Report of the Eminent Persons Group on the ASEAN Charter* of the 10–11th July 2006, Singapore, Ministry of Foreign Affairs.
4. The IMF (1997) defines *kûdôka* as being a long-term decrease in manufacturing employment, whereas a wider definition of the concept implies the loss of domestic competitiveness leading to direct investment and to increased imports (see Guelle, 2001).
5. That is the General Agreement on Tariffs and Trade and World Trade Organization. Note that the 1994 Bogor Declaration committed APEC members to free trade and investment in the region by 2010 for the developed economies (and 2020 for the others).
6. R.A. Mundell is one such advocate of the EU as a model for ASEAN Plus Three; in the view of the Nobel laureate, ASEAN Plus Three should learn from the EU in terms of monetary and trade integration.
7. These are all areas where EU involvement does indeed exist, but where it is marginal; for example, the Stability and Growth Pact (SGP) serves as a *de minimis* measure to avoid major budgetary disruptions and to guarantee price stability, the overriding objective of EMU. The SGP calls for a coordination of budgetary policies in the EU, but it cannot be regarded as a satisfactory replacement for a common budgetary and fiscal policy.
8. Examples include Japan–Singapore, Japan–Philippines, Japan–Indonesia, Japan–Thailand and China–Thailand.
9. Products on the sensitive track list are liberalized according to a mutually agreed timeframe. An early harvest programme covers trade in a limited number of (primarily agricultural) goods. An important feature of the agreement is that it makes use of the ASEAN rules-of-origin mechanism.
10. For some reason, Japan insisted that the text should be simply called a 'framework' and not a 'framework agreement'.
11. Although this provides for putting in place elements of a possible free trade area by 2012, this ten-page document is in essence an 'economic cooperation' agreement dealing with a number of areas where partnership is created or strengthened, such as energy (with co-operation in oil stockpiling, natural gas utilization and promotion of energy efficiency), small and medium enterprises, and tourism and hospitality.
12. See Andreosso and Jacobson (2005), chapter 13.
13. This is according to data provided by the ASEAN Statistical Yearbook, 2004, Chapter 10 — Manufacturing, ASEAN Secretariat, Jakarta.
14. By 2005, Singapore had signed FTAs with Australia, Japan, New Zealand, EFTA, the USA and South Korea, as well as with Jordan and India (Vandoren, 2005).
15. Note that there is still nevertheless an uneasy confusion in the literature in general between FTAs and RTAs (regional trade agreements or arrangements). The RTA concept implies a geographical dimension to integration, a feature not necessarily present in the case of FTAs.
16. A missing variable here is the intensity of financial flows. There are several methods that can be used for measuring financial integration in the different

regions of the world, but the mere existence of the euro would undoubtedly place the EU at the forefront of the league.
17. For more on an assessment of the CEPT, see chapter 2 in Andreosso-O'Callaghan et al. (2006).
18. These are also called Global Production Networks. GSPs take the form of the spatial division of manufacturing and distribution processes in discrete production stages assigned to different countries, according to their host country comparative advantages. Typically, electronics products are amenable to the spatial separation of the manufacturing and assembly processes, and therefore to the constitution of GSPs. A large set of electronic and electrical products (computers, office equipment, TV sets, cameras, instruments, and also machine tools) are today produced and assembled within these GSPs (for the specific case of China's integration in these GSPs, see Sachwald, 2004).
19. According to EUROSTAT data, more than 90 per cent of all intra-EU-15 FDI flows (and more than 80 per cent of stocks) were in service industries in 2003.
20. JETRO is the Japan External Trade Organization.
21. The comparative advantage theory was devised by the nineteenth-century British economist David Ricardo. A comparative advantage exists when one country can produce a product at a lower relative cost than any other partner country.
22. For more on this methodology see Menon (1996).
23. Bearing in mind that nearly 40 per cent of total EU trade in 2005 was with developed (that is, structurally similar) countries, such as the US, EFTA and Japan (EUROSTAT Trade Figures, 2006).

References

Andreosso-O'Callaghan, B. and Bassino, J. P. (2001) 'Japanese Direct Investment in Asia and the European Union: Is There an Interdependence?', in B. Andreosso-O'Callaghan, J.P. Bassino and J. Jaussaud (eds) *The Changing Economic Environment in Asia*, New York: Palgrave/McMillan, pp. 26–51.

Andreosso-O'Callaghan, B., Jacobson, D. (2005) *Industrial Economics and Organization. A European Perspective*, 2nd edition, London, New York: McGraw-Hill.

Andreosso-O'Callaghan, B., Low, L., Nicolas, F., Petschiri, A. and Uprasen, U (2006) *A Qualitative Analysis of a Potential Free Trade Agreement between the EU and ASEAN*, a report commissioned by the European Commission, DG Trade, Brussels, June.

Baharumshah, A., Onwuka Odulukwe, K. and Muzafar Shah, H. (2007) 'Is a Regional Trade Bloc a Prelude to Multilateral Trade Liberalization? Empirical Evidence from the ASEAN-5 Economies', *Journal of Asian Economics* 18. 2, pp. 348–402.

Boisseau du Rocher, S. (2006) 'ASEAN and Northeast Asia: stakes and implications for the EU–ASEAN partnership', *Asia Europe Journal*, 4. 2, June, pp. 229–49.

Chen, C. (1997) 'Foreign Direct Investment and Trade: An Empirical Investigation of the Evidence from China', *Chinese Economic Research Unit*, Working Paper No. 97/11, University of Adelaide.

Dicken, P. (1998) *Global Shift — Transforming the World Economy*, London: Paul Chapman.

Eminent Persons Group (EPG) (2006) *Report of the Eminent Persons Group on the ASEAN Charter*, Singapore: Ministry of Foreign Affairs.
Fong, T. S. (2005) 'European Integration: A Model for Southeast Asia?' *Asia Europe Journal*, 3. 1, pp. 7–11.
Guelle, F. (2001) 'The Links between Japanese Investment in Asia and Deindustrialization in Japan', in B. Andreosso-O'Callaghan, J.P. Bassino and J. Jaussaud (eds) *The Changing Economic Environment in Asia*, New York: Palgrave/McMillan, pp. 52–61.
Helpman, E. (1987) 'Imperfect Competition and International Trade: Evidence from fourteen industrial countries', *Journal of the Japanese and International Economies*, 1, pp. 62–81.
Hou, J. W. (2002) 'China's FDI Policy and Taiwanese Direct Investment in China,' Department of Economics, California State University, available at: http://china-ces.org/HK2002Paper/Jack%20W%20Hou.pdf, accessed 25 June 2006.
Huang, Y. (1998) *FDI in China: An Asian Perspective*, Singapore: Institute of Southeast Asian Studies.
Hyun-Seok, Y. (2005) 'Asian Regionalism: A Post-Crisis Perspective', in W. Moon and B. Andreosso-O'Callaghan (eds) *Regional Integration — Europe and Asia Compared*, Aldershot: Ashgate, pp. 28–45.
IMF (1997) *Deindustrialization: Causes and Implications*, IMF Working Paper 1997-4, Washington, D.C.: International Monetary Fund.
JETRO (1995) *White Paper on FDI*, Tokyo: Japan's External Trade Organization.
Kobayashi, H. (1997) 'Globalization Strategy of Japanese Automobile Industry', paper presented at the conference *The Economic Relations between Europe and East Asia*, Université Paul Valery, Nimes, June.
Menon J. (1996) 'The Dynamics of Intra-Industry Trade in ASEAN', *Asian Economic Journal*, 10. 11, pp. 105–15.
Murray, P. (2005) 'Should Asia Emulate Europe?', in W. Moon and B. Andreosso-O'Callaghan (eds) *Regional Integration — Europe and Asia Compared*, Aldershot: Ashgate, pp. 197–213.
Sachwald, F. (2004) *The Integration of China and East European Countries in Global Networks*, Paris: Les Etudes de l'IFRI, 2, March.
Severino, R. C. (2003) 'Regional Integration in Europe and in Asia — The Future of ASEAN Economic Integration', *Asia Europe Journal*, 1. 4, pp. 475–9.
Tinbergen, J. (1962) *Shaping the World Economy: Suggestions for an International Economic Policy*, Appendix VI, New York: The Twentieth Century Fund.
Vaillant, M. and Ons, A. (2002) 'Preferential Trading Arrangements between the European Union and South America: The Political Economy of Free Trade Zones in Practice', *The World Economy*, 25. 10, pp. 1433–68.
Vandoren, P. (2005) 'Regional Economic Integration in South East Asia', *Asia Europe Journal*, 3. 4, pp. 517–35.
Wakasugi, R. (1997) 'Missing Factors in Intra-Industry Trade: Some Empirical Evidence Based on Japan', *Japan and the World Economy*, 9. 3, pp. 353–62.
Yamazawa, Y. (2000) (ed.) *Asia-Pacific Economic Cooperation (APEC) — Challenges and Tasks for the Twenty-First Century*, London, New York: Routledge.

5
Political Integration in the European Union: Any Lessons for ASEAN?

Edward Moxon-Browne

Introduction

This chapter asks whether, and to what extent, the experience of political integration in the European Union (EU) could be applicable to the Association of Southeast Asian Nations (ASEAN). The argument proceeds in three stages: first, it analyses the manifestations of political integration in the EU; second, it discusses how these manifestations are linked to contextual specificities in the West European political landscape; and, finally, it evaluates the transferability of institutions, policies, and their underlying assumptions to the ASEAN context. At the same time, it is important to emphasize what this chapter does not attempt to do. The evolution of European *economic* integration is deliberately omitted except where, and insofar as, that process impinges upon or directly determines the shape and substance of political integration. Economic integration is dealt with in chapter four of this volume. Likewise, defence and security themes are avoided as these are dealt with in chapter seven, except, again, where these directly reflect or constrain political integration processes. Moreover, the focus here is not with EU–ASEAN relations *per se*. These are after all conceptually quite distinct from the question of whether the EU could provide a model for ASEAN's political integration. One can conceive of conditions where relations between the two organizations might be very close, but no scope for induced integration is deemed possible and *vice versa*.

Political Integration in the EU

A necessary preliminary is discussion of what is meant by 'political integration'. Academic observers are not of one mind on this question.

Nor are they agreed about the relationship between political and economic integration. Clearly, political integration implies a sense of community among people within one political entity, or between several entities since, irrespective of the precise institutional arrangements involved, political integration implies ties of identity, shared values, mutually predictable behaviour, and an implied absence of violence as a method of solving disputes. The notion of a 'security community' (Deutsch, 1966) implies that within a given region people have attained sufficient trust in one another to have dependable expectations of peaceful change. A key feature of political integration thus conceived is the resolution of conflict without resort to violence. Without doubt this applies to the EU, and indeed to many countries lying adjacent in its 'neighbourhood', the latter concept appropriately implying a sense of extended community and a renunciation of violence as a means to solve disputes. However, such an interpretation of political integration may be too narrow to be analytically useful. Political integration, as currently conceived in Europe and elsewhere, also extends to behaviour which has as its object the achievement of common goals designed to benefit the entire community. Thus, political integration can be assessed in terms of the range of activities undertaken in common, and the *significance* of those activities. Common measures undertaken transnationally to benefit butterfly collectors would be far less significant than agreeing on mutual recognition of social security eligibility criteria across the same national boundaries. Deeper levels of political integration could be seen as involving some degree of sacrifice by one part of the population in order to benefit another part. Typically, taxation systems perform exactly this redistributive role in a society that is politically integrated. Only if a sufficient sense of community exists is it possible for these redistributive mechanisms to operate without controversy. In an international 'community' like the EU, the *principle* of redistribution, leaving aside whether it works in practice, is emblematic of political integration across national frontiers.

Writers have also been divided about whether political integration is an outcome or a process. While Haas originally saw it as the 'voluntary creation of larger political units' he later, famously and rather ambiguously, both saw it as a 'process whereby political actors in several distinct national settings are persuaded to shift their loyalties, expectations and political activities towards a new center, whose institutions possess or demand jurisdiction over pre-existing national states' and declared that 'the end result of a process of political integration is a new political community, superimposed over the pre-existing ones'

(Haas, 1968, p. 16). Other writers, despite any evidence of it happening or being likely to happen, have defined political integration as an outcome. Hodges (1972, p. 13) saw 'new political systems' emerging from 'existing political systems', and Harrison (1974, p. 14) envisaged the creation of 'central institutions' with 'binding decision-making powers' successfully allocating values at the regional level.

Although economic integration is not our concern here, and while it can be conceptually distinguished from political integration without difficulty, it is worth saying a few words about their mutual relevance. From a neofunctional perspective, economic integration is seen as providing the bedrock for political integration or for making possible a transition from 'low politics' to 'high politics'. This argument sees political institutions at the regional level resulting from a need to facilitate, coordinate, regulate and extend functional linkages across national borders. It is the success of this functional cooperation across borders that allegedly leads to the new expectations, loyalties and so on, that are characteristic of the neofunctional approach. The story of European integration lends some credence to this line of thinking. From coal and steel to a common market and customs union; from a single market to EU citizenship; from co-decision in policy-making to a role in defence and security, the story has been of sequential achievements and expanded competences: in sum, from the purely economic to the overtly political.

However, other scenarios are conceivable. Political integration may be the *sine qua non* for greater economic intercourse: the fall of the Berlin Wall heralded a tectonic shift in Europe's political landscape, and one which made a reorientation towards economic integration possible. Politics and economics can be kept separate, and the implications of the separation may vary considerably since EU–China relations, for example, are characterized by heavy economic interchange but little political convergence.

The European Context: Institutional Perspectives

A key question that lies at the heart of discourses around European integration theory is the question of Europe's uniqueness. In other words: is the EU *sui generis*? This question has obviously impinged on several longstanding attempts to theorize about integration in various regional contexts. The transferability of the EU model depends to a large extent on whether factors specific to Western Europe are essential prerequisites for the integration process or whether integration could proceed elsewhere based on a different set of factors. This argument requires us to identify factors that are, respectively, necessary or sufficient for political integration to take place. While we can probably identify factors that have guaranteed the success of European integration it is a different matter to say whether these same factors, or merely analogous factors, would be necessary for integration to proceed elsewhere. What is clear, and what makes the question all the more difficult, is that regional integration schemes have nowhere in the world achieved anything like the degree of success that they have in Europe. Thus, it is not known whether this is because factors specific to Western Europe do not exist elsewhere, or for some other reason.

This question is central to the topic under discussion here. If EU political integration is attributable solely to factors that are uniquely present in Europe, the chances of transferability of the EU political project to ASEAN, ASEAN Plus Three or anywhere else for that matter, even as a template, are seemingly very remote. Before addressing that question, one needs to ask whether EU political integration has been highly dependent on conditions that are uniquely present in Europe. Two themes are worth mentioning here.

First, we can trace the roots of integration in Western Europe to what has been termed the 'inadequacy of the state' (Wallace and Wallace, 2000, p. 47). 'Inadequacy' in this context is very different from ways in which the state might be seen as inadequate in some ASEAN countries, as this chapter will demonstrate. In Europe, the postwar reconstruction itself made reliance on cooperation with neighbours an instinctive response, especially in an age where nationalism and exaggerated assumptions about national self-sufficiency had fallen into disrepute. As prosperity and extensive welfare states developed in Western Europe, the state *qua* state found itself under pressure from public opinion to perform its quintessential functions of providing welfare and security to an extent that was increasing exponentially and which lay far beyond its capacity to deliver. In other words, an expectations–capability gap had arisen due largely to notions of a Westphalian state system needing to confront an increasingly post-Westphalian world order. It was therefore almost an instinctive reaction to rely on transnational cooperation for support. In this way, states drew strength from each other and prolonged their own survival. As Milward (1992) has argued, the state was rescued from its own demise by the novel mechanisms of European integration. This was an essentially European phenomenon because nowhere else in the world did public opinion expect so much from the state in terms of welfare and security. The latter concern was exacerbated by the Cold War (until 1990) and thereafter by more diffuse (but no less menacing) threats such as terrorism, environmental degradation, cross-border trafficking and ethnic conflict. By the 1990s a *modus vivendi* had evolved whereby the EU took care of some sectors of policy-making while the nation-state retained control over others. The emergence of subsidiarity in the Treaty on European Union reflected a concern among national elites that the process of delegation to Brussels might have gone too far. By the 21st century, a system of multi-level governance is established in Europe (the 2004 and 2007 enlargements simply widening the geographical scope of a system that was well-rooted in the West), which presupposes a sense of community among citizens in the region which is quite unparalleled anywhere else in the world.

Second, there are a number of factors specific to West Europe which may account for the progress of political integration in this region. First, historical experiences of major conflicts have created a strong desire to devise collective security arrangements, although individual states have pursued contrasting solutions to their own security ranging from neutrality to military alliances. However, behind these apparently divergent security postures lay a neat balance often based on geopolitics. This is best seen in Scandinavia, where Norway's membership of the North Atlantic Treaty Organization (NATO) was balanced by Finland's special relationship with Russia, while Sweden followed strict neutrality between them. Second, Europe has been, and still is, unique in its overlapping confluence of high population density and numerous national borders. Nowhere else in the world can match Europe for this. Linguistic differences, sometimes hardened by conflict, have made functional cooperation necessary as a means to overcome the challenge of geographical proximity. Third, a commitment to liberal democracy became a badge of Europe's identity, separating it from the communist east but then providing the vehicle for a subsequent 'return to Europe'. Earlier, the accessions of Greece, Spain and Portugal were all premised on the need to anchor these recently authoritarian regimes in the bedrock of European liberal democracy. Fourth, notions of the 'welfare state', although differently interpreted in different parts of the Continent, take as their starting point an assumption that the state (or society) has a duty to protect the individual comprehensively from the wilder excesses of the market 'from the cradle to the grave'. On this issue, Europe can be contrasted with the United States where the state is 'kept at arm's length' and the individual is seen as partly responsible for his or her own success and misfortunes. Europe is not unique in espousing the concept of a welfare system (New Zealand and Canada have their own variants) but it is a quintessentially European idea, perhaps (as I have argued elsewhere) *the* defining characteristic of European society (Moxon-Browne, 1997, p. 30). EU social policy has latched on to this theme, by acknowledging that the EU citizen needs protection from the cross-border implications of economic integration. Fifth, despite its imperfections, the concept of EU citizenship as an emblem of political community is a reflection of a value-laden consensus in Europe that does not exist in any other regional organization. Although the precise significance and implications of EU citizenship are still hotly debated (Meehan, 1993; Soysal, 1994; Wiener, 1998; Dell'Olio, 2005) what seems beyond doubt is that European Community law and the role of the European Court of Justice (ECJ) provide a transnational framework for the protection of citizens' rights in the EU without even needing to invoke the concept of citizenship (Moxon-Browne, 2000, p. 190). Again, this transnational system of protection for citizens' rights is unmatched anywhere else in the world.

Transferability of Models of Political Integration

The issue of transferability of models of European integration to new settings has preoccupied students of integration for three decades. Haas identified early three levels of conflict resolution between nation-states that reflect differing degrees of integration. Firstly, that there is that of accommodation by lowest common denominator; secondly, that of splitting the difference; and thirdly that of consciously, or implicitly, upgrading the common interests of the parties involved in the regional grouping (Haas, 1961, pp. 377–8). Reflecting on the European experience we can say that the intensity of political integration is positively correlated with industrialization and economic diversification. Processes which yield optimal progress towards the goal of political community at the European level simply cannot be reproduced in other contexts because the necessary preconditions exist to a much lesser degree. If regional integration proceeds in other parts of the world it is likely that it will do so as a result of factors indigenous to those regions; and this is how it should be. It is a uniquely Eurocentric assumption to expect models developed in a 'contextually specific' process in Western Europe to be appropriate for other regions of the world. Nevertheless, borrowing concepts or labels from the European experience sometimes gives the impression that such transferability is not only possible, but desirable. The African Union consciously borrowed its title from the EU, but it would be difficult to imagine any regional organization less similar to the EU.

ASEAN: Societal Perspectives

When considering the appropriateness of the EU model for Southeast Asia, it is evident that there are a number of reasons why the process of political integration delineated above may not 'fit' easily into the ASEAN reality, never mind any broader grouping. Firstly, society in East and Southeast Asia is religiously and culturally much more heterogeneous than society in West Europe. While most nations in the region are Buddhist, most people in the region are Muslim (due to the preponderant demographic presence of Indonesia); and the Philippines stand out rather anomalously as the only Christian nation in Asia. Ethnically, the picture is even more complicated with significant minorities in most countries exacerbating fissures across the body politic of regimes that, for other reasons, are extremely brittle. Racially, notwithstanding substantial immigrant communities from Africa and the Caribbean, Europe is an overwhelmingly white continent. The picture in Southeast Asia is very different and much more varied. What all this means is that at the fundamental level of cultural homogeneity, a key background condition for political integration, Southeast Asia lacks the societal 'platform' on which a common set of values can be constructed. Admittedly, it can be argued that, in Europe, ethnic and racial heterogeneity has increased sufficiently for this cosy picture of a predominantly white society to have become somewhat dated. Against that, it can be argued that religious and racial minorities in Europe have become assimilated, with varying degrees of willingness, into a consensual acceptance of 'multiculturalism' and liberal democratic values. The strong, yet usually unspoken, reticence regarding Turkish entry into the EU, often disguised as concern about economics or human rights, is in reality a deep reluctance to upset the apple cart of 'Western' democratic values in the existing EU. These values have not been challenged, but perhaps have even been strengthened by the 'return to Europe' of erstwhile communist nations to the east. Their embrace of 'Western values' has had the effect of greatly enhancing the legitimacy of the latter.

Secondly, the nature of the state in Southeast Asia and Europe, respectively, has very different implications for the process of political integration. What might be termed a 'Bonapartist' model of the third world state applies most appropriately to ASEAN states. In this model, the state is a force for cohesion in society by managing and manipulating class struggles without essentially damaging the economic system that preserves the domination of a particular economic class (Nesadurai, 2004, p. 150). This interpretation is perceptive and resonates well with the realities of striking economic growth in the Asian region. Postcolonial societies appeared to have a number of competing bourgeois factions whose conflicts needed to be managed in the long-term interests of capitalist growth and the social institutions on which such development depended, especially private property and the right of accumulation. Most states in ASEAN have been ruled by entrenched elites for decades. In turn, this has led to the evolution of national institutions that tend to favour the status quo (Jayasuriya, 2004, p. 32). It is not surprising that such regimes are unwilling to open themselves to the kind of external scrutiny that international political integration would require or to cede power to external institutions whose diktats could be unpredictable and unwelcome.

As a corollary to this, civil society as understood in Europe is relatively underdeveloped in most Southeast Asian states. Political structures are fragile and the economy is geared towards creating wealth to keep the elites in power. In most of the ASEAN region poverty is still widespread, and any idea that the role of the state is to redistribute wealth is still quite fanciful. In Europe, on the other hand, the state has emerged as purporting to be a neutral arbiter between competing interests in society. Wealth is apparently redistributed within society, although the degree to which this actually happens is often contested. In contrast with Southeast Asia, the state in Europe is buoyed by a vibrant civil society which, in cooperation with the state, seeks strength from a pooling of sovereignty with other states. In Southeast Asia, the notion of pooling sovereignty in order to strengthen national elites is as unimaginable as it is unlikely to occur. If the neofunctionalist analysis is correct in asserting that pluralistic and highly developed societies are most likely to integrate, this pluralism is missing in most ASEAN states despite their high degree of economic development. According to the neofunctional view, the existence of groups in society seeking collaboration with analogous groups in other societies lays the foundations for international political integration. In Europe, this process has been greatly facilitated by geographical proximity and shared (if contrasting) historical experience. In Southeast Asia, geographical distance, cultural divergences and opposing historical experiences militate against the type of political integration that has been possible in Europe.

It also has to be pointed out that although economic and political integration are conceptually distinct and (as argued above) can develop separately at different velocities, economic integration often leads to, or requires, a concomitant process of political integration. In the EU, the main rationale of Community law, and of the policy-making institutions in Brussels, is to facilitate the smooth operation and evolution of the Single Market and all collateral policies that lubricate the processes of economic interchange.

At a much more basic level, moreover, it might be argued that one simple and compelling reason for difficulties in integration among ASEAN countries is the wide divergence in their demographic size. The population of Indonesia, for example, is just over 245 million people and the population of Brunei a mere 380,000. In other words, one ASEAN country has a population that is nearly 1000 times greater than another. In fact, the European experience shows that a huge divergence in population or territorial size is not a barrier to successful integration provided other underlying assumptions can be made. Malta has a population of 360,000 as against a population of 82 million in Germany. The relative unimportance of size (however defined) in the EU is linked to mechanisms that govern decision-making among the member states. As the membership of the EU has increased, recalculations of approximately proportionate voting strengths in the Council, and national representations in the European Parliament, have ensured a balance between the preponderant strengths of the large member states and the sovereignty of small 'micro-states' like Malta or Luxembourg. Indeed, the attraction of EU membership for a country like Malta, or for prospective members like Macedonia or Montenegro, is a guarantee that their interests will be protected as well as their viability as nation-states. Thus, in the European Parliament or in the Council, smaller member states are relatively 'over-represented' in relation to their larger partners. However, it is always a finely balanced calculation, sometimes bitterly contested, as in the long-drawn-out negotiations surrounding the Draft Constitutional Treaty at the 2004 Intergovernmental Conference. Such negotiations can only succeed because of the underlying political consensus and a realization that a successful outcome will 'upgrade the common interest': to fail is to see a setback for everyone — big and small. Although the demographic gap between the smallest and largest country in ASEAN is far greater than the gap between Germany and Malta (about four times greater), it is not this fact alone that explains the failure to make progress on political integration. Instead, it is the lack of an underlying *political* consensus and a spirit of rivalry that is in stark contrast to the sense of solidarity that is well established in Europe. All 27 member states of the EU are multiparty democracies where governments are elected at regular intervals, and political parties alternate sufficiently frequently for the voters to feel empowered by the choices open to them. On a crude right–left spectrum, or even a simple spectrum between democracy and authoritarianism, the gap between EU political systems is much narrower than in ASEAN.

In ASEAN, moreover, there are wide variations in economic prosperity (or poverty) that cut across variations of political ideology. Gross domestic product (GDP) per capita based on Purchasing Power Parities in the ASEAN region ranges from US$1700 in Burma Myanmar to US$28,600 in Singapore. On another measure, the Human Development Index (HDI) Singapore at 0.916 ranks above some EU countries while Laos at 0.553 can be placed among the least developed countries of the world. These stark statistical contrasts mask, rather than reflect, differences of political regime. Brunei has no elections and is effectively a personal fiefdom of its ruler, but its GDP per capita (US$23,600) and its HDI (0.871) place it far ahead of Cambodia (an aspiring democracy with GDP per capita of US$2500 and an HDI of 0.583) and only slightly ahead of Laos (a communist one-party regime with a GDP per capita of US$2500 and an HDI of 0.553). If one looks at all the ASEAN countries one sees that four are multiparty democracies, with Thailand currently a marginal case, while two are communist regimes where only one party is legal, and two (Burma Myanmar and Brunei) are autocracies where political parties are banned or non-existent.

Human Rights

Much of the misunderstanding that has arisen between European and Southeast Asian nations on the topic of human rights revolves around the so-called 'Asian values' debate. The Asian values position was neatly expressed in the Bangkok Declaration of Asian States in April 1993. Here it was stated that, although human rights are universal, they must be considered in a context of different 'national and regional particularities and various historical, cultural and religious backgrounds'. While on the one hand it makes sense to view universalistic notions of human rights through the prism of cultural specificities, it is easy to slide from that position to one justifying authoritarian governments and political regimes that clearly flout human rights standards as generally understood in the rest of the world. This debate continues and its importance for us here is not so much the contrast between Europe and Southeast Asia, which can be justified to some extent on historical and cultural grounds, but the contrasts that exist within the ASEAN group which are discussed below. For any meaningful process of political integration to evolve, an underpinning of values expressed principally, but not exclusively, in common interpretations of human rights seems essential. In the case of the EU, a common system of values is evident in the organic growth of EU law; the increasingly detailed prerequisites for the accession of new member states; stipulations laid down in trade and aid agreements with third countries (even if observed more in the breach than in the observance) and, above all, in 'human rights' provisions associated with the Draft Constitutional Treaty, not the least of which is a complete ban on capital punishment. For good measure, one could add the European Convention on Human Rights, which, although encompassing a wider membership than the EU, provides a series of norms that are consonant with those of the European Court of Justice, the latter having decided to be guided by the former.

A further debate that affects interpretations of human rights in ASEAN countries is the complex relationship between human rights and economic development. On the one hand it can be argued, as it often is in developing countries, that human rights may need to take second place to the overriding need to pursue economic development. The basic human right to share resources equitably is meaningless unless the resources exist in the first place. There is no doubt that China and Singapore have achieved rapid economic success while restricting civil and political rights, but, on the other hand, Zimbabwe has seen increasing political repression accompanied by a collapse of its economy. Alternatively, it can be argued that although human rights may be something of a 'luxury' for developing countries, there are sound arguments for promoting and protecting them alongside progress in economic development. What seems even clearer is that rapid economic progress will, sooner or later, lead to demands for greater political participation, and a concomitant concern to enshrine human rights in constitutional formats. Human rights and economic progress are interdependent at least from the point of view that the achievement of one assists with achievement of the other. As people become more prosperous, they seek to defend their rights and it becomes possible for the state to establish mechanisms enabling them to do so. Likewise, as people increasingly enjoy their rights, economic development becomes easier to manage and foster and, more importantly, the legitimacy of the state is enhanced as citizens increasingly see themselves as stakeholders in its survival.

For evidence that ASEAN countries perceive human rights as being fundamental to the evolution of a 'political community' in their region, we need look no further than the consistent and prolonged attempt to establish a 'Human Rights Mechanism' in the region. Although the word 'mechanism' is deliberately non-committal, avoiding more precise terminology such as 'committee', or 'commission', progress has been painfully slow, and reflects the wide divergences that exist in ASEAN on a theme that is widely regarded elsewhere as having universal significance and evoking a high degree of consensus. In 1993, ASEAN foreign ministers agreed that their organization should consider the establishment of an appropriate regional mechanism on human rights. Subsequently, a 'Working Group for an ASEAN Human Rights Mechanism' was established to cajole ASEAN governments into making progress on this issue. At first, some ASEAN governments argued that no discussion could take place until every country had established a human rights 'commission'. Later, when it transpired that this prerequisite was too burdensome for some countries, a more lenient requirement for a human rights 'focal point' was substituted. A 'focal point' could be a committee or commission, or simply a government office purporting to be concerned with human rights issues. By 2000, all ASEAN countries had set up these 'focal points' and since then the Working Group has been trying to achieve its goal of establishing a 'regional mechanism'.

As recently as 2003, the Working Group expressed disappointment at its own lack of success, stating that ASEAN should now take concrete steps towards the establishment of a regional mechanism. If ASEAN can take only a few months to agree measures against terrorism, the Working Group concluded, it should be possible to act similarly against similar dangers posed by continuing violations of human rights in the region. In December 2006, the Indonesian Foreign Minister Hassan Wirayuda put it more bluntly: 'We can't become the ASEAN Community that we have envisioned for ourselves, until and unless the promotion and protection of human rights is pervasive in our region' (*Jakarta Post*, 21 December 2006). Welcoming this statement, but deploring the lack of progress in ASEAN, the *Jakarta Post* (21 December 2006) made the point quite clearly:

> We fully comprehend the limitations faced by Indonesian diplomats working within the rigid protocols of ASEAN. But how much more gradual can ASEAN be when after 13 years there is little to show in terms of progress towards a rights mechanism? Education and promotion of human rights is an important element, but protection is just as integral. At present, regional efforts on the former are scarce, and on the latter non-existent.... No-one would be friends with someone who was openly abusing his or her family. Should the state not live by equal principles? If Indonesian officials refuse to be more decisive with countries like Myanmar, for example, they should not shy away from engaging in dialogue with opposition groups within that country.

Burma Myanmar is indeed currently viewed as an *enfant terrible* in ASEAN. It embodies in the starkest way dilemmas that exist elsewhere in ASEAN regarding human rights, democratization and the rule of law. The dilemma is between excluding such regimes or tolerating them in the hope of bringing about political change through dialogue and 'carrot and stick' measures of an economic kind. Burma Myanmar, however, appears rather impervious to international opinion, inasmuch as United Nations resolutions, and visits by UN dignitaries to Rangoon, have had little effect. In May 2006, a visit by UN Under-Secretary for Political Affairs Ibrahim Gambari to Burma Myanmar, during which he visited Aung San Suu Kyi and called for her release, resulted in her detention being arbitrarily prolonged a few days later. That said, the human rights situation in some other ASEAN countries is not so significantly better than in Burma Myanmar as to justify any attitudes of moral superiority. Nevertheless, Burma Myanmar stands out as a test-case for ASEAN's political solidarity; and pressure on ASEAN to take action with regard to Burma Myanmar has been increased by the evident dismay of external actors in Washington and Brussels at ASEAN's apparent spinelessness.

In Cambodia, human rights protection is also fragile. Freedom of expression and freedom of assembly remain seriously restricted. Defamation remains a criminal offence, and critics of the government can be charged with 'disinformation' which carries a prison sentence of up to three years. The 2007 local elections and the scheduled 2008 national elections have witnessed an increase of political intimidation and violence, including the deaths of several party activists for which the perpetrators have yet to be brought to justice.

In the Philippines, extra-judicial murders have multiplied. The main targets are political opponents (especially left-wing party activists), human rights campaigners, lawyers, community leaders and trade union officials. Part of the background to this is the inability or unwillingness of the Government to prevent violations of human rights by private companies involved in mining or logging, whose activities impinge on the land of smallholders.

In Vietnam, the principal victims of police persecution are those advocating religious freedom, democracy and minority rights. New laws were introduced in 2006 to curb press freedom, following laws in 2005 to curb the right to demonstrate and to authorize 'administrative detention' (i.e. without trial). A prominent human rights campaigner, Quang Do, who is deputy leader of the Buddhist Church of Vietnam is under house arrest in his own monastery in Ho Chi Minh City with no charges having been made against him. He is forbidden to leave the monastery, and all his communications are censored. He was forbidden by the authorities from going to Oslo to receive a human rights award in November 2006.

Abolition of the death penalty is a characteristic feature of EU member states and reflects an important plank in the wider consensus on human rights. In ASEAN, the situation is very varied, with three distinct groups of countries being identifiable with regard to use of the death penalty: those where it is abolished; those where it can be used but in fact is not; and those where it is still used — sometimes being applied to an increasing range of offences. It is useful to discuss some of these variations within ASEAN if only to underline the divergence of legal traditions and, hence, the lack of a minimal consensus that would be necessary to underpin a value-system on which a sense of political community or an integrated concept of 'citizenship' could be based.

At the outset it is worth emphasising that only two ASEAN countries have legally abolished the death penalty: Cambodia in 1989 and the Philippines in 2006. Otherwise, the ASEAN region is one where, despite a global move in the other direction, the death penalty remains on the statute book. However, in some ASEAN countries, although the death penalty remains legal, it has not been used recently. Brunei has executed no one since 1957; and in Burma Myanmar, Thailand and Laos no executions have taken place in the past two years. In Laos, death sentences are reserved for drug offences only. At the other extreme, Singapore is reckoned to have the highest per capita execution rate in the world. Mandatory death sentences apply (thus allowing no variation for mitigating circumstances) to all convictions for murder and drug-trafficking. In the latter case, possession of drugs assumes knowledge of such possession unless the accused can prove the contrary. In Vietnam, the death penalty is in force for a range of economic as well as criminal and political offences. Execution is by firing squad. In contravention of international law, the identities of those sentenced to death are not made public and even family members have difficulty in obtaining information.

An ASEAN Charter: Light at the End of the Tunnel?

During its 40-year history, ASEAN has found it convenient to adopt a fairly relaxed view towards politics within its member countries while concentrating on the more urgent concerns of economics, trade, aid and development in the region. ASEAN's survival as a regional grouping can be largely attributed to its flexible attitudes towards widely varying political cultures. As the group expanded, political diversity became more pronounced and, in particular, communist regimes in Laos and

Vietnam have contrasted strongly with right-wing authoritarian governments among the founding member states. Only in recent years has ASEAN begun to face up to political problems in its ranks and while the principles of non-interference and consensus remain central to ASEAN's survival, there has been some evidence of the group wanting to emulate the fostering of common political values that characterizes other regional groupings across the globe. All this has taken place in a global context where political 'conditionality' is increasingly seen as part of aid, trade and development relationships at the international level. Most obviously, EU policies implemented through the Cotonou Agreement, through its 'Neighbourhood Policy' in North Africa and Eastern Europe, and through its close monitoring of democratization in the Balkans, have reflected and set new standards for similar policies in other parts of the world. ASEAN cannot escape this if it wants to be taken seriously by other actors, not least by the EU itself. In the case of ASEAN, what seems to have brought matters to a head is the increasingly anomalous position of Burma Myanmar in the group, notwithstanding the distortions of democracy that exist elsewhere in the region. The military government in Burma Myanmar was persuaded to forego its turn at chairing the group in 2006 because of its appalling record on human rights. Admittedly, much of the pressure for this step came from outside ASEAN, but the fact that the group adopted this policy displayed for the first time a determination to draw a line at what political behaviour is unacceptable.

On the other hand, deciding what political behaviour *is* acceptable will be more difficult to determine in the years ahead. The region has a large number of one-party states where opponents of the regime live in fear of persecution; Malaysia and Singapore are two examples. In Vietnam and Laos, one-party communist regimes suppress the same political and civil liberties that the military government in Burma Myanmar was accused of flouting. In Thailand and Cambodia, both would-be democracies, political life is dominated by a single party that makes true alternations of power difficult to achieve. Only in the Philippines and in Indonesia can we say that multiparty democracy is alive and well, although in both countries there are grounds for concern regarding human rights.

At the 38th Ministerial Meeting of ASEAN in Vientiane in 2005, efforts were made to instigate an ASEAN Charter in which common political values would be expressed (Macan-Markar, 2005, p. 2). It is probably no coincidence that this development came only months after the EU had produced a text for a much more ambitious Constitutional Treaty. In the case of ASEAN, an Eminent Persons Group (EPG) comprising distinguished citizens from ASEAN countries was established to make recommendations on a Charter for ASEAN. Indonesia was the prime mover behind this initiative, arguing that unless ASEAN adopted a 'binding constitution' it would not be taken seriously by external actors with which it does business like the EU or the US. The Charter concept will be a tall order for ASEAN given its diverse political perspectives (Conde, 2007, p. 1). By the start of 2007 it became clear what the principal contours of an ASEAN Charter might look like. If this draft charter is agreed upon and implemented, it would allow ASEAN members for the first time to criticize each other's domestic political regimes and to impose sanctions against errant members. However, given that no member-state of ASEAN has an unblemished record, it is unlikely that the language of the Charter will break new ground. Consolidation of the currently cautious conservatism will most likely set the tone of any text agreed.

Conclusion: Political Integration in ASEAN

It is useful to recapitulate our observations on political integration in Europe before attempting an assessment of the prospects for political integration in ASEAN. First, we noted that European political integration was rooted in, and justified by, an impressive level of economic integration. Arguably, the dynamics of the single market required, but also assumed, a degree of political commitment based on a realization that the EU cannot survive in a globalized world unless it forges common policies. As Benjamin Franklin remarked at the signing of the Declaration of Independence: 'We must all hang together or, most assuredly, we will all hang separately'.

High levels of prosperity in Europe, linked in the popular imagination to integration, mean that populations identify with the integration process and support it. There is a widespread awareness of the EU in the 27 member states, and even though Euroscepticism is apparent in parts of the EU, it rarely advocates a complete dismantling of the European project. The notion of EU citizenship, despite its imperfections, reflects a plausible community of values, interests and aspirations that reaches beyond the nation-state. To paraphrase Haas, 'shifts in the loci of authority and power would be accompanied by patterns of loyalty transference where groups ceased to direct their activity towards national governments and would look to the developing supranational arena' (cited in Rosamond, 2000, p. 56). Geographical proximity and a high incidence of national frontiers in a relatively small geographical space tended to focus European minds on the benefits of collaboration. In a literal sense as well, infrastructure communication developments such as railways, roads, mass travel and a common currency have all contributed to creating a new awareness of an 'imagined community' and solidarity in Europe.

In ASEAN, almost all these prerequisites are absent. Geographically, the region is disparate and members are often separated by oceans, political incompatibilities and economic rivalries. It can be remarked, without exaggeration, that the only communal value in ASEAN is a fierce attachment to national sovereignty, and this has been well expressed through the ASEAN principles of non-interference and consensus in decision-making. Economic integration in ASEAN has not progressed to the level where political integration is seen as necessary, or useful. Economic success in the popular mind is linked to national effort, not to transnational cooperation. Foreign direct investment comes into the region not because it is a region but because individual national economic policies are highly conducive to investment, such as Singapore in ASEAN or South Korea outside it.

As we have seen, poverty is widespread in ASEAN. Popular awareness of ASEAN is virtually non-existent. Thus, a quintessential feature of political integration, that it be underpinned by widespread popular legitimation, is absent in ASEAN. To achieve durable political integration, a sense of ownership of the process needs to reach down into the constituent societies. Economic success, where it has been achieved in ASEAN, affects elite minorities, and these attribute economic success to policies that are autarchic rather than open or international. Very little has been done to elaborate policies that might attract investment more broadly or on a transnational basis. As this chapter has demonstrated, in ASEAN there is no community of values such as that underpinning the integration process in Europe (Fong, 2005, pp. 7–11). Therefore, it would be difficult if not impossible to compose a 'constitution' analogous to the European model, the efforts at an ASEAN Charter notwithstanding.

This chapter discussed political integration in the EU at two levels: institutional and societal. At the institutional level, it was argued that EU institutions provide a possible template for the ASEAN region, but that the degree of sovereignty pooled in the EU is unlikely, for several reasons, to be replicated in ASEAN. Nevertheless, representative and executive institutions in the EU could provide a basis for more concerted decision-making in ASEAN, if the political will existed.

At the societal level this chapter was concerned with notions of citizenship and reciprocal rights, and it was argued that, in the EU, a high degree of mutual responsiveness exists across national boundaries. However, in the ASEAN region, despite there being scope for recognition of mutual rights on the back of labour mobility and foreign direct investment, little has been achieved. In the area of human rights there exist wide divergences among ASEAN countries, and the prospects for achieving a meaningful 'charter' were at best problematic.

References

Conde, C. (2007) 'ASEAN puts charter with punitive powers high on agenda', *International Herald Tribune*, 4 January.
Dell'Olio, F. (2005) *The Europeanization of Citizenship*, Aldershot: Ashgate.
Deutsch, K. (1996) *Nationalism and Social Communication*, Cambridge, MA: MIT Press.
Fong, T. S. (2005) 'European Integration: A Model for Southeast Asia', *Asia Europe Journal*, 3. 1, pp. 7–11.
Haas, E. B. (1961) 'International Integration: the European and the Universal Process,' *International Organisation* 15. 3, pp. 366–92.
Haas, E. B. (1968) *The Uniting of Europe*, Stanford: Stanford University Press.
Harrison, R. J. (1974) *Europe in Question*, London: Allen and Unwin.
Hodges M. (ed.) (1972) *European Integration*, Harmondsworth: Penguin.
Jayasuriya, K. (2004) 'Embedded mercantilism and open regionalism: the crisis of a regional political project', in K. Jayasuriya (ed) *Asian Regional Governance: Crisis and Change*, London: Routledge.
Macan-Markar, M. (2005) 'ASEAN Searches for Common Political Values', *Global Policy Forum*, 1 August, 1. 3, available at http://www.globalpolicy.org/nations/sovereign/integrate/2005/0801asean.htm, accessed 28 January 2007.
Meehan, E. (1993) *Citizenship and the European Community*, London: Sage.
Milward, A. (1992) *The European Rescue of the Nation-State*, Berkeley: University of California Press.
Moxon-Browne, E. (1997) 'Eastern and Western Europe: towards a new European identity?', *Contemporary Politics* 3. 1, pp. 27–34.
Moxon-Browne, E. (2000) 'The Europeanization of Citizenship: A Passport to the Future?', *Yearbook of European Studies* 14, Amsterdam: Rodopi, pp. 179–96.
Nesadurai, H.E.S. (2004) 'Asia-Pacific approaches to regional governance: the globalization–domestic politics nexus', in K. Jayasuriya (ed.) *Asian Regional Governance: Crisis and Change*, London: Routledge.
Rosamond, B. (2000) *Theories of European Integration*, London: Palgrave.
Soysal, Y. N. (1994) *Limits of Citizenship: Migrants and Post-National Membership in Europe*, Chicago: University of Chicago Press.
Wallace, H. and Wallace, W. (2000) *Policy-Making in the European Union*, 4th edition, Oxford: Oxford University Press.
Wiener, A. (1998) *European Citizenship Practice*, Boulder: Westview.

6
The Origins and Development of ASEM and EU–East Asia Relations
Yeo Lay Hwee

Introduction

The Asia–Europe Meeting (ASEM) is the latest and the most ambitious attempt to provide a framework for EU–East Asia relations. It complements long-standing instances of cooperation such as the European Union–Association of Southeast Asian Nations (EU–ASEAN) partnership, the expanding EU–China relationship, the relationship between the EU and Japan, and the relationship between the EU and South Korea (the Republic of Korea). ASEM was launched in 1996 with an inaugural summit of leaders from the EU member states, the European Commission, ASEAN, China, Japan and South Korea. A constellation of factors provided the backdrop to the conception and birth of ASEM. These factors included Europe's reaction to APEC and the fears of a fortress Europe on the part of East Asia.

This chapter examines what ASEM has achieved to date. It asks whether the ASEM framework has provided a significant boost to EU–East Asia relations. It explores whether EU–East Asia relations have strengthened since the creation of ASEM. It analyses whether ASEM has been of mutual benefit to the two regions and contributed in any way to global governance. Have the EU and East Asia defined and enhanced their roles as global players as they become increasingly involved in each other's regions? The chapter commences with a brief examination of EU–East Asia relations before ASEM and explains the reasons behind ASEM's creation. The chapter then discusses the development of the ASEM process and evaluates its impact on the EU–East Asia partnership. In the process, it will also explore questions about the EU's strategic interest and vision and the future of ASEM vis-à-vis the other frameworks the encompass EU–East Asia relations.

EU (EEC)–East Asia Relations before ASEM

When the European Economic Community (EEC) was formally established by the Treaty of Rome in 1957, many countries in East Asia were emerging from struggles for independence and were in the process of transforming from colonies into independent states. European attention was turned inward, on reconstruction, reconciliation and regional integration. There was no concerted 'European' external policy towards East Asia, because in the EEC's early days of integration the focus was on creating a common market. Foreign policy as a whole remained very much in the hands of member states. Similarly, the East Asian countries also focused their attention on national and regional affairs, particularly their own experience of post-World War Two decolonization and nation-state building.

As the EEC developed, integrated further, and then enlarged to include the United Kingdom, Ireland and Denmark, its power as an international trading partner grew. The key instrument that makes the European Community an international trading power is the common external tariff. The European Community conducted its bilateral cooperation with East Asian countries (as with other third countries) through the framework of Trade and Cooperation Agreements. There was also structured political dialogue between member states and most partners in East Asia through ministerial meetings or meetings at political director level.

The European Community began to slowly explore and deepen relations with East Asia in the 1970s. These relations were conducted with individual countries, rather than regions, and varied significantly in depth, attention and focus. For example, development aid constituted a major focus of relations with Southeast Asia.

In terms of bilateral relations, those between the European Community and Japan are the longest established. The European Commission (EC) Delegation office was established in Tokyo in 1974. However, EC–Japan political relations have not been particularly strong, due in large part to Japan's special relationship with the United States. Their two-way trade relationship, whilst dynamic, was also fraught with various trade conflicts, particularly in the 1980s. Cooperation has been strongest in technical areas ranging from industrial policy, science and technology, and research, to executive training and environmental protection.

Diplomatic relations between the Community and China were formally established in 1975, although official relations did not effectively develop until the mid-1990s. The EC Delegation was only established in Beijing in October 1988. The following year, diplomatic relations were suspended in response to the brutal events at Tiananmen Square. EC–China relations were normalized in 1992, and have since continued to expand, driven by China's huge and growing markets and its increasing diplomatic clout.

The first regular ministerial meeting between the Community and South Korea took place in 1983, but it was only in 1989 that the Commission established a Delegation in Seoul. The 1990s saw European involvement in the Korean Peninsula through the Korean Energy Development Organization (KEDO) and cooperation between the European Community and South Korea began to both diversify and strengthen. Of these three bilateral EC relationships, that with South Korea remains the least developed.

Similarly, in the early days of the Community, there was no bilateral dialogue with individual countries of ASEAN. Informal dialogue between ASEAN and the Community first took place in 1972. Initially, the dialogue focused primarily on market access for ASEAN's exports into the EC, and a price stabilization scheme for ASEAN's primary products. Relations were formalized in 1980 with the signing of the ASEAN–European Community Cooperation Agreement during the second ASEAN–European Community ministerial meeting in Kuala Lumpur. This was the first bloc-to-bloc interregional dialogue that the European Community had with a part of Asia. Bilateral relations between the Community and individual East Asian nations remained relatively underdeveloped.

The early 1980s saw increasing economic challenges posed to the European Community by Japan and the newly industrializing economies (NIEs). The Community developed political dialogue with East Asia, (particularly with ASEAN) because of concern over the possible expansion of the Soviet Union's influence into Asia through its Vietnamese ally and the Soviet invasion of Afghanistan. The Community, however, remained largely self-absorbed as it prepared for the Single Market. It was not until the 1990s that the Community became cognizant of the tremendous changes in East Asia and the need to re-acquaint itself with the region. Coupled with its own internal changes after the Treaty of European Union (the Maastricht Treaty), which entered into force in January 1993, was the need to review existing foreign relations instruments towards external parties, particularly a region that was fast becoming one of the key engines of growth. This led to the first Communication from the Commission to the Council on a new strategy towards Asia.

The 1994 New Asia Strategy paper, as discussed in chapter nine of this volume, was essentially reactive. It was a response to the increasing economic dynamism of the Asian region, particularly the impressive performance of the four Asian tigers (Hong Kong, Singapore, South Korea and Taiwan); the opening up of the Chinese market; and the unilateral liberalization of several Southeast Asian economies. While the 1994 New Asia Strategy recognized the tremendous changes taking place in Asia and acknowledged the need for the European Union to enhance its engagement with, and increase its economic presence in, Asia, it did not offer any clear, concrete ideas on how to go about achieving its objectives beyond some general guidelines. It was, however, clear that economic objectives were the motivation for the New Asia Strategy as the very beginning of the document noted, 'The rise of Asia is dramatically changing the world balance of economic power. ... The Union needs as a matter of urgency to strengthen its economic presence in Asia in order to maintain its leading role in the world economy.' (European Commission, 1994, p. 1)

It was left to ASEAN, and in particular Singapore, to seize on the New Asia Strategy, which clearly recognized EU relations with ASEAN as a cornerstone of its dialogue with East Asia, to push for the European Community to 'upgrade' its relations with East Asia through a high-level summit meeting of leaders. This was to be the genesis of the Asia–Europe Meeting process.

The Development of ASEM

The Asia–Europe Meeting was initially conceived as an informal forum and process for developing dialogue and cooperation between East Asia and the EU. One of ASEM's most noticeable characteristics lies in its composition of its regional representation, particularly in the case of 'Asia'. On the one hand, Asia, stretching as it does from Turkey to Australasia, was represented until 2006 by only three Northeast Asian countries (China, Japan and South Korea) and the seven Southeast Asian countries that then made up ASEAN (Brunei, Indonesia, Malaysia, the Philippines, Singapore, Thailand and Vietnam). On the other hand, 'Europe' was initially represented by the 15 European Union member states at the time and the European Commission. ASEM's membership has since expanded to include the new EU member states and new members of ASEAN, Laos, Burma Myanmar and Cambodia, the ASEAN Secretariat, India, Pakistan and Mongolia.

The idea of having a meeting of leaders from Asia and Europe originated at the Europe–East Asia Economic Summit held in Singapore in September 1994. Then Prime Minister of Singapore Goh Chok Tong further developed this initiative in a trip to Europe where he canvassed support. He convinced the French of the need for such a meeting by emphasizing the developing economic links between the US and Asia in the context of Asia-Pacific Economic Cooperation (APEC). On the European side, the New Asia Strategy's concern that the EU was losing out on the many economic opportunities in East Asia due to strong competition from Japan and the US was evident.

Goh's efforts to bring about an Asia–Europe meeting of leaders were motivated by two factors. First, with the end of the Cold War there was greater fluidity in the regional political and economic landscapes in the Asia-Pacific. China's economic potential had been unleashed with its open door policy. In the Southeast Asian subregion various states were uncertain about the implications of a rising China. Japan, although still an economic powerhouse, appeared to be in a state of decline and was also unclear about its own strategic role in the region. The US's commitment to and engagement with the region were also called into question as the Cold War's ideological battle ceased and the US appeared to be turning inward. Engaging the EU, then, was part of a strategy conceived by a small state, Singapore, to bring as many key players into the region as possible. It was anticipated that this could keep all major powers engaged in the region, while at the same time mitigating the possibility that any one single power could become too dominant. With an EU expansion in 1995 to 15 members, a single market of 350 million, and the development of a Common Foreign and Security Policy, the potential for the EU to become a global actor and major player in the region was welcomed in East Asia at the time.

Second, Singapore and ASEAN also regarded the EU's New Asia Strategy as a clear indication of the EU's interest in increasing its engagement and raising its profile in Asia. A leaders' meeting, with its considerable political symbolism, would send a clear signal of the EU's intention to upgrade its relations with Asia.

The alacrity with which the proposal for an Asia–Europe Meeting was taken up and the prompt launch of the first summit in Bangkok in March 1996 suggested that this was an idea whose time had come. So what were the underlying regional and global conditions and factors which provided the impetus and hastened the maturation of the idea of ASEM?

Realist analysts in international relations emphasize the systemic change in the distribution of power with the emergence of East Asia as an economic powerhouse in the early 1990s, and the desire for an increasingly integrated and expanding EU to become a global actor in the emerging new world order. They also examine the possible convergence of narrow national interests — the commercial race towards East Asia by many European companies and the emerging East Asian economies' need to attract European investments and to expand trade.

Liberal institutionalists, on the other hand, focus on the resurgence in interest in regionalism in the 1980s and regard ASEM as reflecting the increasing trend towards interregional dialogue as an alternative to traditional bilateralism, which is seen as inadequate to cope with global problems, and universalism, which is hampered by the multiplicity and diversity of actors involved. They see ASEM as part of the rising trend of regionalism to cope with the challenges of globalization.

There are merits in both perspectives as ASEM was a result of various constellations of forces and interests. The emergence of rapidly growing East Asian economies and the further integration of Europe in the early 1990s; the growing spectre of an increasingly unilateral America; and the fear that the world economy would be fragmented into three separate blocs — all of these provided the underlying structural explanations that realists used to explain ASEM. For the Europeans, ASEM was also to be a counterbalance to the Asia-Pacific Economic Cooperation (APEC). In the early 1990s, APEC, which links the US with 17 other Asia-Pacific economies, was seen as moving rapidly towards free trade in the Asia-Pacific. This created some concern among Europeans that they might be disadvantaged in the lucrative Asia-Pacific markets. At the same time, East Asians saw engagement with the EU through ASEM as a means to diversify their economic dependence on the US and Japan. There were also fears of a Fortress Europe following the Maastricht Treaty (Yeo, 2003, pp. 5–17).

At the same time, the early to mid-1990s — the initial years of the post-Cold war period — heralded a sense of optimism and faith in international cooperation and international institutions to deal with growing interdependence. Institution-building, multilateralism, and multi-level governance were seen as the means to advance transnational cooperation to deal with both the opportunities and the challenges of globalization.

The role of ASEAN in driving the development of ASEM is worthy of recognition, particularly in the context of a wider ASEAN–EU relationship. The established ASEAN–EU link in some ways provided a model on which ASEM was based. Indeed, Dent has noted that among the ASEAN states, 'ASEM was generally seen as the projection of its pre-existing interregional ties with the EU onto a broader canvas' (Dent, 1999, p. 246).

ASEAN's identity as a successful diplomatic community since its years of being involved in bringing about an international resolution of the Cambodian crisis in its own neighbourhood, and its economic dynamism of the 1980s and early 1990s, have brought about a sense of confidence and assertiveness in safeguarding its interest in the wake of changing power relations in the broader Asia-Pacific region. In response to the economic competition from other emerging markets around the world, particularly China, ASEAN announced in 1992 the establishment of an ASEAN Free Trade Area (AFTA) and also commenced work on a common ASEAN Investment Area (AIA). In response to the uncertainties of the politico-security situation in the immediate years of the post-Cold War period, ASEAN proposed a pan-Asia-Pacific multilateral framework, the ASEAN Regional Forum (ARF), to encourage dialogue in politico-security matters. This was also closely linked to the impact of a rising China, and the desire to bring China into a multilateral setting in order to socialize it into the regional norms of peaceful and cooperative engagement.

Following Goh's initiative in proposing an Asia–Europe meeting to then French Prime Minister Eduoard Balladur, the task of ASEM's establishment on the 'Asian' side was carried out by ASEAN. France, in turn, used its presidency of the EU Council, in the first half of 1995, to persuade its European colleagues to participate.

The Singapore ministry of foreign affairs drafted a position paper on the need for an Asia–Europe Meeting and presented it to the ASEAN Senior Officials Meeting (SOM) in March 1995. The paper proposed an informal meeting between Asian and European leaders to engage in a wide-ranging dialogue. While the general principle was one of inclusiveness, to facilitate the early launching of the proposed meeting, the paper suggested that participation would be based on the principle that the EU would select the European participants and ASEAN, the East Asian participants. The paper also added that, for East Asia, the important consideration was to include dynamic economies which had contributed to the region's prosperity and growth.

From this position paper, it was clear that economic considerations were the primary justifications for ASEM, at least for the ASEAN nations. The paper established that the three major regions of economic power — North America, Europe and East Asia — were likely to dominate global trade and investment activities well into the 21st century. While noting that there were strong transatlantic ties and also strong links between East Asia and North America through APEC and a series of bilateral linkages, it pointed out that what was palpably absent was a strong link between East Asia and Europe.[1] Beyond the clear economic agenda, the strategic reason for ASEM was presented in the context of closing the triangle — balancing the relations and creating strong links between the three engines of growth — in order to safeguard the continued openness of the global economic order and thereby contribute to global peace and prosperity.

In its recognition of the confidence of ASEAN in seizing the opportunity to drive the process, the paper suggested that preparatory work for the Asia–Europe Meeting could begin with the ASEAN–EU SOM in May 1995. Once participation had been agreed by ASEAN and EU, other relevant officials could then be invited to join in the preparatory meeting.

During the ASEAN–EU SOM, the EU indicated that European participation at the first Asia–Europe Meeting would be restricted to the 15 EU member states. On the Asian side, ASEAN indicated that it would invite China, Japan and South Korea. All three Northeast Asian countries accepted the invitation to attend the first meeting (Serradell, 1996, pp. 190–5). There were initially some reservations from Japan, which wished to include Australia and New Zealand in the first meeting. However, again reflecting the influence of ASEAN, particularly Malaysia and Indonesia, it was decided that Australia and New Zealand would not be included in the inaugural meeting.

Preparations for the first summit meeting intensified after the ASEAN–EU SOM. There were intense negotiations regarding its format and agenda. There were some differences initially over the specific agenda. For example, the Europeans wanted to use the Asia–Europe meeting as a platform for discussing a range of issues related to the World Trade Organization (WTO) such as the social clause, intellectual property rights and the investment code, and secured East Asian support for a Multilateral Agreement on Investment sponsored by the Organization for Economic Cooperation and Development (Smith, 1998, p. 309). As the inaugural ASEM was scheduled for March 1996, it seemed opportune for the Europeans to have this as a platform to discuss WTO issues and secure the support of key East Asian partners before the first WTO ministerial meeting to be held in December 1996.

The East Asians, however, were not keen to have the inaugural Asia–Europe Meeting turned into a pre-negotiation round before the WTO ministerial meeting. Their main interest was to get European governments to encourage European businesses to invest in Asia, particularly in long-term infrastructure projects that would bring about greater human resource development and more technology transfers. Another priority for the East Asian governments was developing economic relations with the EU and increasing market access. They wanted the EU to lessen the use of discriminatory trade measures such as the anti-dumping law and quotas on Asian products (Smith, 1998, p. 310).

There were also different emphases placed on the importance of political dialogue. Several East Asian countries wanted the dialogue to focus on economic issues and omit political issues. However, in order to conform to the general consensus that the dialogue should be wide-ranging, political dialogue was to be included. A compromise was reached whereby the major focus of meetings would be on issues of common interest, rather than the more contentious issues such as human rights and the situation in East Timor.

After much intense negotiation, all parties agreed that the inaugural meeting should be informal in character (with the emphasis on dialogue) and comprehensive in scope, covering all aspects of relations between the two regions. The most informal type of gathering — a forum with a broad, indicative list of topics for discussion — was adopted. Thus, ASEM was born in March 1996 in Bangkok (Yeo, 2003, pp. 25–6).

Since its birth, ASEM has evolved into a process and forum of meetings with a rudimentary structure comprising three pillars — economic, political and sociocultural. The summit represents the highest decision-making level and is held biennially. The summit is in itself the culmination of various meetings involving ministers and senior officials from the foreign, economic and finance ministries. Over the years, the ministerial meetings have broadened to include environment ministers, education ministers and others, depending on the initiatives and projects that are adopted at each summit. Initiatives and projects form an important and integral part of the visible output of ASEM. These initiatives and projects are clustered around the three pillars and thus far, the economic pillar has the densest cluster.

The foreign ministers and their senior officials are responsible for the overall coordination of ASEM activities. They are assisted by four coordinators: two from the EU side coming from the EU presidency and from the Commission; and two from the Asian side, one representing Northeast Asia and the other representing Southeast Asia. The idea of having a virtual ASEM secretariat has been approved and is being developed but is not yet fully functioning.

ASEM's beginning was certainly promising. The inaugural summit in Bangkok was hailed a success, with more concrete outcomes than originally envisaged. The Bangkok Summit agreed on a very detailed work programme and a process was established with commitments to hold subsequent summits in London and Seoul. Meetings among foreign ministers and economic ministers were also agreed to. Other proposals included the creation of an Asia–Europe Business Forum (AEBF) to promote business interests; an Asia–Europe Foundation (ASEF) to promote cultural and intellectual exchanges; and an Asia–Europe Environmental Technology Centre to undertake research and development in the area of environmental issues and policy.²

As an acknowledgement that developing Asia–Europe relations was a long-term process, the leaders also requested that their senior officials prepare an Asia–Europe Cooperation Framework (AECF) to establish long-term principles of cooperation.

There was much enthusiasm immediately after the Bangkok Summit and over a span of two years various meetings took place and several projects were initiated. Within a year of the inaugural summit, ASEF, the single concrete institution dedicated to promoting cultural, intellectual and people-to-people exchange between Asia and Europe, was launched.

However, enthusiasm for ASEM dampened later in 1997 with the Asian Financial Crisis. There were fears that the ASEM process might be derailed as several East Asian countries lost their economic lustre and struggled to cope with the broader socioeconomic malaise that accompanied the stalling of their economies. These fears were not realized. However, it was clear that the Europeans were now driving the process, while ASEAN was consumed by the crisis. The second summit in London took place as scheduled and the Europeans extended assistance to the key East Asian countries affected by the crisis through the ASEM Trust Fund.

By the third ASEM summit in Seoul in 2000, the countries affected by the crisis had begun to show signs of recovery. However, another issue had cropped up as a challenge to the ASEM process. This concerned the issue of enlargement of ASEM membership. The EU sought to expand its membership to the former communist states in Central and Eastern Europe, and EU practice dictated that all members of the EU would automatically become partners in its external dialogue process. Asian members of the ASEM process also wanted to include all three new ASEAN members — Cambodia, Laos and Burma Myanmar — into the ASEM process, should EU enlargement take place. However, the poor human rights record and the oppressive regime of the military junta in Burma Myanmar had led to sanctions by the European Union. The EU was thus reluctant to have Burma Myanmar become a member of ASEM.

The issue of enlargement and membership was finally resolved at the fifth ASEM summit held in Hanoi 2004, as a compromise was reached for Burma Myanmar to attend the summit in Hanoi at a lower level of representation. During the protracted negotiations over Burma Myanmar's membership, two ministerial meetings were cancelled. However, the fact that a compromise was finally reached, to allow the fifth Summit to take place, in some ways reflected the desire of Asians and Europeans alike to keep the ASEM process alive and intact.

At its tenth anniversary in 2006, regular official meetings within the ASEM process involved not only the biennial meetings of heads of state, but also meetings between ministers and senior officials from the foreign, trade, economics, finance, and environment ministries. Meetings also took place between customs officers, experts in trade and investment promotion. There are also dialogue and meetings on topics ranging from human rights, inter-faith relations, counter-terrorism, transnational crimes and money laundering to the issues of a digital divide, water resources management and public debt management.

An Assessment of ASEM's Impact on EU–East Asia Relations

Since its inauguration, ASEM has been criticized by some analysts as a 'talking shop', a forum where dialogue has been broad but not deep, and where there is a lack of tangible results and concrete achievements. It has also been criticized for placing too much emphasis on form rather than substance.[3] One could respond to these critics by countering that, at the initial stage, East Asia–EU relations were starting from a low base and that East Asia and Europe needed to 'rediscover' each other, so symbolism was as important as substance. However, there is a real need to take stock of the progress of ASEM and how it has influenced EU–East Asia relations. Assessing it on the basis of the dozens of initiatives, hundreds of meetings, the establishment of ASEF, and its momentum for self-perpetuation, it would be natural to assume that there should be some tangible benefits and a positive impact on EU-East Asia relations. Indeed, it can be argued that perhaps the most concrete and obvious achievement of ASEM, in addition to increased economic cooperation, has been the Asia–Europe Foundation (ASEF), which attempted to reach a broad audience through a large number of activities involving students, young leaders, parliamentarians, academics, artists and the media.

A study commissioned by the Japanese and Finnish foreign ministries to look into ten years of ASEM, reached the conclusion that while progress has been made in improving dialogue between East Asia and the EU on a wide range of issues, the dialogue, while broad, has not been deep. The dialogue process has remained at information-sharing level and has not moved into substantive cooperation.[4] Furthermore, ASEM's potential to bring about a significant change in the quality of EU–East Asia relations, contributing to multilateralism and global governance, had not yet been realized. There were also few measurable tangible benefits emanating from the numerous initiatives and activities beyond 'mutual understanding'. This was because the focus of most meetings is on information-exchange and stating each other's position on various issues.

In the months leading to the sixth ASEM Summit in Helsinki in September 2006, South Korea produced a report assessing ASEM initiatives to assess the impact of ASEM. The report noted that in its first decade a total of 96 initiatives, 11 under the Political Pillar, 46 under the Economic Pillar and 39 under the Socio-cultural Pillar had been implemented. ASEM members promoted dialogue and cooperation through these initiatives over a wide range of issues. However, many of these initiatives were in the form of seminars or conferences, and were held just once or twice with insufficient follow-up or impact, and had not necessarily contributed towards longer term cooperation. There was also considerable overlap and duplication in initiatives. The report also found that public awareness of these initiatives was extremely low. The Korean study confirmed several of the criticisms of the ASEM process that appeared over the years. In particular, it called into question the effectiveness and efficiency of 'initiatives-led approaches' in achieving the overall objectives of ASEM.

These objectives conceived of ASEM as one of the overarching frameworks for promoting EU–East Asia relations. In the European Commission Working Document of 18 April 2000, it is stated that the key characteristics of the ASEM process are its informality; its multi-dimensionality carrying forward equally a political, economic and socio-cultural dimension; its emphasis on equal partnership, that is eschewing any aid-based relationships in favour of a more general process of dialogue and cooperation; and its high-level focus stemming from the summits themselves. ASEM was not designed to replace or duplicate, but instead to complement the work already being carried out in other bilateral and multilateral forums. These characteristics were reiterated as key principles and objectives enunciated in the Asia–Europe Cooperation Framework adopted during the third ASEM summit in Seoul. Specifically, the AECF noted that the ASEM process should be multi-dimensional and conducted on a basis of equal partnership, mutual respect and mutual benefit. It should not be institutionalized and as an informal process should stimulate and facilitate progress in other forums. In addition, the key principles and objectives, as they appeared in the AECF, also called for ASEM to enhance mutual understanding and awareness between the two regions through a process of dialogue and cooperation on mutually identified priorities for action. Dialogue and cooperation would, according to the AECF, go beyond governments to include business, the private sector and the people.

Many of these 'principles and objectives' in the AECF are too general and ambiguous, and inevitably place limitations on the achievement of tangible results. An examination of all of the Chairman's statements emanating from the ASEM summits, is one means of evaluating ASEM's progress. As ASEM is not a static entity but an evolving process, one would assume that its broad objectives will evolve and crystallize into more specific goals as interaction among the member states deepens. From the various Chairman's statements, one can infer that the ASEM dialogue process is aimed at strengthening the relationship between East Asia and the EU so as to lead to more trade and investments between the two regions (under the economic pillar); greater cooperation in multilateral forums such as the WTO and the UN, which would contribute to multilateralism and global governance (under the political pillar); and more dialogue in socio-cultural areas going beyond governments and involving the different sectors of society (under the socio-cultural pillar).

Closer examination of the range of ASEM activities under the economic pillar illustrates that while this pillar has the most initiatives (as reflected in the study sponsored by South Korea) the impact of these initiatives and how much they have actually led to increased trade and investments between EU and East Asia is not clear. For example, the Trade Facilitation Action Plan and Investment Promotion Action Plan identified obstacles to trade and investment and made recommendations on how to remove these barriers. However, due to the non-binding nature of these recommendations and the fact that not many people in the business sector were even aware of these plans, it is difficult to directly attribute any increase in trade and investments between the two regions to these plans. Indeed, research by European researchers during the decade of ASEM's evaluation study showed that while two-way trade (in absolute volume) between the EU and Asian ASEM member states increased, the EU exports to Asian ASEM countries as a proportion of the EU's total exports dropped by 1.16%. Outward European FDI into all Asian ASEM countries (except China) steadily decreased during the period 1999–2002 (in part due to the Asian financial crisis). FDI into the ASEAN countries continued to fall through 2003–04.[5]

The Asia–Europe Business Forum (AEBF), which was one of the very first initiatives taken up after the inaugural Summit in Bangkok, has taken place annually since 1996. It provides a forum for dialogue, exchanges and networking between a small group of Asian and European business people and the opportunity for consultation and input into the ASEM official process. The extent to which these initiatives translate into significant influence on policies is a matter of conjecture.

Dialogue under the political pillar of ASEM has broadened to include parliamentarians and young leaders. The topics ranged from human rights to transnational crimes and terrorism. There have been useful exchanges of information and clarifications of positions. However, actual cooperation to tackle some of these issues such as anti-terrorism and anti-corruption has not taken place within the broad ASEM domain. Instead, more concrete cooperation is usually transferred to another level. For example, in the area of combating terrorism, more cooperation is undertaken at the ASEAN–EU level, whilst concrete projects and assistance are targeted at country level.

ASEM never quite lived up to the *raison d'être* of strengthening the weakest side in the triangle of North America, Europe and East Asia, and its contribution to global governance for peace and prosperity. It has not been able to enhance the balance of power in the triangle, and its relevance in the broader international context has been questioned. While it is true that ASEM was conceived only as a informal forum for dialogue and not a negotiating forum for problem-solving, the fact that it has not been successful in coordinating or harmonizing the interests of its partners efficiently *vis-à-vis* larger international bodies and that actual cooperation only takes place at bilateral and subregional levels has made its repeated commitment to multilateralism sound somewhat hollow.

In the socio-cultural pillar, the establishment of the Asia–Europe Foundation (ASEF) is a significant achievement, and reflects a commitment by ASEM leaders to promote understanding and to broaden the dialogue beyond the level of governments. As noted in the Korean report, ASEF has played a pivotal role in adding value to the ASEM process through its activities to encourage cultural, intellectual and people-to-people exchanges. However, there is overlap and duplication between ASEF-led activities and ASEM initiatives in the socio-cultural pillar and more should be done to streamline activities. An informal survey conducted by East Asian researchers also pointed out that, despite all these activities and initiatives, awareness about the ASEM process in the media and wider public remains low.[6] Beyond a small group of academics, researchers, students and civil society activists responsible for organizing a parallel Asia–Europe People's Forum back to back with ASEM summits, knowledge about the ASEM and its objectives remains low. Lack of visibility and of public profile is, therefore, a major problem for ASEM in its purported attempt to broaden the dialogue beyond government officials.

These assessments of ASEM lead one to question its impact on EU–East Asia relations. The argument that ASEM has acted as a catalyst and stimulated and strengthened cooperation in other strands of EU–East Asia relations, such as EU–ASEAN and EU–China, would be difficult to prove. The increasing importance of EU–China relations cannot in any way be attributed to ASEM, but rather to the meteoric rise of China in its own right and hence the need for the EU to step up its engagement with China. The EU's recent obsession with China is evidenced in the five policy communications on EU–China relations, in contrast to two such documents for an overall EU–East Asia strategy.[7]

EU–ASEAN relations are improving after a few years of acrimonious relations following Burma Myanmar's admission into the Association in 1997. The EU was deeply concerned about the situation in Burma Myanmar and had since 1996 adopted a common position which included an embargo on exports that may be used for repression, denial of visas for many military officials and freezing of funds held by these Myanmar Burmese officials abroad. When Burma Myanmar became part of ASEAN, EU–ASEAN relations stalled. Meetings were cancelled and the 13th ASEAN–EU ministerial meeting, due to be held in 1998 and hosted by the EU, could not take place because of the visa ban on Burmese Myanmar leaders. It was only after the EU was allowed to send its first Troika mission to Burma Myanmar in July 1999 to have a meeting at senior official level with Aung San Suu Kyi that changes were made in Spring 2000 to the common position on Burma Myanmar. While strengthening some sanctions, the changes made in the common position opened up the possibility for Burma Myanmar's participation in the 13th ASEAN–EU ministerial meeting in December 2000. The venue of the meeting was also shifted to Vientiane instead of Europe to allow Burma Myanmar's participation.

However, the issue of Burma Myanmar continued to cloud relations. It was not until 2003 that the European Commission, in its Communication on 'A New Partnership with Southeast Asia' acknowledged that it was probably not wise to allow the particular case of Burma Myanmar to continue to stall its relations with ASEAN as a whole. While the EU remained deeply concerned about the political situation in Burma Myanmar, the 2003 policy communication stressed the need to have a flexible approach to avoid EU relations with the ASEAN and the Southeast Asian region as a whole being hampered by the Burma Myanmar issue. The communication recommended a new approach towards

Southeast Asia that is similar to the multi-layered regional cooperation taking place within Asia. While recognizing the importance of supporting ASEAN's regional integration, it also noted that not all development assistance and cooperation programmes are best achieved through a strictly region-to-region approach. Concrete programmes and projects should be implemented through bilateral or subregional channels and with a more sectoral focus. This opened up the possibility that the EU and any two ASEAN members could initiate a specific project and go ahead to implement the initiative according to an agreed plan, while it remains open to all ASEAN members to join later when they are ready (European Commission, 2003).

Towards a New Partnership?

The EU has drawn up two frameworks — the Trans-Regional EU–ASEAN Trade Initiative (TREATI) for dialogue on all trade and investment issues; and the Regional EC–ASEAN Dialogue Instrument (READI) for dialogue on all other areas — to further reinvigorate ASEAN–EU relations.

While recognizing the lack of deep or imbedded integration within ASEAN, the EU remains committed to support ASEAN regionalism through its ASEAN–EC Project on Regional Integration Support (APRIS). This project aims to draw lessons from the experience of the EU in forging regional economic integration, contribute to improving ASEAN mechanisms and support capacity building activities for the ASEAN Secretariat and ASEAN member states. More importantly, it is hoped that through APRIS and through the EU's participation in the Initiatives for ASEAN Integration programme, development gaps between the richer and poorer ASEAN member states might be reduced, which could in turn facilitate the further integration of ASEAN.[8]

What is evolving from the search for a new partnership between the EU and ASEAN is a pragmatic, multi-layered and multi-pronged approach towards cooperation. Three layers of cooperation are worked on simultaneously; the first involves the EU with various ASEAN member states; the second operates through the EU-ASEAN inter-regional framework; and thirdly there is the ASEM process. ASEM's position in the overall schema of EU–East Asia relations is not that of a central or key framework, but rather that of one of the many strands of EU–East Asia cooperation.

ASEM leaders during the 2006 ASEM summit in Helsinki reaffirmed ASEM's importance as a 'multi-faceted dialogue facilitator' and welcomed it as a 'platform for policy development between Asia and Europe'

(Chairman Statement of the 6th Asia–Europe Meeting, 2006). There is clearly no strong desire from the ASEM leaders to change the Meeting's current informal, loose character. It appears likely that ASEM will remain as a forum for exchanging views, and concrete cooperation will take place mainly within the other frameworks of EU–East Asia relations.

ASEM will also be obliged to compete with bilateral links such as EU–Japan, EU–China, EU–Korea and EU–ASEAN relations, for both attention and resources. The EU appears to have adopted of 'variable geometry' approach to international relations and cooperation. Recognizing Asia's great diversity and the lack up to now of a clear East Asian regional entity,[9] the EU has opted for a flexible, multi-layered strategy to extract the most out its partnerships with the various East Asian countries. The EU's own enlargement and its increased diversity perhaps also facilitated the acceptance of the practicality of such an approach. As for the East Asian countries, such a multi-level and multi-pronged pragmatic approach is certainly not alien to them, and would be happily embraced. The different national interests and the lack of a distinctive pan-East Asian regional identity, has meant that the bilateralism has been the norm rather than the exception.

There is no doubt that EU–East Asia relations will remain important and continue to strengthen, due to growing trade links and increased strategic linkages. In the economic sphere, Asia has recently surpassed the North American Free Trade Agreement to become the EU's main trading partner. Beyond economics, the growing interdependence means that no global or transnational challenge can be effectively managed without deeper and closer engagement between Asia and Europe. However, ASEM is unlikely to be a key engine in propelling EU–East Asia relations and deepening the engagement. As noted earlier, the EU–China partnership is gaining in importance — both strategic and economic. EU–ASEAN relations are certainly improving after years of neglect. The commencement of negotiations for an EU–ASEAN free trade agreement confirms this trend. EU–South Korea relations also look set to move forward, with the negotiations for an EU–South Korea free trade agreement. EU–Japan relations, although appearing low-key, remain an important aspect of the EU's links with East Asia. During the 10th EU–Japan Summit held in Brussels in 2002, a ten-year action plan for EU–Japan joint cooperation was endorsed. ASEM with its rather inchoate configuration on the side of 'Asia' is likely to become less important as all these other strands of the EU–East Asia relations gather momentum.

Conclusion

Despite the initial optimism about the potential of the Asia–Europe Meeting ASEM) in strengthening Asia–Europe relations and enhancing the global roles of the EU and East Asia in the triangular relationship among the three key power centres — North America, Europe and East Asia, the reality has not lived up to the high expectations.

ASEM is one of the multilateral fora that bring East Asia and EU together without the domineering presence of the Americans to allow for a more honest and open dialogue and to open the possibility for the two to play a more active role in shaping a new multilateral world order. However, although ASEM has generated many meetings, activities and initiatives and even established a concrete institution, the Asia–Europe Foundation (ASEF) to encourage more exchanges and interactions between the peoples of Asia and Europe, the reality is that ASEM today remains essentially an informal inter-governmental forum without any mechanisms and institutions capable of actual problem solving (Yeo, 2004, pp. 20–1). ASEM is still not a tool capable of enhancing multilateralism and global governance capacity directly. It is primarily an instrument used for networking, information gathering and confidence building.

For ASEM to enhance its importance as an interregional forum or tool that can contribute to global governance and help shape the new world order, two things need to happen. First, East Asia must integrate further to become a distinct regional and global actor. Second, the EU must be willing and prepared to shoulder more global responsibilities. Unfortunately, despite the recent trends of regionalism and increasing regional cooperation, East Asia is still far from being a coherent regional entity. ASEM's recent expansion to encompass India, Pakistan and Mongolia further dilutes the ability of Asian ASEM members to act as one. The EU's enlargement to 27 members has also led to a concern that the EU will remain self-absorbed and inward-looking as it continues to seek a better way to manage its own internal policies and processes. This is likely to leave it with little time and resources to play an active global role beyond its immediate backyard.

In conclusion, EU–East Asia relations will continue to grow, but through an *ad hoc* multi-layered and multi-pronged approach. ASEM is unlikely to be a key engine in propelling EU–East Asia ties and enhancing the global roles of EU and East Asia. It will remain as an entity in the broad gamut of inter-regional fora and summit meetings that will give significance to low-intensity cooperation or so called flexible cooperation which is shallow and opportunistic and does not provide or contribute to real solutions of global problems.

Notes

1. The Position Paper on the Asia–Europe Meeting was prepared by the Singapore Ministry of Foreign Affairs in March 1995 (obtained through interview). It set out the rationale for such a link; and discussed the principles for participation, the possible theme and agenda for the meeting, timing and venue and frequency of the meeting.
2. Chairman's Statement of the Asia–Europe Meeting, Bangkok, 2 March 1996, available online at http://ec.europa.eu/external_relations/asem/asem_summits/ index_sum.html, accessed February 2007.
3. This was the general sense from a study done by a group of researchers from Asia and Europe commissioned by the Japanese and Finnish Foreign Ministries. The evaluation report on ten years of ASEM is published by the Finnish Ministry for Foreign Affairs entitled "ASEM in its tenth year: Looking Back, Looking Forward". Available at www.aseminfoboard.org/content/documents/060504_ASEMInItsTenthYear.pdf, accessed November 2006.
4. The author was involved in the research and evaluation. First Asian country studies were made in which researchers carried out an informal survey to determine the awareness and knowledge of the ASEM process. Two conferences were also held to discuss the different research surveys and findings.
5. Please refer to the European Background Study done by the University of Helsinki Network for European Studies (which is part of the study commissioned by the Japanese and Finnish Foreign Ministries to look into ten years of ASEM) http://www.aseminfoboard.org/content/documents/EuropeBgroundStudy.pdf, accessed November 2006.
6. Please see Asian Country Reports (which is part of the study commissioned by Japanese and Finnish Foreign Ministries on 10 years of ASEM) http://www.jcie.or.jp/thinknet/forums/asem10/asia.pdf, accessed November 2006.
7. The five policy communications on EU–China relations are: A Long Term Policy for China–Europe Relations (1995); Building a Comprehensive Partnership with China (1998); EU Strategy towards China: Implementation of the 1998 Communication and Future Steps (2001); A Maturing Partnership: Shared Interests and Challenges in EU–China Relations (2003); Closer Partners, Growing Responsibilities (2006).
8. Drawn from the EU's 2005–06 Regional Indicative Programme for ASEAN. This document is available on the European Commission's External relations website (http://ec.europa.eu/external_relations/asean/csp/rip_05-06_en.pdf), December 2006.
9. The ASEAN+3 framework came very close and had the potential to coalesce as an East Asian Community, but regional rivalries and differences have slowed the process, and another entity, the East Asia Summit (EAS) comprising ASEAN+3 plus Australia, New Zealand and India has appeared

in the horizon complicating the process of institution and identity-building in East Asia.

References

Dent, C. (1999) *The European Union and East Asia: An Economic Relationship*, London/New York: Routledge.

European Commission (1994), *Towards a New Asia Strategy*, Brussels: European Commission.

European Commission, (2000) *Perspectives and Priorities for the ASEM Process into the new decade* (Working Document COM 2000 241), Brussels: European Commission.

European Commission, (2003) *A New Partnership with South East Asia* (Communication), Brussels: European Commission.

Finnish Ministry of Foreign Affairs, (2006) *ASEM in its Tenth Year: Looking Back, Looking Forward*, Helsinki: Publications of the Ministry of Foreign Affairs, Finland.

Serradell, V. P. (1996) 'The Asia–Europe Meeting (ASEM): A Historical Turning Point in Relations between the Two Regions', *European Foreign Affairs Review*, 2, pp. 185–210.

Smith, M. (1998) 'The European Union and the Asia-Pacific', in A. McGrew and C. Brook (eds) *Asia-Pacific in the New World Order*, London and New York: Routledge, pp. 289–315.

Yeo, L. H. (2003) *Asia and Europe: The Development and Different Dimensions of ASEM*, London/New York: Routledge.

Yeo, L. H. (2004) 'Dimensions of Asia–Europe Cooperation', *Asia–Europe Journal*, 2. 1, pp. 19–31.

7
The Economic Geography of Regionalization in East Asia and Europe

Christopher M. Dent

Introduction

The density of regionalized economic activity is significantly high in both East Asia[1] and Europe. This so-called 'regionalization' derives from various transnational business and infrastructural linkages that have deepened in both regions over time. Intra-regional trade and investment flows in both Europe and East Asia have not only increased, but also have become more systemically integrated, mainly through the expansion of international production and distribution networks. These networks represent an important micro-level foundation to regional integration in East Asia and Europe on which state-led projects of regionalism, such as the Single European Market, and the Association of Southeast Asian Nations (ASEAN) Free Trade Area have been built. Conversely, these projects have further spurred the development of international production networks (IPNs), thus suggesting a symbiotic relationship.

International production networks are also inextricably linked with the economic zonal development of East Asia and Europe. Core urban-industrial zones of development (for example industrial districts, metropolitan conurbations, transborder 'growth polygons', development corridors) may be considered the most important network nodes of economic development in both regions. Linkages within and between these core zones are fundamental features of East Asia and Europe's economic geography. This chapter examines the economic geography of regionalization in East Asia and the European Union (EU), concentrating on micro-level developments in regional integration. It analyses the reasons behind the growth of international production networks in both regions and also the zonal dimension to their regional economic development. Contrasts and comparisons between East Asia and Europe are made therein.

Regionalization in East Asia and Europe: Geographic Perspectives

Regionalization and Economic Geography

We may define *regionalization* as a regional integration process that derives from the micro-level activities of private or civil sector actors, these primarily being firms. This may be contrasted, then, with state-led projects of *regionalism* whereby regional integration is driven by public policy initiatives, such as a free trade or financial co-operation agreement. Of course, a prime aim of such projects is to foster the regionalization process itself, with the objectives of improving the region's resource efficiency and economic competitiveness. Regionalization furthermore represents the economic geography of regional integration, or the actual physical manifestation of what binds a regional economy together in a coherent and structural sense.

The micro-perspectives of regionalization require us to look at the regional integration process in quite different spatial and territorial terms in relation to the conventional macro-level perspectives of regionalism. One thinks of Europe and East Asia as both being relatively integrated economic regions through the development of pan-regional systems of trade, investment and finance. One also still tends to think of nation-states as being the main 'container boxes' of economic activity, or that the European and East Asian regional economies comprise a set of 'national' component parts, for example the German economy, the Japanese economy. This is still relevant to the extent that certain forms of economic activity and systems are defined by national parameters, for example in terms of legal and regulatory systems and other delineations of state policy governance. However, the EU is now a very defined regional economy in its own right at the macro-level, especially after the introduction of the Single Market and euro common currency. More importantly, though, if we look at the micro-level we see patterns of economic activity and linkage that look very different from the neat macro-box perspective of national economies. On the one hand, micro-level economic activities are becoming more transnational in nature, forging more functional integrative linkages in East Asia and Europe on a region-wide scale. Multinational business, through the spread of international production and distribution networks, is the prime agent of this process.

On the other hand, there is a tendency in the economic landscape of both regions for many important forms of activity to be geographically concentrated or agglomerated in 'core zones' of development. At one end of the spatial scale, these tend to be urban–industrial areas, mostly city-based and working up to the extended metropolitan region area. Industrial districts or clusters are a particularly important manifestation of this development. Further up the geographic scale, these zones can transcend national borders and incorporate a number of sub-national regional economies in a symbiotic development relationship. Together these micro-level centres of economic activity also serve as network nodes in the regionalized integration of Europe and East Asia. There exists, then, a complementarity between the centrifugal forces associated with expanding IPNs and the centripetal forces of agglomerated economic and industrial development. For example, it is generally the case that IPNs function on operational linkages that involve industrial districts from different countries.

Rising Intra-Regional Trade

Europe experienced a pattern of rising intra-regional trade during the deepening internationalization (or proto-globalization) of the period 1860–1914, and then a contraction of this trade during the inter-war years. However, with the reconstruction of the West European economies and the strong economic growth of core national economies like Germany and France, West Europe's intra-regional trade soon began to rise again, hence indicating a return of regionalized linkages. Historic data provided by Anderson and Norheim (1993) suggests that West Europe had the world's highest levels of intra-regional trade for many decades before the inception of the European Economic Community (EEC). In 1958, West Europe's intra-regional trade ratio was 53 percent. By the 2000s, this had reached well over 60 percent for the EU. East Asia's intra-regional trade ratio has also gradually increased since the 1960s, and especially fast from the 1980s onwards. Its overall intra-regional trade ratio was roughly 15 to 20 percent in the early 1960s, rising to around 25 to 30 percent in the early 1980s and then to 52 percent by 2003.

Electronics, machinery, automobiles, transport equipment and information technology (IT) products together account for the significant majority share of East Asia's intra-regional trade. The growth of component trade is indicative of the growth of international production networks in East Asia (Borrus et al., 2000). The share of components in East Asia's total manufacturing exports was 32 percent in 2000 compared to 28 percent for NAFTA and 19 percent for the EU (World Bank, 2003). Japan acts as an important hub of production-sharing operations, originating about one third of all regional exports of components for assembly. Indonesia imports 70 per cent of its component products from Japan, and for South Korea, Taiwan and the Philippines this is at least 50 percent (Ng and Yeats, 2003). China accounts for around a quarter of the region's total component trade exports (Sakakibara and Yamakawa, 2004).

International Production Networks in East Asia and Europe

What Are International Production Networks?

Regional economic interdependence in East Asia and Europe has moved increasingly beyond deepening intra-regional trade. Economic links within both regions at the micro-level have become more functionally integrative on a subregional and pan-regional scale. The recent growth of international production networks represents an important development in the East Asian and European regionalization processes through the creation of regionalized systems of business activity. As this chapter will demonstrate, IPNs can differ significantly in their organizational and spatial nature. They are closely associated, or even synonymous, with multinational enterprise (MNE) activity. Yun (2003, p. 173) defines an IPN as 'an international division of labour, in which each function or discrete stage of a value chain is spatially or geographically relocated in the most efficient site, and undertaken by different firms including MNEs and local firms'.

Configuring an IPN entails a combination of intra-firm and inter-firm linkages, or service links. In this process, firms must consider how the marginal cost savings of fragmentation are offset by the service link costs of operating the network (Jones and Kierzkowski, 1990). Advances in communication and transportation technologies have both gradually reduced service link costs and enabled firms to more effectively manage IPNs on larger organizational and geographic scales. Improvements in production technology have also enabled an ever finer slicing of the production process into separate blocks or fragments (Athukorala, 2003). This has lead to wider geographic IPN configurations. Competition between countries for attracting IPN investments are made less on cost considerations and more on skills capability, managerial and technical capacity, supply logistics, infrastructural provision and providing investor firms with access to world-price inputs and capital factors. East Asian governments in particular have implemented 'industrial cluster' policies with this in mind, developing or building upon specialized facilities and capabilities (such as pools of skilled labour) located in particular zones or 'industrial districts' within their country.

Types of International Production Network

Some forms of international production can have a much stronger networking and integrative effect than others. Figure 7.1 presents four different types of international production (network).

The different types of IPN shown in Figure 7.1 are explained here in turn:

- *Platform Production for Regional Market (type I)*: This type involves minimal input from international sources. Value-added activities are concentrated in just one country and served by local suppliers. The main assembly production is likely to be situated in an industrial district that provides the 'platform' from which the assembly or core firm exports to the regional market.
- *International Vertical Production (type II)*: International sourcing occurs, but in a mostly uni-directional manner, whereby suppliers of materials and components serve the needs of assembly firms, such as automobile and electronics manufacturers. These vertical production links do not involve mutual exchanges or cooperation between the core firm and its local and international suppliers, or much interaction amongst supplier firms. Both types I and II have low network characteristics.
- *Subregional Production Network (type III)*: A high degree of networked activity between a number of firms but geographically concentrated in a particular trans-border zone, often involving just two countries or economies.
- *Regional Production Network (type IV)*: Operates on a high level of network interaction among firms from multiple countries across the region. Tends to apply to larger MNE producers in sectors such as electronics, computers, automobiles and machinery industries. This is the most regionally integrative of the four types.

These are generalized types of international production that are devised to illustrate key principles and methods by which IPNs can be organized. Not all IPNs neatly fit into this categorization but rather lie in between types, or have different characteristics from a number of types. For example, there are many IPNs that generally fall into the *type IV* category that only involve two or three countries. There are also subregional scale IPNs that are more based on vertical production links (*type II*) than

127

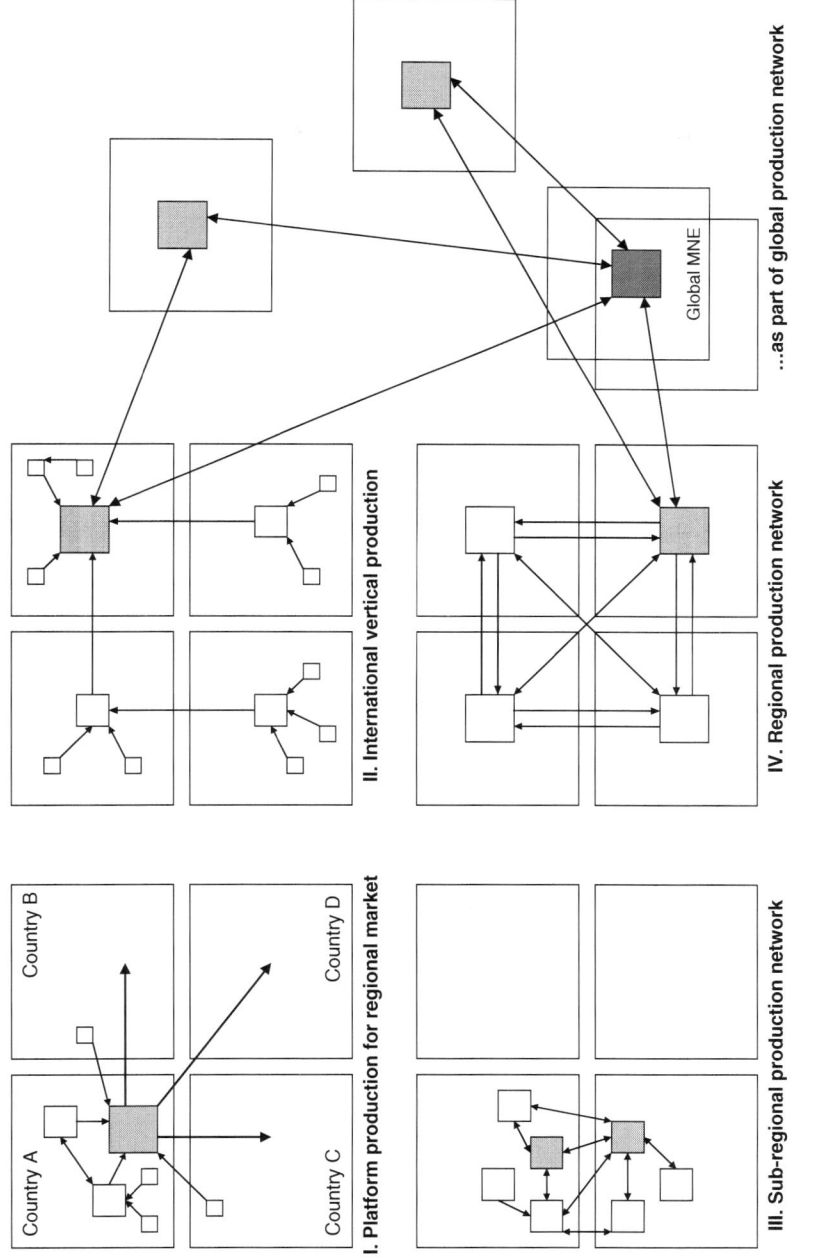

Figure 7.1 Types of international production within a regional economic space.

interactive networked links (*type III*). Figure 7.1 also shows how a region's international production networks are often embedded within larger global production networks (GPNs). This represents an important interface between regionalization and globalization, and is especially relevant to East Asia given its IPN density.

IPN Activity in East Asia

Of all the world's regions, East Asia is host to the highest concentration and also greatest variety of IPN activity (Henderson et al., 2002; World Bank, 2003, Yun, 2003; Kimura and Ando, 2004; Yusuf et al., 2004). Japan's 'flying geese' model is often cited as the modern antecedent of East Asian IPN development (Tsui-Auch, 1999; Peng, 2000). Akamatsu (1935) first developed this model or theory in the 1930s. Companies such as Nissan and Mitsubishi constructed production plants across the region, linked together to other plants, both back in Japan and elsewhere. The flying geese concept was revived in the 1960s to explain a re-emergent Japan's role in the East Asian regional economy. From this time, Japanese MNEs began to make substantial investments in other parts of East Asia, first in South Korea and Taiwan, and then into Southeast Asia. This involved the relocation of labour-intensive industries (such as textiles, basic electronics) to take advantage of East Asia's much lower unit-labour costs. Meanwhile, American firms were developing their own overseas investments and basic production networks in East Asia, partly under procurement contracts to support US military operations in the Korean and Vietnam wars.

As the techno-industrial foundations of East Asia's first-generation 'tiger' economies (Singapore, South Korea, Taiwan, Hong Kong) strengthened, so these in turn evolved into overseas investing countries, joining Japan, the US and also European countries as foreign investors in less developed parts of East Asia. This was the flying geese dynamic that initial investments from 'leading geese' economies had a positive multiplier effect on regional economic development, with less developed countries following in the slipstream of stronger leading economies (Feenstra, 1998). The revaluation of the Japanese yen, as a consequence of the 1985 *Plaza Accord* between the G7 countries, led to a notable surge of Japanese outward FDI during the late 1980s. The revaluation (the deliberate raising of a currency's exchange rate value) meant not only that Japanese firms relocated more production overseas in East Asia and elsewhere, but also that Japan-based firms regionalized their procurement strategies more widely as it became cheaper to import components and other inputs. This gave a significant spur to IPN development in East Asia.

There are two main explanations for why IPNs are more extensively developed in East Asia than any other part of the world. First, East Asia's development asymmetry, and hence heterogeneity of country competitive advantages, broadens the scope for IPN divisions of labour. This ranges from higher value-added activities (design, high-tech production) being generally conducted in the region's more advanced economies like Japan, South Korea, Taiwan and Singapore, while more labour-intensive, lower-end activities are undertaken by less developed countries such as Vietnam and Cambodia. Second, the improving technological and industrial capabilities of East Asian countries as a whole over recent decades have made the region an important workshop of the world. East Asia now accounts for major shares of production in big global industries like electronics, automobiles, textiles, machinery, computers and other information and communication goods. The production of these multi-component products are increasingly organized in IPN configurations.

IPN Activity in Europe

High levels of MNE activity have been prevalent in Western Europe for some considerable time. Many key industries in the region have been organized on an international division of labour basis. The macro-level integration (regionalism) of Europe has created increasingly coherent regional economic spaces that have spurred the development of pan-regional corporate networks. Historically speaking, Europe's automobile sector has been at the forefront of the region's IPN activity (Lagendijk, 1997). European car manufacturers as well as American companies such as Ford and General Motors have been operating at least some basic forms of IPN in the region for many decades. Ford's regional strategy in Europe has always been closely aligned to the macro-level integration process. In 1967, a year before the EEC introduced its customs union arrangement, the company expanded its production network to include a larger number of countries. In the late 1970s, it established a new assembly production plant in Spain in anticipation of the country's accession into the European Community a few years later. Linkages between macro-level integration and IPN development are apparent in the regional strategies of other automotive firms too. For example, General Motors extended its Europe regional production network into Central and Eastern Europe in the 1990s to prepare for the EU's eastward enlargement, establishing a new engine plant in Hungary and a new assembly plant in Poland. On the eve of the euro's launch, Toyota announced in 2001 that it would set up a second assembly plant in northern France rather than extend its first plant based in Britain, primarily because of Britain's decision to not join the single currency.

Amin (2000) asserted at the turn of the millennium that, 'the EU can be seen as a gigantic international production complex made up of networks of transnational corporations which straddle across national boundaries and form trade networks in their own right' (p. 675). Dicken (2003) argues that supply-side forces are leading to pan-regional operations in production and distribution being created to take advantage of scale efficiencies in a more integrated Single European Market that is evolving at the macro-level. But at the same time, 'demand-side factors are still being articulated primarily at the country-specific level, where linguistic and cultural differences play a major role in the demands for goods and services' (Dicken, 2003, p. 271). Consequently, much production in Europe is still geared at the national level to serve local or national markets. While post-Fordist flexible production systems permit nationally customized production to occur within the same regionally dispersed production network, Europe's IPNs generally do not operate in the same region-extensive and functionally integrative manner across as many industries as East Asia's do. Most IPN activity in Europe tends to involve just a small handful of countries. One reason for this has been West Europe's relatively lower degree of development asymmetry, and hence there is a less clear division of labour apparent when compared to East Asia.[2] However, the EU's enlargement into Central and Eastern Europe (CEE) has brought greater economic diversity to the Single Market area. Much of the new foreign investment attracted by countries such as Poland, Hungary and the Czech Republic has developed new production network linkages with the EU's core economy.

There remain, nevertheless, far fewer examples of *type IV* regional production network in Europe than in East Asia. Even in the automobile sector *types I* and *II* international production remains the norm for many large car producers. Dicken (2003) has argued that, with the exception of the Volkswagen group, most European car manufacturers remain very embedded in their home nations. Fiat, Peugeot-Citroen and Renault still produce a large majority of their units in their originating countries, and Fiat only produce cars in one other country (Poland) apart from Italy. Japanese firms — Nissan, Honda and Toyota — have too adopted more of a *type I* international production arrangement whereby production has been concentrated in Britain with some international sourcing. Established second-tier and third-tier suppliers from Japan in the *keiretsu* network of these core assembly firms have followed them to Britain to work in the same 'just-in-time' logistical systems as back home.

Volkswagen's take-over of Skoda in the early 1990s did, though, help spearhead the extension of Europe's IPN activity into Central and Eastern Europe. Volkswagen matched roughly a third of Skoda's domestic suppliers with foreign automotive suppliers in new joint venture operations (for example with Lucas from Britain and Siemens from Germany) and developed the company's regional and global sourcing network based on Volkswagen's on supplier network platforms (Meyer, 2000). Many of the EU's new CEE member states have the advantage of possessing relatively high-skilled yet low-cost labour and good infrastructure, especially Central European countries like the Czech Republic, Hungary and Poland. A steadily growing number of European companies (Philips, Siemens, ABB and Ericsson), as well as American firms (General Electric and IBM) have been extending their regional production networks into the CEE subregion, the key sectors being mechanical engineering, electronics, automobiles, textiles and clothing. The EU's an-European System of Cumulation model for rules of origin also allowed for widespread diagonal cumulation in pre-accession trade agreements signed with CEE countries that have been conducive to the development of pan-regional production systems (Augier et al., 2005).

A. Smith (2004) has observed with regard to the textiles industry that CEE countries are becoming incorporated into the 'outward processing trade' systems of IPNs in this sector. Pre-accession free trade arrangements with the EU (Europe Agreements) helped facilitate this process through lowering the transaction costs of creating these more pan-regional networks (Pellegrin, 2001). Outward processing trade here entailed EU-based textiles manufacturers and retailers contracting out work to CEE producers for re-export to the EU. This circular trade was permitted tariff-free conditions under EU trade and customs regulations. It was also not subject to any relevant quota regulations if the original materials derived substantially from EU-based sources. Yet, the CEE textile and clothing producers still remain on the periphery of IPN arrangements in this sector, being locked in generally subservient relationships with Europe's big textile and clothing firms (Smith, A., 2004).

One should also note that much of Europe's labour-intensive production in particular has been gradually transferred and incorporated into East Asia's own IPN systems. Furthermore, Europe and East Asia are increasingly linked by global production network arrangements. Many European firms that have set up production networks that serve the East Asian market have linkages with their core-based operations back home in Europe. The same applies for Japanese and Korean production networks based in and serving the European market. This is especially prevalent in the automobile, electronics, and information and communication technology (ICT) product sectors.

Industrial Districts and Agglomerated Integration

Industrial Districts in Perspective

Industrial districts may be considered as spatially dense agglomerations of industry-related firms, or concentrations of specialized industries in particular localities. They can also be viewed as the physical building blocks of core and dynamic economic development within a regional economy or the world economy generally, being the centre of many of important global industries, for example, Silicon Valley and the ICT sector. To Dicken (2003), they form an essential part of the world economy's 'global mosaic' of densely concentrated regional economies. Industrial districts are based on a cluster or agglomeration dynamic where spatial concentrations of firms and their activities confer particular competitive advantages. Studying their development provides an important insight into the zonal economic development of the East Asia and European regional economies.

In all regions, patterns of economic development have been determined by 'path dependence' factors. Localized socio-economic and geographic factors have shaped historic trajectory of development in both Europe and East Asia. Examples include: a proximity to resource elements, such as iron ore (steel production), coast (maritime trade, fishing); traditional craft skills historically located in an area; expanding urbanized human capital (educated, skilled) that spurs particular industry development; and the evolutionary growth of socio-institutional resources (craft guilds, industry associations, research and design centres) that, amongst other things, help produce the 'social capital' necessary for dynamic industry development (Putnam, 1993). Furthermore, certain agglomeration effects can ensure that 'core' economic development remains geographically concentrated in particular areas or localities. This works on the basic principle that a critical development mass attracts more mass over time, this process being both cumulative and self-reinforcing.

Storper (1997) analysed this process through the combined working of traded and untraded interdependencies. Advantages derived from the geographic proximity that exist between networked firms performing different but linked functions in the production chain (for example, autos and electronics) are one instance of traded interdependency. This proximity helps to achieve symbiotic cost efficiencies, and makes possible a higher intensity of inter-firm transactions and collaboration. Untraded interdependencies are born from less tangible, socio-economic benefits that are strongly associated with external economies of scale factors. Examples include how all firms in the locality benefit from the pool of skilled workers, the provision of specialized infrastructure to serve the area, and technological and knowledge spillovers.

Markusen (1996) has categorized industrial districts into four main types. Those of the Marshallian variety (named after British economist, Alfred Marshall) are characterized by dense networks of local small to medium enterprises and high degrees of inter-firm co-operation among them. Examples include Third Italy (Emilia-Romagna), Baden-Württemberg, Rhône-Alpes, and Kangwan (South Seoul). Many Marshallian industrial districts have deep historic roots that derive from a locality's craft traditions and accumulated skills, such as the silverware and kitchenware makers of Tsubame, Japan, the cane furniture producers of Cebu, Philippines, and the ceramic tile firms clustered around Sassuolo (Porter, 1990; Yamawaki, 2001; World Bank, 2003). Sassuolo is actually part of the 20 to 30 mini-district cluster that makes up the larger Third Italy (Emilia-Romagna) district. Other mini-districts here include Modena (machine tools, sports cars), Prato (fashion textiles) and Brianza (designer furniture). Third Italy districts are founded on craft-design competitive advantages and high value-added inputs. It has similarities with the Baden-Württemberg industrial district in Southwest Germany, whose industrial core is based around Stuttgart and is home to Bosch, Porsche and Daimler-Benz. These firms are served by a cluster of mechanical and electrical engineering, and automotive sector suppliers. Moreover, it is the most research-and-development-intensive region in Germany and approximately 40 percent of the workforce is employed in manufacturing, almost twice the national average.

The second type, the 'hub–spoke' or 'core–ring' industrial district, is based around the core operations of one or two large firms in a particular area (for example Toyota and Toyota City in Japan) and is defined by networked relations developed among firms in the district. A third type, 'satellite platform' industrial districts, rely heavily on foreign investment and are founded on congregations of branch facilities from externally based multi-plant firms. These districts are characterized by low levels of intra-district trade and contractual relationships among the district's firms, but their high levels of extra-district production chain linkages are normally constituent elements of IPN activity. Examples include Jurong (Singapore), Kumi (South Korea), and China's 'Special Economic Zones'. Lastly, 'state-anchored' industrial districts arise from either state-developed industrial parks or estates (such as Hsinchu Science Park in Taiwan or 'Silicon Fen' around Cambridge in Britain) or are based around one or several government institutions (military bases, universities) served by dense networks of localized suppliers in a public–private partnership relational context, for example the Tsukuba research complex in Japan and the Biopolis estate in Singapore.

Embedded within a Broader Urbanized Development Process

Most industrial districts are located in areas of significant urbanization because they can draw upon high levels of human, infrastructural and technological resources. For example, a key factor behind the clustering of Japan's many high-tech industrial activities around the Tokyo area is that most of the country's prestigious universities and research institutes that have established strong links with high-tech firms are located in the area. Many industrial districts do not have well-defined spatial boundaries, and moreover can be embedded within wider metropolitan areas or city conurbations. Examples include Tokyo–Nagoya–Osaka in Japan, Taipei–Hsinchu in Taiwan, Seoul–Inchon in South Korea, Manila–Quezon City in the Philippines, Milan–Genoa–Turin in Italy, the Rhine–Ruhr area in Germany, and the Leeds–Manchester–Liverpool corridor in North England (Scott, 1998; Smith, A., 2004).

Moreover, the general commercial interaction between these zones represents the majority of intra-regional trade, finance and other forms of regional economic exchange in East Asia and Europe. In East Asia, capital city districts often account for over 50 percent of their respective national gross domestic products. East Asia's larger and more powerful cities (such as Tokyo, Hong Kong, Shanghai, Beijing, Singapore, Seoul, Taipei, Bangkok) have played an important role in East Asia's regional economic integration. As D.A. Smith (2004, p. 400) observed, such cities perform various coordinating and decision-making functions for 'geographically dispersed business networks of finance, manufacturing, retailing, and transport'. Sassen (1991) has argued more generally that global cities (such as London, Paris and Tokyo,) serve as the prime 'command and control centres' in the global economy, being the headquartered locations of large powerful firms and also the main infrastructural hubs of the region (Keeling, 1995; Sassen, 1998). In sum, the networked links woven over time amongst cities, industrial districts and other forms of economic zones (see pan-regional development corridors examined later) are a prime foundation of East Asia and Europe's regionalization.

IPN Connections with Industrial Districts

Industrial district agglomeration may work for and against IPN fragmentation and development, depending on the nature of the IPN itself (Ando and Kimura, 2003; Kimura and Ando, 2004). At the broader level, the agglomeration represented by industrial districts is an important element of the new economic geography in which economic activity is generally defined in zonal terms, for example concentrated in subnational, urban–industrial zones, or cutting across national borders in a transnational manner (see the following section on cross-border regional integration). On the one hand, the salience of industrial districts suggests that there may be limits to IPN growth, and hence to pan-regionalized integration generally. Put alternatively, economic activity is 'sticky', remaining highly concentrated in particular localized zones within macro-regional economies such as Europe and East Asia. On the other hand, one might take the view that IPNs are ultimately founded on linking into the specialized local economic assets of industrial districts and other kinds of localized economic zones. We saw that the connections between IPNs and industrial districts can vary according to the respective nature of both forms of economic activity. For example, Marshallian industrial districts, which are generally more prevalent in Europe than East Asia, are comparatively more self-contained with relatively few externalized linkages. Satellite platform industrial districts, which in contrast are more prevalent in East Asia, may be extensively plugged into IPN operations because they consist mainly of hosted foreign-investing enterprises. Industrial district development and IPN development may thus in certain cases work in a complementary fashion in advancing economic regionalization.

Cross-Border Regional Integration

Growth Polygons in East Asia

Cross-border regional integration is another important trend in economic regionalization in East Asia and Europe. In East Asia's case, this has concerned various 'growth polygons' that have emerged across the region over the last two or three decades (Thant et al., 1995). East Asia's 'growth polygons' are essentially subregional economic zones that encompass concentrations of transborder economic relationships and activities, and hence are closely associated with *type III* configurations of international production (see Figure 7.1). They may, however, span a subregional group of countries and not just two. Many are founded on transnationalized production chains within a subregional locale that exploit the specific comparative advantages of each participating economic zone.

The advance of economic liberalization — which has broken down international barriers to trade, investment and finance — has assisted this integrative process. In recognizing the emergence of growth polygons, many governments in East Asia have undertaken measures to further assist their development, for example through infrastructure investments (construction of new transport links, energy generation provision and communication hubs and networks) and general policy cooperation to manage the economic interdependence between their countries where subregional integration is apparent. Many growth polygons are also supported by international agencies such as the Asian Development Bank (ADB). In some cases, growth polygons may be considered more as constructs of inter-state development policy rather than dense geographic concentrations of transnationalized business activity. The ADB sponsored Greater Mekong Subregion is a good example of this. The region's main growth polygons are:

- *Indonesia-Malaysia-Singapore Growth Triangle (IMSGT)*: linking Singapore to Indonesia's Riau province and Malaysia's Johor province.
- *Greater Mekong Subregion (GMS)*: Myanmar, Cambodia, China (Yunnan Province), Laos, Thailand and Vietnam. Sponsored by the ADB.
- *Brunei-Indonesia-Malaysia-Philippines East ASEAN Growth Area (BIMP-EAGA)*: involving Brunei Darussalam, and a number of provinces from Indonesia, Malaysia, and the Philippines. Sponsored by the ADB.
- *Tumen River Area Development Programme (TRADP)*: involving North Korea's Rajin-Sonbong Economic and Trade Zone, Eastern Mongolia, China's Yanbian Korean Autonomous Prefecture in the Jilin Province, the Russian Far East's Primorsky Territory and South Korea.
- *Yellow Sea Rim Subregion*: the coastal areas facing the Yellow Sea of North and Northeast China, North and South Korea, and southern Japan. Overlaps geographically with the above but based more on a natural density of international business interactions than any joint policy initiative.
- *South China Sea Growth Triangle (SCSGT)*: Chinese business community linkages between southeast coastal China, Taiwan and Hong Kong.
- *Indonesia-Malaysia-Thailand Growth Triangle (IMTGT)*: established in 1993 and centred on the Straits of Malacca, a historic trading route. This has expanded from an original 10 participating provinces to 25 and is sponsored by the ADB.

In general, then, growth polygons involve contiguous or neighbouring economic zones from different nation-states participating in a symbiotic development relationship. Sometimes they engage whole countries in combination with subnational territories. The role of each zone or country will depend upon its comparative level of development, access to factor resources, position in international production networks, and so on. Similar to IPNs, the transborder nature of growth polygons leads one to question the notion that the East Asian regional economy consists simply of series of unitary nation-state components. As examined earlier, particular districts and zones of the East Asian economy are often more integrally linked with districts and zones from other countries than with those inside the same country. The same principle applies to growth polygons that like IPNs have created new integrative economic spaces and constitute an important layer to East Asia's regionalization.

Growth polygons can be categorized into three broad types in accordance to the particular evolutionary path of their development. These are:

- *Trans-border metropolitan spillovers*: this type of growth polygon is centred on an urban growth pole (industrial city, industrial district, or city-state such as Singapore and Hong Kong) whose development 'spills over' into neighbouring territories from other countries, thus creating a transnational economic space around its core. The Singapore-centred IMSGT represents a good example of this type.
- *Joint natural-resource-based or infrastructure-based development projects*: these centre on the co-management of a shared transnational resource like a river, the GMS and TRADP being prime examples. This entails developing frameworks of subregional diplomacy between involved local and national governments to manage transborder economic interdependence issues, as well as to minimize disputes arising from economic activities derived from the common resource or resources concerned.
- *Outgrowth of internationalizing, inter-firm networks*: at their core, these are clusters of export-oriented firms within a particular subregional locale that generally has wide sectoral coverage. These networks are generally founded on cross-border kinship or socio-cultural ties, and Chinese *guanxi* connections tend to be especially relevant here. The SCSGT, incorporating southeast coastal China, Hong Kong and Taiwan, is a prime example of this growth polygon type (Chen and Ho, 1995).

As with IPNs, each growth polygon may not neatly fall into one of the types above but rather exhibit characteristics from different types.

Cross-Border Regions (CBRs) in Europe

For some time, the EU's supra-national agencies such as the European Commission have promoted the idea of a 'Europe of the Regions'. Indeed, most economic geography discourses on Europe's regionalization focus on subnational regional development rather than its pan-regional development (MacLeod, 1999, Smith A., 2004). One strand of this analysis of Europe's regional economic geography concentrates on the formation of cross-border regions (CBRs) among European countries. There are integrational similarities with East Asia's 'growth polygons' here. Perkmann (2003, p.156) defines a cross-border region as 'institutionalized collaboration between contiguous sub-national authorities across national borders' and identifies more than 70 CBRs that have emerged across Europe. He generally notes the important part played by public agencies in CBR development, and thus comparisons may be made with East Asia's more state-led growth polygons like the IMSGT, BIMP-EAGA and GMS projects.

The CBR trend began in the late 1950s, the first project being EUREGIO, established in 1958 on the Dutch–German border and incorporating the areas of Enschede and Gronau. Scandinavian countries were also significantly involved in the early phase of Europe's CBR development, initiating a number of projects in the 1960s and 1970s with the financial support of the Nordic Council. Other EUREGIO-type projects, such as the Euregio Rhein–Waal and Euregio Maas–Rhein, were formed in the mid-1970s[3] (see Table 7.1). Perkmann (2003) notes that the macro-level integration process was a key facilitator of CBR cooperation and development. The Council of Europe helped provide the institutional framework for inter-agency cooperation, the 1980 Madrid Convention being particularly useful in this regard, creating the legal and regulatory conditions in which local authorities from different countries could embark on CBR projects. The Convention has been signed by 20 countries and updated by two additional protocols. Meanwhile, the European Commission has provided financial assistance primarily through the Interreg Community Initiative funds.[4] This micro-level integration was seen to underpin the wider macro-level integrational process, especially where extant functional interdependencies among participating CBR regions could be further developed.

Like East Asia's 'growth polygons', Europe's CBRs can vary in terms in geographic scope, cooperation intensity and types of actors involved.

Table 7.1 Cross border regions (CBRs) in Europe: Selected projects

Year	Name	Countries	Type	Scale
1958	EUREGIO	Ger, Neth	iC	loc
1964	Orensundskomiten	Den, Swe	Sc	reg
1971	Nordkalottkommitten	Nor, Swe, Fin	Sc	reg
1973	Euregio Rhein – Waal	Ger, Neth	iC	loc
1976	Euregio Maas – Rhein	Bel, Ger, Neth	iC	loc
1978	Alps-Adriatic	Aus, Ger, Ita, Swi, Cro, Slo, Hun	WC	reg
1980	Granskommiten Ostfold – Bohuslan	Nor, Swe	Sc	loc
1982	Western Alps	Fra, Ita, Swi	WC	reg
1982	Pyrennes	Fra, Spn	WC	reg
1987	Transmanche Region (Kent/Nord Pas de Calais)	Fra, UK	eC	reg
1990	Danube Countries	Aus, Ger, Hun	WC	reg
1991	Euroregion Neisse-Nisa-Nysa	Cze, Ger, Pol	eC	loc
1992	Euroregion Euskadi – Navarre – Aquitaine	Fra, Spn	eC	reg
1993	Carpathian Euroregion	Pol, Hun, Svk, Rom, Ukr	WC	reg
1994	Euregio Bayerischer Wald – Bohmerwald – Sumava	Aus, Cze, Ger	eC	loc
1995	Euregio TriRhena	Fra, Ger, Swi	iC	reg
1995	Region Insubrica	Ita, Swi	eC	reg
1996	Euregion Glacensis	Cze, Pol	eC	loc
1996	Upper Silesia – Northern Moravia	Cze, Pol	eC	loc
1996	Euregion Tatry	Svk, Pol	eC	loc
1997	Sonderjylland – Slesvig	Den, Ger	iC	loc
1998	Euregio Baltyk	Den, Est, Lat, Lith, Pol, Swe	WC	reg
1998	Europaregion Tyrol	Aus, Ita	eC	reg
1998	Danube-Drava-Szava Euro-Regional Initiative	Bos-Her, Cro, Hun	eC	reg

Source: Perkmann (2003)
Notes: For CBR types: iC (integrated micro-CBRs), eC (emerging micro-CBRs), Sc (Scandinavian groupings), WC (Working Communities). For prime CBR actors involved: loc (local authorities), reg (regional authorities).

Some projects involve local authorities and some larger regional authorities. Some are based on already well integrated transborder economic linkages and while others may be considered emerging CBRs (see Table 7.1). Certain CBRs incorporate a number of subnational regions, this applies especially to the various 'Working Community' associations created in the 1970s and 1980s, including the Western Alps, Danube Countries, Alps–Adriatic, Atlantic Arc and the Pyrenees groupings. These are based on an organizational structure of a general assembly, executive committee and thematic work programmes. However, Working Community CBRs have varied significantly in terms of their integrational aspirations, and have tended to achieve relatively limited results overall (Aykac, 1994). On a country-specific level, high levels of cooperation intensity tend to be achieved in CBRs that involve German participation, which may be mainly attributed to the strong executive powers exercised by the country's regional Länder governments. Strong 'region-states' from federated nation-states — such as Germany, Austria, Italy and Switzerland — have generally been able to embark on substantive transborder integrational projects. German public authorities are also behind many of Europe's smaller, local-scale and highly integrative CBR initiatives (see Table 7.1). Similar levels of cooperation are also found in Scandinavian projects where local municipalities enjoy comparable levels of policy autonomy (Bergman-Windberg, 1998). By contrast, those involving France tend to be at a lower level owing primarily to the relatively weak and small-scale character of localized government. In East Asia, it has been central governments, however, that have provided the guiding hand behind growth polygon projects.

In further linkage to Europe's macro-level integration process, Austria's engagement in CBR projects accelerated after it acceded to the EU in 1995. There was also a substantial growth in CBR activity involving Central and Eastern European countries after the end of the Cold War, thus contributing to the wider pan-European regionalization process. But as with East Asia's growth polygons, the private sector's enthusiasm for Europe's CBR projects has often been lacking, with firms being more oriented towards their own national economic spaces. Furthermore, local CBR governing authorities have lacked the necessary policy competence and funds to develop substantive integrational links, such as cross-border infrastructural systems (Harding, 1997; Brenner, 1999). Most CBR projects are also much more likely to flourish where close social, cultural and ethnic ties exist in the cross-border zone. This also applies to East Asia's cross-border regional integration, where such linkages are particularly strong, for instance, in the South China Sea Growth Triangle between China, Taiwan and Hong Kong. Where these ties are weak, then this can lead to a 'low trust' relational environment and undermine the integrational project. Kratke (1998) argues this has applied to German–Polish CBRs initiated in the 1990s.

Part of Europe's CBR trend has been the promotion of wider interregional collaboration inside Europe. Here, interregional alliances have been forged among subnational governments with common industrial interests and associations. The most high-profile example has been the 'Four Motors for Europe' regions project involving Baden Württemberg (Germany), Rhône-Alps (France), Catalonia (Spain) and Lombardia (Italy). This alliance was formed in 1988 with the support of the European Commission and based on industrial collaboration in the automotive and related sectors, such as machine tools and electrical/electronic products. The Four Motors for Europe project seeks to foster technological infrastructural linkages and cooperation among each region's dense networks of university and research institutes in all these regions (Borras, 1993, Wolfe, 2000). In many ways this may be viewed as an international collaborative venture between sector-related industrial districts, and there is also an international production network perspective to consider, as inter-firm (and thereby international production) networking among the four regions is actively promoted by the project. This, then, is another demonstration of the overlaps that exist among different regionalization processes.

The CBR phenomenon is a good example of where micro-level integration in Europe is being fostered within a dense institutional context. Not only have the European Commission and the Council of Europe played a key role in supporting CBR development, but agencies such as the Council of European Municipalities and Regions and the Assembly of European Regions and the Association of Border Regions have also performed facilitating roles in promoting greater collaboration among the subnational regions across Europe. Further additions to this institutional architecture were made in the 1990s, with the establishment of the Consultative Council of Regional and Local Authorities and the Committee of Regions after the ratification of the Maastricht Treaty (Grasse, 1999). Overall, then, Europe's CBRs are more institutionally constructed entities than East Asia's growth polygons, most of which have flourished with relatively limited public agency involvement with the exception of the IMSGT.

East Asia and Europe's Pan-Regional 'Development Corridors'

At the highest end of the geospatial scale of cross-border regional integration are the pan-regional 'development corridors' of East Asia and Europe. These are broader subregional economic spaces than either growth polygons or CBRs, which stretch across a whole macro-region. Development corridors generally comprise the macro-region's densest concentration of infrastructure development, high-tech industry clusters, and high-income markets. They thus represent its main spine or 'growth axis' of core economic development, and are generally where regionalized linkages are also the strongest. From the position of the main development corridor(s) one can also get some kind of idea of a macro-region's prime core and periphery zones, and can thereby assess over time the patterns of regional development convergence and divergence, that is, where the main concentration of higher value-added economic activity and main infrastructural linkages within the region are concentrated.

East Asia's pan-regional development corridor stretches from Japan down through the Korean peninsula, then along coastal China taking in Taiwan, and eventually down to Singapore at the bottom of the Malay Peninsula (see Figure 7.2). This has emerged out of the deep historic processes of regionalization noted earlier in the chapter. It is no coincidence that East Asia's development corridor takes in many of the region's ancient trading posts located in Japan, coastal China and Southeast Asia. Similarly, Europe's main development corridor — often referred to as the 'Blue Banana' — is historically founded on the medieval Alpine–Rhine trading routes, and moreover was the core zone of Europe's industrial revolution centuries later (Cappellin, 1993; Heidenreich, 1998). The 'Blue Banana' zone is densely populated (accounting for around 40 percent of the EU's population in the late 1990s) and highly urbanized. It stretches from Northern Italy, arching banana-like along the Franco-German border into the Low Countries (Belgium, Netherlands, Luxembourg) and then extending into mid-England (Figure 7.3). It has Europe's highest concentration of motorways (hence the 'blue' banana), other transportation linkages and also socio-cultural facilities (Dunford, 1998; Hospers, 2002).

Conclusion

This chapter has tried to present a geospatial perspective on Europe and East Asia's regional integration. It has studied various micro-level integrational processes that have been knitting together the regionalization of the European and East Asian economies. These macro-regional economies are not 'bloc-like' but rather based on a patchwork of multi-scale economic zones and business networks that involve various forms of transnational or cross-border linkages. The geospatial dimensions and patterns of regionalized development studied by this paper enable us to see how regional integration in both East Asia and Europe is occurring

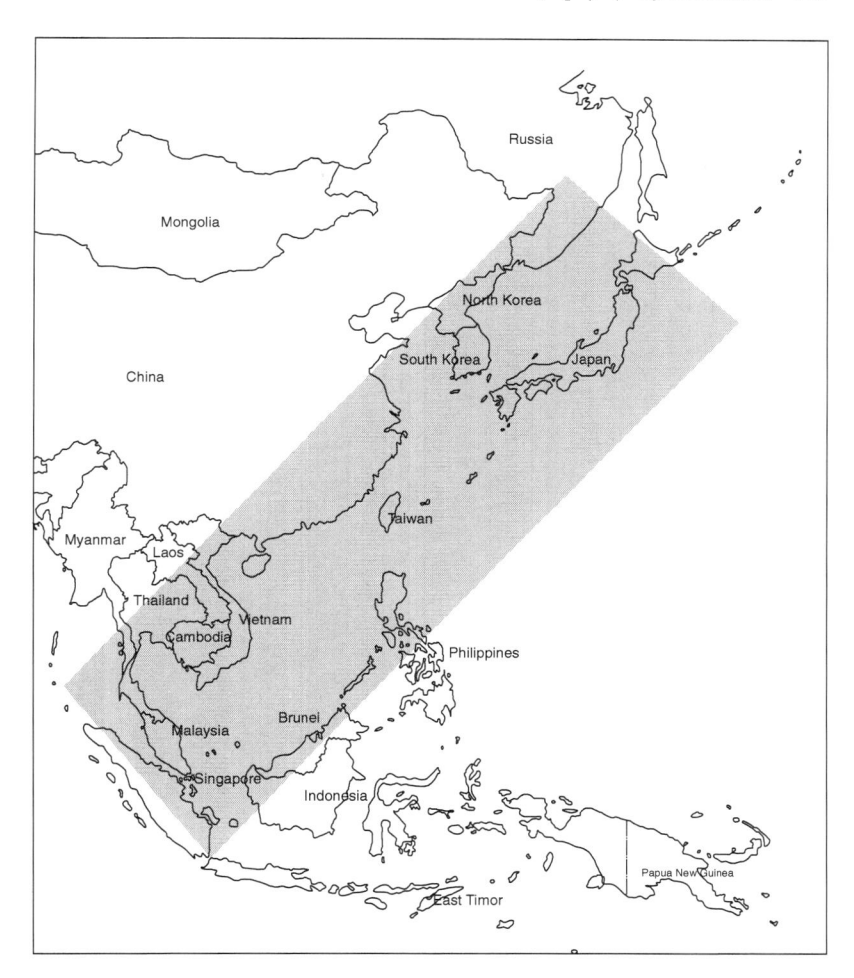

Figure 7.2 East Asia's pan-regional development corridor.

at the 'ground level' so to speak. This was first examined in relation to international production network activity in East Asia and Europe with reference to the development of more functionally integrative economic and business linkages being forged across both regions at the micro-level. It was argued that IPN activity has been an important binding force in the regionalization of East Asia and Europe, creating new transnational business systems across and between national economies, but that this more strongly evident in the former than the

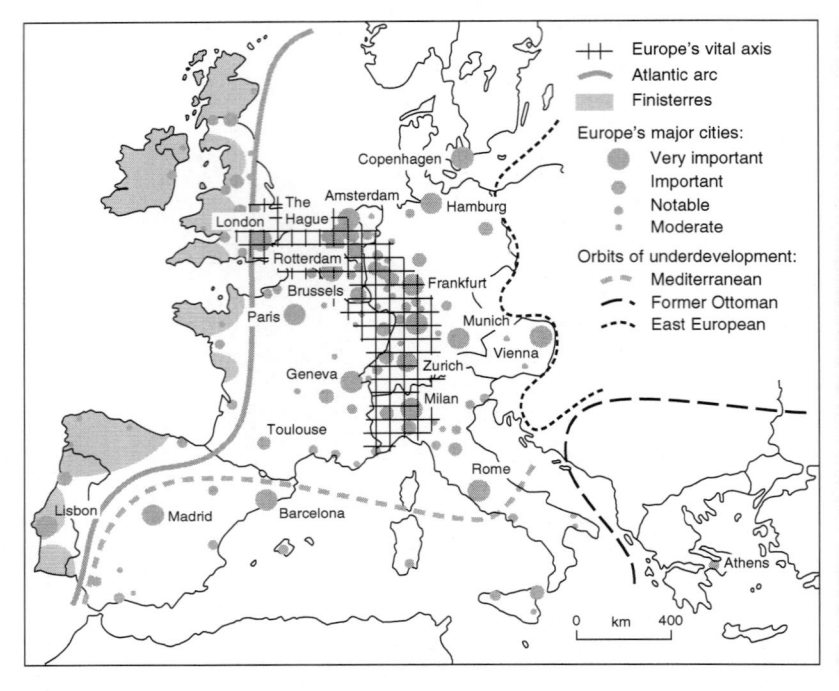

Figure 7.3 Europe's vital axis.

latter. International production networks have played a critically important role in the regional economic development of East Asia generally, thereby shaping the region's economic geography more significantly. In contrast, Europe is more a 'region of regions', where localized competitive advantages tend to be embedded in region-based industrial districts such as Third Italy and Baden Württemberg. However, it is not just a matter of the centripetal forces of industrial district agglomeration being ranged against the centrifugal forces of IPN dispersion. Industrial districts can serve as the essential network nodes on which IPNs are locationally rooted. This represents the interface between the networked and zonal development aspects of East Asia and Europe's economic regionalization. The analysis on cross-border regional integration concerning East Asia's growth polygons and Europe's cross-border region projects examined this relationship further. Dense concentrations of cross-border networked relationships can create new economic zones or spaces in themselves between countries at the subregional level. The integrational factors thus far mentioned can all in turn form the basis of a pan-regional development corridor at the highest end of the geospatial scale. It was noted how East Asia and Europe's development corridors may be considered the prime 'core' or growth axis of each macro-region, and thereby the main spine of their regionalized economic activity.

This chapter has identified the similarities and contrasts in the economic geography of regionalization in East Asia and Europe. Many of the constituent linkages of both regionalization processes derive from the same integrative factors (transnationalized business operations) and universal dynamics (the drive for economic efficiencies). Moreover, East Asia and Europe's regionalization are both embedded within the same broader globalization process as, for example, was examined in relation to IPNs and their position within wider global production networks. In general, though, and as with macro-level regionalism, micro-level regionalization has advanced in a stronger institutionalized context in Europe compared to East Asia. Europe's local and regional authorities, as well as local civic institutions, have played an important role in industrial district and CBR project development. EU-based firms have also formulated their regional corporate strategies in accordance to macro-level integration projects such as the Single European Market, the euro single currency and EU enlargements. One can expect to see a similar pattern of alignment in East Asia if its own macro-level integration progresses in the future.

Notes

1. By East Asia I am referring to the two subregional groupings: (i) Southeast Asia, comprising Brunei, Cambodia, East Timor, Indonesia, Laos, Malaysia, Myanmar, Philippines, Singapore, Thailand, Vietnam; (ii) Northeast Asia comprising Japan, China, South Korea, North Korea, Hong Kong SAR, Macau SAR, Mongolia and Taiwan.
2. Another reason cited by Zysman and Schwartz (1998) concerns Europe's relatively extensive legal restrictions on labour reorganization and lay-offs that could, in certain cases, constrict the IPN reconfiguration options of firms when re-strategizing production in response to changing market-related and other factors.
3. These were based on the original EUREGIO project, as their name suggests.
4. Interreg III (2000–06) has a total budget of €4.9 billion, which CBR development draws from.

References

Akamatsu, K. (1935) 'Trend of Japanese Trade in Woollen Goods', *Journal of Nagoya Higher Commercial School*, 13, pp. 129–212.

Amin, A. (2000) 'The European Union as More than a Triad Market for National Economic Spaces', in G. L. Clark, M. P. Feldman and M. S. Gertler (eds) *The Oxford Handbook of Economic Geography*, Oxford: Oxford University Press, pp. 671–685.

Anderson, K. and Norheim, H. (1993) 'History, Geography and Regional Economic Integration', in K. Anderson and R. Blackhurst (eds) *Regional Integration and the Global Trading System*, Hemel Hempstead: Harvester Wheatsheaf, pp. 19–51.

Ando, M. and Kimura, F. (2003) *The Formation of International Production and Distribution Networks in East Asia*, National Bureau of Economic Research Working Paper No. 10167, Cambridge MA: NBER.

Athukorala, P. (2003) *Product Fragmentation and Trade Patterns in East Asia*, ADB Working Paper No 2003/21, Manila.

Augier, P., Gasiorek, M. and Tong, C. L. (2005) 'The Impact of Rules of Origin on Trade Flows', *Economic Policy*, 43, pp. 567–624.

Aykac, A. (1994) *Transborder Regionalisation: An Analysis of Transborder Cooperation Structures in Western Europe within the Context of European Integration and Decentralisation Towards Regional and Local Governments*, Sindelfingen: Libertas.

Borras, S. (1993) 'The Four Motors for Europe and its Promotion of R&D Linkages: Beyond Geographical Contiguity in Inter-Regional Agreements', *Regional Politics and Policy*, 3. 3, pp. 163–76.

Borrus, M., Ernst, D. and Haggard, S. (eds) (2000) *International Production Networks in Asia: Rivalry or Riches?*, London: Routledge.

Brenner, N. (1999) 'Globalisation as Reterritorialisation: The Re-scaling of Urban Governance in the European Union', *Urban Studies*, 36. 3, pp. 431–51.

Cappellin, R. (1993) 'Inter-regional Co-operation in Europe: An Introduction', in R. Cappellin and P. Batey (eds) *Regional Networks, Border Regions and European Integration*, London: Pion.

Chen, E. K. Y. and Ho, A. (1995) 'Southern China Growth Triangle: An Overview', in M. Thant, M. Tang and H. Kakazu (eds), *Growth Triangles in Asia: A New Approach to Regional Economic Co-operation*, Oxford: Oxford University Press.

Dicken, P. (2003) *Global Shift: Reshaping the Global Economic Map in the 21st Century*, London: Sage.

Dunford, M. (1998) 'Economies in Space and Time: Economic Geographies of Development and Underdevelopment and Historical Geographies of Modernisation', in B. Graham (ed.) *Modern Europe: Place, Culture, Identity*, London: Arnold, pp. 53–88.

Feenstra, R. (1998) 'Integration of Trade and Disintegration of Production in the Global Economy', *Journal of Economic Perspectives*, 14. 4, pp. 31–50.

Grasse, A. (1999) 'The Myth of Regionalisation in Europe: Rhetoric and Reality of an Ambivalent Concept', *Journal of European Area Studies*, 9. 1, pp. 79–92.

Harding, A. (1997) 'Urban Regimes in a Europe of the Cities', *European Urban and Regional Studies*, 4. 4, pp. 291–314.

Heidenreich, M. (1998) 'The Changing System of European Cities and Regions', *European Planning Studies*, 6, pp. 315–32.

Henderson, J., Dicken, P. Hess, M., Coe, N. and Yeung, H. W. C. (2002) 'Global Production Networks and the Analysis of Economic Development', *Review of International Political Economy*, 9. 3, pp. 436–64.

Hospers, G. J. (2002) 'Beyond the Blue Banana: Structural Change in Europe's Geo-Economy', paper presented at the *42nd European Congress of the Regional Science Association*, 27–31 August, Dortmund.

Jones, R. and Kierzkowski, H. (1990) 'The Role of Services in Production and International Trade: A Theoretical Framework', in R. Jones and A. Krueger (eds) *The Political Economy of International Trade: Essays in Honour of Robert Baldwin*, Oxford: Blackwell, pp. 31–48.

Keeling, D. J. (1995) 'Transport and the World City Paradigm', in P.L. Knox and P.J. Taylor (eds) *World Cities in a World System*, Cambridge: Cambridge University Press, pp. 115–131.

Kimura, F. and Ando, M. (2004) 'The Economic Analysis of International Production/Distribution Networks in East Asia and Latin America: The Implication of Regional Trade Arrangements', paper presented at the *APEC Study Centres Consortium Meeting*, Vina del Mar, Chile, 26–9 May.

Knox, P. and Agnew, J. (1998) *The Geography of the World Economy*, London: Arnold.

Kratke, S. (1998) 'Problems of Cross-Border Regional Integration: The Case of the German-Polish Border Area', *European Urban and Regional Studies*, 5. 3, pp. 249–62.

Lagendijk, A. (1997) 'Towards an Integrated Automotive Industry in Europe: A "Merging Filiere" Perspective, *European Urban and Regional Studies*, 4. 1, pp. 5–18.

MacLeod, G. (1999) 'Place, Politics and "Scale Dependence": Exploring the Structuration of Euro-Regionalism', *European Urban and Regional Studies*, 6, pp. 231–53.

Markusen, A. (1996) 'Sticky Places in Slippery Pace: A Typology of Industrial Districts', *Economic Geography*, 72. 3, pp. 293–313.

Meyer, K. (2000) 'International Production Networks and Enterprise Transformation in Central Europe', *Comparative Economic Studies*, 42. 1, pp. 135–50.

Ng, F. and Yeats, A. (2001) 'Production Sharing in East Asia: Who Does What for Whom, and Why?' in L. Cheung and H. Kierzhowski (eds) *Global Production and Trade in East Asia*, Boston: Kluwer Academic, pp. 63–109.

Pellegrin, J. (2001) *The Political Economy of Competitiveness in an Enlarged Europe*, Basingstoke: Palgrave.

Peng, D. (2000) 'The Changing Nature of East Asia as an Economic Region', *Pacific Affairs*, 73. 2, pp. 171–91.

Perkmann, M. (2003) 'Cross-Border Regions in Europe: Significance and Drivers of Regional Cross-Border Co-Operation', *European Urban and Regional Studies*, 10. 4, pp. 153–71.

Porter, M. (1990) *The Competitive Advantage of Nations*, London: MacMillan.

Putnam, R. D. (1993) *Making Democracy Work: Civic Traditions in Modern Italy*, Princeton: Princeton University Press.

Sakakibara, E. and Yamakawa, S. (2004) 'Market-driven Regional Integration in East Asia', paper presented at the workshop *Regional Economic Integration in a Global Framework* sponsored by the European Central Bank and the People's Bank of China, Beijing, China (September 22–23).

Sassen, S. (1991) *The Global City: New York, London, Tokyo*, Princeton: Princeton University Press.

Sassen, S. (1998) 'The Impact of New Technologies and Globalization on Cities' in Lo, F. C. and Yeung, Y. M. (eds) *Globalisation and the World of Large Cities*, Tokyo: United Nations University Press, pp. 391–411.

Scott, A.J. (1998) *Regions and the World Economy. The Coming Shape of Global Production, Competition and Political Order*, Oxford: Oxford University Press.

Smith, A. (2004) 'Regions, Spaces of Economic Practice and Diverse Economies in the New Europe', *European Urban and Regional Studies*, 11. 1, pp. 9–25.

Smith, D.A. (2004), 'Global Cities in East Asia: Empirical and Conceptual Analysis', *International Social Science Journal*, 56. 3, pp. 399–412.

Storper, M. (1997) *The Regional World: Territorial Development in a Global Economy*, London; New York: Guildford Press.

Thant, M., Tang, M. and Kakazu, H. (eds) (1995) *Growth Triangles in Asia: A New Approach to Regional Economic Co-operation*, Oxford: Oxford University Press.

Tsui-Auch, L. S. (1999) 'Regional Production Relationships and Developmental Impacts: A Comparative Study of Three Production Networks', *International Journal of Urban and Regional Research*, 23. 2, pp. 345–59.

Wolfe, D. A. (2000) 'Networking among Regions: Ontario and the Four Motors for Europe', *European Planning Studies*, 8. 3, pp. 267–84.

World Bank (2003) *Major Trade Trends in East Asia*, Policy Research Working Paper 3084, Washington, D.C.: World Bank.

Yamawaki, H. (2001) *The Evolution and Structure of Industrial Clusters in Japan*, Working Paper 37183, Washington, DC: World Bank Institute.

Yun, C. (2003) 'International Production Networks and the Role of the State: Lessons from the East Asian Development Experience', *European Journal of Development Research*, 15. 1, pp. 170–93.

Yusuf, S., Altaf, M. A. and Nabeshima, K. (eds) (2004) *Global Production Networking and Technological Change in East Asia*, Oxford: World Bank/Oxford University Press.

Zysman, J. and Schwartz, A. (1998) 'Reunifying Europe in an Emerging World Economy: Economic Heterogeneity, New Industrial Options, and Political Choices', *Journal of Common Market Studies*, 36. 3, pp. 405–29.

8
European and Asian Security and the Role of Regional Organizations in the Post-9/11 Environment

Nicholas Rees

Introduction

The focus of the chapter is on the impact of the September 11 terrorist attacks (9/11) and the War on Terror on the approaches to security adopted by the European Union (EU) and the Association of Southeast Asian Nations (ASEAN), and on whether regional security arrangements have provided an effective means of responding to such threats. The chapter examines the responses of the two regions to terrorism, focusing specifically on the impact that heightened concern over security has had on the regional organizations in the respective regions, as well as on interregional cooperation between the EU and ASEAN with regard to security. It addresses three key questions. First, how and in what ways did regional organizations in Europe and Asia respond to the events of 9/11 and the subsequent terrorist attacks. Second, what impact has this had on regional security cooperation in Europe and Asia? Finally, what are the prospects for EU–Asian security cooperation, especially with regard to combating terrorism?

This chapter suggests that 'new' security threats such as terrorism have challenged the ability of regional organizations to respond to such problems and that this reflects the underlying weaknesses of the respective organizations as security actors. It focuses largely on the role of the EU and ASEAN, and to lesser degree on other regional organizations and forums, in international security and their response to the War on Terror. It looks at these developments within the EU, including its response to terrorism and the adoption of specific anti-terrorism measures. In Asia, the response among states was fragmented, reflecting different foreign policy outlooks and values and the weak level of security cooperation in regional organizations. The chapter argues that the lack of strong regional security cooperation in Asia reflects a very different approach to security issues among the states in the region, the emphasis being on informal norm-building rather than institutionalization. The lack of strong institutionalization and resources has made regional cooperation in Asia problematic, although attitudes have been changing, given a range of economic, environmental and security shocks and the prospects of deepening cooperation. Security matters are increasingly discussed in Asian regional organizations and fora and form part of the dialogue with the European Union.

Understanding European and Asian Approaches to Security

Europe: The EU and NATO

Security arrangements in Europe still depend overwhelmingly on the nation-state, although states have been willing to adapt and change their individual approaches to security by participating in a range of regional organizations that plays a role in European and international security. The EU's role in security matters has grown since the end of the Cold War, following concerns about the inability of the EU to influence events in Bosnia-Herzegovina and then in Kosovo. The development of a more elaborate common foreign and security policy (CFSP) and the framing of a European security and defence policy have considerably enhanced the EU's desire and ability to play a global role beyond its borders. This has been underpinned by the development of a political and military institutional infrastructure within the Council Secretariat, as well as through the elaboration of a strategic concept of operations. The EU has developed a European Security Strategy, which calls for an increased cooperation in defence and an improvement of military capabilities (Solana, 2003).

In contrast to the EU, the North Atlantic Treaty Organization (NATO) has continued to play an important role in European security and beyond. Early initiatives included the North Atlantic Cooperation Council (1991) and the Partnership for Peace (1994); both of which helped to prepare the way for enlargement (1999, 2004). It has moved beyond being an organization committed to the collective defence of Europe to one that has become an international security player within and outside of Europe since the agreement on 'out of area' activities at the Prague Summit in 2002. NATO remains the primary security actor in which European states cooperate with their North American counterparts. The United States, in particular, continues to rely and depend on NATO as Europe's principal security provider. An early indication of the alliance's resolve lay in Kosovo (1999), where NATO engaged in a military operation on humanitarian grounds, but in which the prime objective was to oppose and oust President Slobodan Milosevic. Similarly NATO had previously provided a peacekeeping force in Bosnia-Herzegovina (the International Implementation Force, subsequently renamed the Stabilization Force). Outside Europe, NATO has participated in Afghanistan, where it has been involved in leading the international stabilization force since August 2003; it has also contributed logistical support to the African Union peacekeeping force in Darfur and delivered humanitarian relief after the earthquake in Pakistan (2005).

Asia: ASEAN, ASEAN Plus Three, ARF and APEC

The complex geography of Asia and especially East Asia, with a diverse range of states with very different interests and security outlooks, inevitably makes security cooperation difficult in this broad 'region' (see Narine, 2002). In contrast to Europe, where the states are largely liberal democracies, the states in Asia are characterized by very different types of political regime. There are democracies, ranging from strong to weak, authoritarian regimes and military-dominated state structures, all with significant differences in their levels of economic development. It is important to be aware of these differences as they influence and shape the response of the states to terrorism, given the different domestic institutional machineries, legal systems and administrative capacities. Asian states have predominantly addressed security concerns through a mix of bilateral agreements (of which those between Australia and Indonesia, and the Philippines and the US are notable examples) and through participation in security alliances. As Katzenstein suggests, 'Absent in Asia are the pooling of sovereignty and far-reaching multi-lateral arrangements that typify Europe's security order' (2005, p. 125). External actors, such as the US, China, Russia and Japan, have all historically played a role in the region and continue to influence developments today. The Cold War made regional cooperation difficult, given the series of bilateral alliances, the ideological divisions and the posturing between the major powers, China and the US. Indeed, China had an indirect influence on the establishment and evolution of ASEAN, as well as more recently being involved with ASEAN and ASEAN Plus Three. The US has and continues to play a significant role, developing strong bilateral relationships, which may have constrained the development of regionalism, rather than enabling it as in Europe (Beeson, 2005, p. 979). In contrast Japan has played a limited leadership role in the region, despite, or perhaps because of, its economic development and its dependence on the US (Okawara and Katzenstein, 2001).

ASEAN's approach to security has been different from that of the European Union, reflecting the core values and nature of the organization, its limited role and functions and its lack of commitment to collective security (Acharya 2003a; 2003b; Cabellero-Anthony, 2006). ASEAN states were committed to policies of national resilience such as developing their national economies, strengthening national identities and safeguarding borders — and by extension, to regional resilience (against external actors) and regional stability. In effect, this added up to a comprehensive approach that covered political, economic and socio-cultural security as well as military security (Caballero-Anthony, 2006, p. 267). The security cooperation within the region was based on informal norm-building rather than institutionalization. The so-called 'ASEAN Way' placed an emphasis on national sovereignty and non-interference in other states (Haacke, 2003a, p. 214). The approach rested on informality (private discussions and confidence-building measures) and consensus building (broad agreements and legal procedures) (Archarya, 2001; Sharpe, 2003). ASEAN has been slow to change its approach to security matters, despite some proposals aimed at adopting the idea of flexible engagement, and in October 2003 the adoption of the Declaration of ASEAN Accord II (Bali Concord II) which committed ASEAN, among other things, to establishing a Security Community (Haacke, 2006).

In addition, ASEAN Plus Three, which includes Japan, China and South Korea, has since 2002 also embraced security issues. Other fora that have focused on security and terrorism have included the ASEAN Regional Forum (ARF), which has extended ASEAN's cooperation to its dialogue partners (Garofano, 2002). ARF has also provided the main forum in which China was able to engage with the US, Japan and Australia, while ASEAN has viewed the inclusion of China as a useful means of keeping it 'on-board' (Koo and Smith, 2005; Kurlantzick, 2006). Security issues have also been included and discussed within the Asia-Pacific Economic Cooperation (APEC) forum (see chapter four in this volume). APEC was at the outset focused on regional economic cooperation (Lee, 2003), but it has since 2001 discussed security matters at its summit meetings and sought to link economic and security issues. At the APEC summit in 2001 it was suggested that terrorism was a direct threat to economic development; likewise it was seen as a threat to peace and stability at APEC summit in 2002. The limited nature of these activities in the security arena, however, reflect the fact that many APEC members are already engaged in security cooperation either at a bilateral level via specific security agreements or within other regional organizations such as ASEAN and NATO (Dent, 2003; Hughes, 2003; Bowring, 2006).

What Security Threats Face Europe and Asia?

The types of security threats facing European and Asian states have tended to differ, given very different historical and geo-strategic considerations, although some threats are more likely to be of common concern in both regions (such as environmental issues, terrorism and organized transnational crime). The perception and understanding of what constitutes threat has also differed, reflecting different domestic and regional considerations in Europe and Asia. It is in cases where there is a common understanding and agreement on the nature of the threat that common action is going to be most likely, especially through regional organizations, such as the EU and ASEAN. As the following analysis suggests, the EU was more readily able to agree that terrorism was a threat, in Europe and elsewhere, than was the case in ASEAN, where states were more reluctant to identify it as a threat and agree on common action. However, ASEAN did change its position, notably after the Bali bombing in October 2002, and did begin to agree on joint initiative and to increase cooperation across the region and externally with other states and regional organizations.

The EU faced relatively few traditional security threats, such as those associated with territorial disputes, and itself largely comprises a stable group of democracies that rely upon peaceful means to resolve their differences. The end of the Cold War and break-up of the Soviet Union removed Europe's main traditional security concern. The EU has identified in the European Security Strategy five threats to international stability and security: terrorism, weapons of mass destruction (WMD) proliferation, regional conflicts, state failure and organized crime. The EU's immediate focus has been on maintaining order and stability on its borders, as is evident in the development of the European neighbourhood strategy, and the focus on the Balkans. The EU has been particularly concerned and involved in addressing security issues in Bosnia-Herzegovina, Serbia, Kosovo, Macedonia and Albania. Other conflicts of concern that are now closer to Europe include those in Moldova, Chechnya and Georgia. The Israeli/Palestinian conflict, the war in Iraq and relations with Iran, all constitute major security concerns, but are not necessarily threats to Europe.

In contrast to Europe, conventional security issues in Asia continue to be prominent and affect a number of states, with ongoing disputes over borders and maritime areas, some of which have re-emerged since the end of the Cold War. There have also been various separatist rebellions in states such as East Timor, Aceh and West Papua, as well as Myanmar, the Philippines (Moro Islamic Liberation Front (MILF) and Abu Sayyaf) and southern Thailand. Outside of traditional security issues, the Asian financial crisis highlighted the growing impact of globalization on regional security (Hughes, 2003, p. 44). Other major threats to ASEAN have been poverty, health threats (HIV/AIDS, SARS and Avian Influenza), environmental degradation, natural disasters, and transnational crime.[1] The region is known for money laundering and three states (the Philippines, Malaysia and Indonesia) are on the Organization for Economic Cooperation and Development's Financial Action Task Force black list. Drug trafficking remains a problem, with Thailand at the centre of many activities, including money laundering. The degree of connection between these issues is hard to establish, although there is some evidence of linkage.

The threat of terrorism in Asia is evident from the horrific events that have taken place since 9/11, but it needs to be put in context and not overplayed, given that a number of the terrorist threats in states such as Indonesia are seen by Asian specialists as home grown (Abuza, 2002). Rüland (2005), for example, notes that in Indonesia the millenarianist Darul Islam movement dates from the 1950s and that while there may be links between terrorist groups they do not constitute a 'second front'. He suggests that while there are Islamic extremists who may be dangerous, the vast majority of those involved in the revival of Islam are not a threat. Abuza notes that 'Muslims in Southeast Asia have long been characterized as secular, tolerant, modernist, and development orientated' (2002, p. 428). However, he suggests that many individuals from groups such as Kumpulan Mujaheddin Malaysia, Jemaah Islamiah (JI), the Moro Islamic Liberation Front (MILF) and Laskar Jihad, who did fight in Afghanistan and have since returned to their home countries in Asia, have shared resources, undergone joint training and engaged in money laundering and financial transfers.

When EU and ASEAN responses are compared, it is evident that the threat perception regarding terrorism differed. In the EU there was early state agreement that terrorism constituted a significant threat, whereas in ASEAN there was less common agreement on this, reflecting differing national positions (Chow, 2005, p. 302). In ASEAN, discussion of terrorism was divisive; terrorism was considered by some states to be a domestic matter, precluding discussion and external involvement. Nevertheless, ASEAN did reach some agreement that terrorism did constitute a threat, as reflected in the November 2001 ASEAN Declaration on Joint Action to Counter Terrorism.[2]

European and Asian Responses to 9/11 and the War on Terror

The events of 9/11, the Madrid Bombing (March 2004) and London Bombing (July 2005) were mirrored in Asia — Bali (October 2002), Jakarta (August 2003/September 2004) and the Philippines (February 2003 and 2004) — all of which received high levels of coverage in the Western media and generated considerable political discourse on the 'threats' posed by international terrorism. The focus on Al Qaeda, as well as on what are considered related terrorist movements, has led to differing degrees of international response, both from international and regional organizations and individual states and politicians. The EU, while agreeing on the need to develop a common approach, encountered numerous practical problems in adopting EU-level measures to counter terrorism. Asian responses were more piecemeal, reflecting differing perceptions of these threats and the complex make-up of the Asian region. Some states adopted very stringent anti-terrorist regulations and took a proactive attitude in identifying and arresting terrorists. Other states in the region were more cautious, given their sizeable Islamic populations as well as their fragile state structures.

The EU's Response

The events of 9/11 and the threat of terrorism challenged the EU to develop its capability as a security actor; both externally in regard to the fight against terrorism, and internally in terms of security (Hill, 2004). The EU immediately expressed its support for the US, holding an emergency meeting of the EU General Affairs Council on 12 September, and issuing a joint declaration on the terrorist attack on the US. The EU expressed its horror at the events, stressed its solidarity with the United States with whom it was seen as sharing common values and declared a European Union national day of mourning (Den Boer and Monar, 2002). On 20 September 2001, the EU and US issued a joint ministerial statement on combating terrorism in which they highlighted the fact that they shared common values and ideals in relation to democracy and freedom (Dubois, 2002). On 21 September an extraordinary meeting of the European Council took place in Brussels to assess the situation. It called for a broad coalition against terrorism under the auspices of the United Nations (UN Security Council Resolution 1368): 'The member states of the European Union are prepared to undertake such actions, each according to its means. The actions must be targeted and may also be directed against states abetting, supporting or harbouring terrorists' (European Council, 2001). The Council noted that the US had the right to self-defence, as accorded under Article 51 of the UN Charter. The EU, in a highly symbolic move, also supported the invocation of Article 5 of the North Atlantic Treaty on 12 September. The Council endorsed the Justice and Home Affairs Action Plan. The Plan of Action on EU counter-terrorism strategy included enhanced police and judicial cooperation, developing international legal instruments, putting an end to the funding of terrorism, strengthening air security and coordination of the EU's overall action.[3]

On 7 October 2001, the US began bombing suspected Taliban and terrorist bases in Afghanistan, following the failure of the Taliban to hand over Osama bin Laden. The EU's support for the US military campaign in Afghanistan was, at the outset, relatively united, with EU foreign ministers declaring their support at their meeting in Luxembourg on 8–9 October. However, attempts by the three larger states, France, Germany and the United Kingdom (UK), to discuss military matters prior to the summit meetings raised some concerns among the smaller states. The response to the War on Terror highlighted both the EU's immediate support for the US as well as illustrating its continuing difficulties over time in maintaining a united front amongst its members to the crisis.

9/11 did provide the EU with the impetus to make further progress on anti-terrorist measures. There already existed a degree of police cooperation, a European police office, legal instruments to allow for extradition, and contact between the security service heads. The European arrest warrant was given added impetus by these events, although it still encountered member state opposition, especially from Italy. The EU also worked on a definition of terrorism, which had previously been absent as agreement had proven impossible, although there were still difficulties in agreeing on a list of terrorist offences and organizations. A final agreement was reached and the Justice and Home Affairs meeting in December adopted a Common Position, a Regulation and a Decision.[4] The EU also set up a 24-hour counter-terrorist unit in Europol and authorized the director of Europol to open negotiations with the US on the transmission of personal data. This was further supported by the EU decision in December to establish Eurojust, which was given a mandate to deal with terrorism. A range of other measures were agreed, aiming to ensure greater European cooperation on anti-terrorist activities. However, EU cooperation with the US encountered problems in areas, such as in police and judicial cooperation (date protection), where differences between them surfaced (Dubois, 2002, p. 330).[5]

The US-led War on Terror, while initially endorsed by European leaders, proved to be divisive in the long run. At the outset European states, especially Britain, supported UN Security Council Resolution 1373 and the US-led attack on Afghanistan, the aim of which was to overthrow the Taliban and the Al Qaeda regime. However, President Bush's comments in the State of the Union address to Congress in January 2002, in which he accused the 'axis of evil' (Iran, Iraq and North Korea) of being the sponsors of terrorism, raised concerns in Europe. The EU, unable to do much, largely stood by; as the US and the UK mounted a diplomatic offensive against Iraq during the early part of 2002 (Hill, 2004). Both claimed that the ambiguous UN Security Council Resolution 1441, adopted on 8 November, authorized the use of force; a claim opposed by the French and Russians. The US decision to undertake military action against Iraq in March 2003 ended up deeply dividing the EU and NATO, highlighting the divisions between supporters and opponents of US foreign policy. There was a marked divide between Germany and France, on the one hand, and the US; while other European states such as Britain, Spain, Italy and the Netherlands, closely aligned themselves with the US. The French government was particularly critical of US actions, with then President Chirac and the French Foreign Minister de Villepin making public statements opposed to US–UK actions. In the UN Security Council the UK and France clashed in the debate on Iraq in March 2003.

At the Seville European Council in June 2002, a declaration was adopted on the contribution of EU CFSP against terrorism.[6] The Declaration identified the range of EU activities against terrorism, including strengthening the EU instruments for long-term conflict prevention; political dialogue with third countries on the fight against terrorism, non-proliferation and arms control; assistance to non-EU states in order to reinforce their capacity to respond to the threat of terrorism (including an anti-terrorism clause in EU agreements); re-evaluating relations with states depending on their attitudes to terrorism; and the implementation of UN Security Council Resolution 1373. The Danish Presidency in October 2002 commissioned a report on the study of extreme fundamentalism and terrorism, which was discussed at the Thessaloniki European Council in June 2003. The European Council also reviewed all EU actions in the fight against terrorism, as well as adopting a Declaration on Non-Proliferation of Weapons of Mass Destruction.

However, within the EU, the terrorist attacks on Madrid and then London further galvanized the EU into action. Following the Madrid attacks, the Union adopted at its March 2004 meeting a Declaration on Combating Terrorism and appointed an EU Counter Terrorism Coordinator, the former Dutch minister, Gijs de Vries, to ensure implementation of common measures. In June 2004 the European Council endorsed the revised EU Plan of Action on Combating Terrorism. The Council also agreed on a number of priority areas for action: prevention and management of terrorist attacks, protection of critical infrastructures, and finance of terrorism. Later in November, the European Council adopted the Hague Programme on Strengthening Freedom, Security and Justice in the EU, part of which aimed to ensure the effective prevention and combating of terrorism by ensuring cooperation among the member states in the interests of the security of the Union as a whole. It also charged the EU Situation Centre in the Council Secretariat with providing the Council with strategic analysis of the terrorist threat based on member states' intelligence and security services and information from Europol with effect from January 2005. In December 2005 the European Council adopted the EU Counter-Terrorism Strategy, which was aimed at providing a framework for preventing radicalization and the recruitment to terrorism, protecting citizens and infrastructure, pursuing and investigating terrorists, and improving the response to attacks. In September 2006 a comprehensive Strategy for Combating Radicalization and Recruitment into Terrorism was agreed by the EU.

In summary, the EU's response to the War on Terror was highly comprehensive and consistent over time, highlighting the strength of the EU as an actor in terms of its legal and institutional instruments and its commitment to combating terrorism at home and abroad. The challenge of implementing EU policy in this arena and ensuring that the member states worked together was a difficult task, which in part explains why the EU appointed a champion in this area. The EU's aims as regards the exchange of information, development of a common legal framework and working with partners have been achieved, thereby enhancing its capacity to combat terrorism (De Vries, 2006).

The Asian Response

In comparing the response of states and regional actors in Asia to terrorism in the post 9/11 period, it is evident that these events tended to reinforce bilateralism, a key tenet of Asian diplomatic and security relations, while having a more varied impact on regional organizations and fora. In particular, the external influence of the US on the region was highly significant, making regional cooperation more difficult, given that the US approach was largely focused on developing its own bilateral and regional security alliances. In contrast to the ASEAN response, the EU was able to adopt at an early stage a unified approach to supporting the US and opposing terrorism. In Asia, the divisions among the members of ASEAN, with varying degrees of support for the US, limited ASEAN's response to 9/11 and the broader threat of terrorism. ASEAN did issue a Declaration on Terrorism in November 2002, although it said little about how the states would respond to terrorism. The situation changed after the bombing in Bali on 12 October 2002, which killed over 180 people, many of whom were Australian tourists, and led ASEAN members to take a more assertive and proactive response to the presence of terrorists within their states.

At a relatively early stage (November 2001), US officials met ASEAN representatives to explain that the US viewed East Asia as a strategically important region and a major front in the War on Terror (De Castro, 2004, p. 198). The US emphasized that it would provide logistical and other support to those fighting terrorists, including intelligence support and information on radical groups. The response of Asian states to the War on Terror was ambiguous, reflecting the varying concerns and domestic interests of Asian states (Haacke, 2002, p. 113). A number of Asian governments including Singapore, Thailand and the Philippines officially supported the US War on Terror and later the US-led invasion of Iraq. The Philippines under President Gloria Macapagal Arroyo was one of the first states to endorse the US War on Terror and proved to be a strong supporter of the US, expressing a willingness to provide aid and send troops to Afghanistan and later on to Iraq (Francia, 2003, p. 21). In return for its support, the Philippines received from the US a $100 million package of military training and equipment plus 660 US troops to address its own internal insurgency problems. Other states were more cautious, including Indonesia and Malaysia, both with large Muslim populations, and there was a fear that it could lead to a war against Islam (Abuza, 2002). The President of Malaysia supported the fight against terrorism, but was unwilling to support US actions in Afghanistan and sought a peaceful resolution to the problems (Putzel, 2003, p. 176). The Thai Prime Minister was supportive of the US, although the Foreign Minister asked the UN to replace the US as the lead nation, fearing a backlash at home. Thailand was cautious, perhaps concerned that the US might request use of its military bases and aware of its own small Muslim population. Vietnam and Laos had relatively few Muslims and there was therefore less of a concern about a backlash from internal dissidents, although there were also concerns over US actions.

The War on Terror and the US-led campaign in Afghanistan posed particular problems in Indonesia. Indonesia, which has long been considered to be a critical regional player given the size of its Muslim population (85 per cent), remained a weak and fragile state following the downfall of President Soeharto in May 1998 and democratic elections in June 1999. President Megawati Sukarnoputri, who had been appointed in June 2001, was still in a relatively weak position in Indonesia, as was her party, the Indonesian Democratic Party of Struggle. The Vice President, Hamzah Haz, a leading Muslim and head of the United Development Party, was opposed to US actions in Afghanistan and had also supported a jihad in Maluku (Davis, 2005). Other Muslim organizations organized anti-US demonstrations. A number of these organizations were believed to have links with Al Qaeda, including Darul Islam, Laska Jihad and Jemaah Islamiah. The US and other regional states were concerned about Indonesia, which was seen as centre of terrorist activity and was considered to have been slow to act on terrorism. The situation changed after the bombing in Bali, following which the US and Australian authorities called on the Indonesian government to take action. The Indonesian President passed a decree increasing the powers of the police, who then arrested Abubakar Ba'asyir, a Muslim cleric and leading member of Majelis Mujahadin Indonesia, as well as other Islamic radicals. The Indonesian government proceeded to pass an Anti-Terrorism Law and took further measures against terrorists. The US also restored its military ties with Indonesia and provided an aid package of $657.4 million (Chow, 2005, p. 312).

The War on Terror led to renewed external interest by the US in the region, which is no great surprise given its long-standing historical ties and the fact that it views the region as strategically important. The US has designated the Philippines, Taiwan, and Thailand as major non-NATO allies (de Castro, 2004). It has, therefore, sought to reassert its influence in the region by bolstering its bilateral security alliances with key states. It has also provided an opportunity for some Asian states to re-engage the US and benefit from external assistance. Some Asian states, such as those with whom the US had strong links, were offered significant incentives to support US policy, including economic and military assistance. The Indonesian President Megawati was offered $600 million in US economic assistance within a week of 9/11, while further economic and military assistance was offered to the Philippines (Haacke, 2003b, pp. 114–5). The US has also engaged in a number of joint military exercises with selected Asian states. It transited US troops via the Philippines to Afghanistan, signed the Mutual Logistics Support Agreement (2002) with them and US armed forces trained personnel of the Armed Forces of the Philippines so as to enable them to tackle the 'threat' from insurgent movements such as the Moroa National Liberation Front and the Abu Sayyaf group. The US also held a military exercise with Thailand and intensified security cooperation with Singapore. In the broader Asia-Pacific region America revitalized its links with Australia, an ally that has strongly supported it in Afghanistan and Iraq.

The challenge to ASEAN was to consider how it might respond to the US's call for support in the War on Terror and to terrorism. Individually the Asian states were likely to respond in different ways; given the mix of domestic considerations, intra-ASEAN rivalries and ties to the US. Nevertheless, ASEAN needed to respond so that its credibility as a regional organization would not be challenged. In October 2001, at the Third ASEAN Meeting on Transnational Crime in Singapore, foreign ministers issued a joint communiqué in which they condemned all acts of terrorism. The statement, however, went on to repudiate any direct link between terrorism and Islam, given the sizeable Muslim populations in some of the states. At the seventh Annual ASEAN Summit in November 2001, leaders adopted a Declaration on Joint Action to Combat Terrorism, which outlined how it would seek to cooperate in an effort aimed at practical counter terrorism measures. The Declaration went on to outline a number of measures including increased cooperation among ASEAN states aimed at combating terrorism through cooperation between law enforcement agencies and the sharing of good practice and support for the early signing and ratification of the International Convention for the Suppression of the Financing of Terrorism. ASEAN's response was ambiguous, which is hardly surprising given the dynamics of ASEAN and its members' positions and priorities (Haacke, 2003b).

ASEAN's efforts to combat terrorism were intensified during 2002, first at the informal meeting of foreign ministers in Phuket in February and then at the Special ASEAN Ministerial Meeting on Terrorism in May, during which a concrete work programme aimed at fighting transnational crime, including terrorism, was agreed. At a practical level the ASEAN work programme focused on information exchange, cooperation in legal matters, cooperation in law enforcement, institutional capacity building, training, and extra-regional cooperation. In addition, Indonesia, Malaysia, the Philippines, and later on Thailand and Cambodia signed an Agreement on Information Exchange and Establishment of Communication Procedures aimed at helping them to cooperate in the fight against transnational crime, including terrorism. A critical element of this agreement was the exchange of intelligence, which lead to the arrest of terrorist suspects. Other elements of this cooperation included an ASEAN agreement on cooperation in the area of non-traditional security issues with China, a Joint Declaration for Cooperation to Combat International Terrorism with the US and further cooperation through ASEAN Plus Three and ARF. The bombing in Bali served as a wake-up call leading to renewed ASEAN attempts to counter terrorism though transnational cooperation.

The first ASEAN Plus Three Consultation on Transnational Crime was held in Ha Noi in June 2003. Subsequent meetings have adopted a concept plan to address transnational crime in eight areas, with an ASEAN state leading in each area. On the ground a number of the Asian states engaged individually in a range of internal activities aimed at countering terrorism, including the arrest and detention of suspected terrorists in Malaysia, Singapore, the Philippines, Thailand and Indonesia (Haacke, 2003b. p. 116). There was also closer intelligence cooperation within ASEAN amongst the members (Rüland, 2005, p. 551), with intelligence sharing with the US leading to the capture of suspected al-Qaeda and JI terrorists.

The effectiveness of ASEAN as an organization, already in doubt after the Asian financial crisis, was challenged by the events of 11 September and the Bali Bombing. The nature of ASEAN as a weak regional organization and its approach to security meant that it faced practical problems in rising to meet the challenges of these types of security crises, including 9/11, the Bali bombing and the SARS outbreak. This does not mean that it is ineffective as an organization, but it has to depend on the actions of its members, who vary in their level of ability, capacity and willingness to act. The slowness with which Indonesia responded to the terrorist threat on its own territory was a cause of concern to other Asian states and the US, but the eventual actions of ASEAN, its joint declaration with the US on combating terrorism (May 2002) and the individual actions of its member states somewhat offset this problem. Nevertheless, the response of ASEAN highlights its limitations as a regional security organization and, as one commentator noted, 'ASEAN's performance as a security regime has been less inspiring', in contrast to its diplomatic role, which is seen by some academic commentators as having been quite effective in coordinating its members approach to terrorism (Haacke, 2003b, p. 126).

Other Asian regional fora that sought to address terrorism encountered similar problems. ASEAN Plus Three adopted Joint Communiqués on Terrorism (2002) and Transnational Crime (2004) and a work programme to implement the ASEAN Plan of Action to combat transnational crime (2002). At the ninth ASEAN Plus Three summit in Kuala Lumpur (2005), foreign ministers discussed the challenges facing the region; including terrorism, maritime security and transnational crimes, avian influenza and natural disasters. However, little further concrete action was proposed — beyond an expressed commitment to cooperation.

The Asia Regional Forum (ARF) provided a further forum for discussion and agreement on measure aimed at combating terrorism in the region. In 2002 ARF adopted a Statement on Measures Against Terrorist Financing; as well as measures on freezing terrorist assets, implementation of international standards, and cooperation on exchange of information, outreach and technical assistance. ARF held a yearly Inter-Sessional Meeting on Counter-Terrorism and Transnational Crime at which it discussed the challenges of information and intelligence sharing, combating document fraud and police and law enforcement cooperation. It sought to enhance cooperation amongst its members to combat terrorism and transnational crimes through information sharing and intelligence exchange, combating document fraud and law enforcement cooperation.[7] ARF's effectiveness, however, is limited given that ASEAN has been the driving force behind the forum and that the forum's focus has been on confidence-building measures. Also, like ASEAN, it has been adversely affected by the US' emphasis on bilateral cooperation, which undermines any potential ARF role.

Interregionalism: EU–ASEAN Relations and ASEM

There has also been a degree of interregional security dialogue between the EU and Asia, which, while limited, has been growing and has provided some responses to terrorism. This is in line with the broader EU–ASEAN engagement, which has been growing since the early 1990s, albeit largely in relation to trade links (Gilson, 2005). EU–ASEAN ministerial meetings, which are held every two years, have provided a focus for such discussions, although the issue of Burma Myanmar's participation in ASEAN remains an ongoing problem from the EU's perspective (see Dent, 1999).[8] The EU's growing interest in security matters and the UN's commitment to fighting terrorism means that such issues now regularly arise on EU-ASEAN agendas. There are concrete examples of such cooperation. The EU and ASEAN signed a Joint Declaration for Cooperation to Combat International Terrorism at the fourteenth ASEAN–EU Ministerial Meeting in Brussels in January 2003. It has also signed an ASEAN–European Commission (EC) Regional Programme on Counter-Terrorism, aimed at border management and document security. The

EU has also committed itself to supporting regional efforts at combating terrorism, including the International Law Enforcement Academy in Bangkok, the Southeast Asia Regional Center for Counter Terrorism in Kuala Lumpur and the Jakarta Center for Law Enforcement Cooperation in Semarang, Indonesia.[9] Another notable example of cooperation has arisen as a result of the Aceh Peace Accord in August 2005. The EU, through the former Finnish President Martti Ahtisaari, played a leading role in negotiating between the Government and the Free Aceh Movement. The EU also dispatched a small European Security and Defence Policy mission to Aceh, which, with ASEAN, formed the Aceh Monitoring Mission. Most recently the EU Commission deployed an election observer mission to Aceh, in response to a request from the Indonesian government, to observe the local elections in December 2006.

The engagement of ASEAN with the issue of terrorism did spawn new forms of cooperation with extra-regional partners. For example, in March 2003 ARF convened the first annual meeting on Counterterrorism and Transnational Crime, which included the EU, US, Japan, China, Australia and Russia. This reflected a growing agreement on the threat of terrorism and a willingness to engage partners in discussions and coordinated action. As one Commission official has suggested, 'The EU has gained in stature in the Asian security community by upgrading its commitment in the ARF, resulting in its recognition as a meaningful actor'.[10]

The value of the EU–ASEAN interface lies in the European experience of developing common policy responses to issues such as terrorism and the ability of European officials to share their experiences with Asian counterparts, including the possibility of policy transfer. The problem and challenge for ASEAN is that it lacks the legal–institutional base that characterizes the EU, and therefore its ability to respond to such situations is limited. This is significant as the states that form ASEAN are likely to find security cooperation difficult to achieve, given their own differing legal systems and security priorities. Achieving concrete border and transnational cooperation between immigration, customs and police forces is difficult and there is much to be learnt from the European experience.

The Asia–Europe Meeting (ASEM) has provided a further forum in which security issues and international terrorism have been discussed between Europe and Asia. It provides an important opportunity for networking and for informal discussions between state representatives from the two regions, although concrete actions can be few and far between. In the wake of 9/11 the leaders meeting in Copenhagen at the fourth ASEM did broaden their discussions to focus on security matters, with the issue of a Declaration on Cooperation against International Terrorism. The sixth Asia-Europe Meeting, which took place in Helsinki on 10–11 September 2006, focused on issues such as trade, Lebanon, Iraq, Afghanistan and nuclear proliferation. However, the effectiveness of ASEM has been questioned: some see it as a talking shop, whereas others see it as an opportunity for the states to discuss issues of major importance and a counter-balance to US–Asian dialogue (Reiterer, 2006, see also chapter seven in this volume). Most studies suggest that ASEM's main role has been that of a balancing function, with some limited institution building and identity formation. (Reiterer, 2006) It has also provided a voice in favour of multilateralism and served as a means for Europe and Asia to agree on issues to be discussed in forums such as the UN, the World Trade Organization and other global forums (Rüland, 2006, p. 58). ASEM has begun to address non-traditional security threats, such as organized crime, terrorism, pandemics, energy and environmental issues at its meetings. Finally, it has reinforced the ASEAN Plus Three process, thereby enhancing intra-regional cooperation among the Asian member states.

Conclusion

As this chapter has shown, European and Asian regional organizations, largely the EU and ASEAN, have responded to terrorist threats in very different ways, reflecting very different organizational structures and attitudes to terrorism. The EU adopted a coordinated approach to terrorism, based on a broad consensus and agreement amongst its members on the need to combat terrorist threats, as well as addressing other security threats as outlined in the European Security Strategy. The EU adapted its behaviour and that of its members, adopting a mix of legal instruments and practical measures such as intelligence exchange and the European arrest warrant aimed at countering terrorism. It coordinated its approach with the US, third-country partners and regional players such as ASEAN, and initially adopted a united front in the UN.

In contrast, the types of security threat in East Asia were different from those in Europe, reflecting the nature of the region. The East Asian approach to security cooperation and terrorism in the region was based on developing dialogue, consultation and building consensus, rather than through the actions of regional institutions and legal measures. The states did not agree on what constituted security threats and largely sought to preserve and protect national sovereignty. After 9/11 the states did condemn terrorist activities and engage in some cooperative measures aimed at combating terrorism, but the external influence of the US was a major consideration. This approach largely reflected the traditional 'ASEAN Way', which has been pragmatically adapted to avoid intra-ASEAN disputes, while ensuring a degree of coordination among ASEAN members in addressing largely regional terrorist threats. ASEAN states also had to confront domestic security challenges, including separatist movements and terrorist organizations, some of which have been linked to groups outside the region.

ASEAN is made up of a diverse grouping of states, who face a wide range of domestic and regional security challenges. As a regional organization, ASEAN is markedly different to the European Union, where most member states do not face domestic security challenges and remain relatively secure. ASEAN's member states responded differently to the 'war on terror' reflecting a mix of domestic considerations and regional concerns, as well as bilateral commitments and alliances. Some Asian states and ASEAN itself have been past masters at balancing larger states in the broader region (China, Japan and India) and external security actors, such as the US and Russia; and the War on Terror provided a further example of this approach. The different approaches of the EU and ASEAN, and other forums such as the ARF and ASEAN Plus Three, to security and terrorism reflect the very different circumstances of the East Asian region and the varying levels of security threats arising in it.

In the case of the European Union, the high degree of coordination and adoption of common measures played a significant role in ensuring that the Union was a credible security actor with the tools and instruments to address terrorist threats. In a number of instances, EU institutions and some member states used the occasion to push through measures in justice, security and home affairs that had previously languished, and, in some cases, had been opposed by particular member states. The EU was therefore able to address fundamental questions with regard to what constituted terrorist acts and identification of terrorist organizations. Its relationship with the US, however, whilst initially highly cooperative, deteriorated following US actions in Iraq, with some EU states strongly opposed to US actions. In the case of ASEAN, the War on Terror had an adverse impact on the organization; with many member states taking their own national actions and/or cooperating directly with the US — thereby limiting ASEAN's role in the War on Terror. ASEAN did serve as a useful forum in which issues associated with the War on Terror could be discussed and provided the basis for some degree of coordination of ongoing activities by its member states aimed at combating terrorism.

A growing intra- and inter-regional dialogue between the EU and ASEAN provided the regional organizations with an opportunity to learn from each other in the way they approached security matters with examples of the EU transferring policy and practice to ASEAN. This is evident in the degree of security dialogue that exists between the EU and ASEAN, which has grown and developed since the events of 9/11 and the War on Terror. The EU has funded specific initiatives in Asia aimed at combating terrorism and has supported ASEAN efforts to tackle terrorism. However, many states in East Asia still look more to the US rather than Europe and the EU for assistance on security matters, although the EU's growing interest in security matters and the UN's commitment to fighting terrorism means that such issues are regularly discussed on EU–ASEAN agendas and that the states do engage in some practical cooperation with regard to organized crime and terrorism. Finally, from an ASEAN perspective the EU is one of a number of actors with which it needs to balance its interests, including the US, China and Japan, as well as the broader Asia-Pacific.

Notes

1. See ASEAN Regional Security: the threats facing it and the way forward, ASEAN Secretariat, 10 April 2006. www.aseansec.org/18395, date accessed 27 November 2006.
2. ASEAN Declaration on Joint Action to Counter Terrorism, November 2001, accessible at http://www.aseansec.org/5620.htm, date accessed 27 November 2006.
3. It was not, however, until 10 December that the EU adopted a two Common Positions and a Council Regulation to give effect to UN Security Resolution 1373.
4. Common Position of 27 December on the application of specific measures to combat terrorism, 2001/931/CFSP, 28 December 2001; Council Regulation (EC) No 2580/2001 of 27 December 2001 on specific restrictive measures directed against certain persons and entities with a view to combating terrorism, 28 December 2001; Council Decision of 27 December 2001 establishing the list provided for in Article 2(3) of Council Regulation (EC) No 2580/2001 of 27 December 2001, 2001/927/EC, 28 December 2001.
5. The EU negotiated four agreements with US on container security, airline passenger name records, extradition and mutual legal assistance.
6. Counil of the European Union, Annex V, EU Presidency Conclusions, Seville, 21–2 June 2002, Brussels, 13463/02.
7. ARF Statement, 19 May 2005.
8. The EC–ASEAN Agreement dates from 1980 and covers all of the ASEAN states, with the exception of Myanmar.

9. The EU has bilateral agreements with Bangladesh, Cambodia, India, Laos, Macao, Nepal, Sri Lanka, South Korea and Vietnam. EU–Japan relations are managed under an annual EU–Japan Action Plan. Relations with China were governed under the 1985 Trade and Economic Cooperation Agreement, although a new Partnership and Cooperation Agreement is in the offing.
10. 'Europe raises its Asian game: new directions in EU-Asia relations', Commission Official, External Relations, DG, 7 December 2006, CERC Conference, Melbourne University, Australia.

References

Abuza, Z. (2002) 'Tentacles of Terror: Al Qaeda's Southeast Asian Network', *Contemporary Southeast Asia*, 24. 3, pp. 427–65.

Acharya, A. (2001) *Constructing a Security Community in Southeast Asia: ASEAN and the Problem of Regional Order*, London: Routledge.

Acharya, A. (2003a) *Regionalism and Multilateralism: Essays on Cooperative Security in the Asia Pacific*, 2nd edition, Singapore: Eastern Universities Press.

Acharya, A. (2003b) 'Will Asia's Past be its Future?', *International Security* 28. 3, pp. 149–64.

Beeson, M. (2005) 'Rethinking Regionalism: Europe and East Asia in Comparative Historical Perspective', *Journal of European Public Policy*, 12. 6, pp. 969–85.

Bowring, P. (2006) 'APEC's last chance to matter', *International Herald Tribune*, 17 November.

Caballero-Anthony, M. (2006) 'Regional Institutions and Regional Crises in East Asia', in B. Fort and D. Webber (eds.) *Regional Integration in East Asia and Europe: Convergence or Divergence?* London: Routledge.

Chow, J. T. (2005) 'ASEAN Counterterrorism Cooperation since 9/11', *Asian Studies* 45. 2, pp. 302–21.

Davis, M. (2002) 'Laskar Jihad and the Political Position of Conservative Islam in Indonesia', *Contemporary Southeast Asia*, 24. 1, pp. 12–32.

De Castro, C. R. (2004) 'Addressing international Terrorism in Southeast Asia a matter of Strategic or functional approach', *Contemporary Southeast Asia* 26. 2, pp. 193–217.

Den Boer, M. and Monar, J. (2002) '11 September and the Challenge of Global Terrorism to the EU as Security Actor', in G. Edwards and G. Wiessala (eds) *The European Union: The Annual Review 2001/2002 (Journal of Common Market Studies)*, Oxford: Wiley-Blackwell, pp. 11–28.

Dent, C. M. (ed.) (1999) *The European Union and East Asia: An Economic Relationship*, London: Routledge.

Dent, C. M. (2003) *Asia Pacific Economic and Security Cooperation: New Regional Agendas*, Palgrave Macmillan.

De Vries, G. (2002) 'The Fight Against Terrorism — Five Years After 9/11', paper presented at the Annual European Foreign Policy Conference, LSE, 30 June 2006.

Dubois, D. (2002) 'The Attacks of 11 September: EU–US Cooperation in the Field of Justice and Home Affairs', *European Foreign Affairs Review*, 7. 3, pp. 317–36.

European Council (2001) 'Conclusions and Plan of Action of the Extraordinary Meeting on 21 September', Council Document SN 140/01.

Francia, L. H (2003) 'Meanwhile in Manila...', *The Nation*, 27 October 2003 pp. 21–6.
Garofano, J. (2002) 'Power, Institutions, and the ASEAN Regional Forum', *Asian Survey* 42. 3, pp. 502–21.
Gilson, J. (2005) 'New Interregionalism? The EU and East Asia', *European Integration*, 27. 3, pp. 307–26.
Haacke, J. (2002) ASEAN's Diplomatic and Security Culture: Origins, Developments and Prospects, London: Routledge Curzon.
Haacke, J. (2003a) *ASEAN's Diplomatic and Security Culture: origins, developments and prospects*, London: Routledge.
Haacke, J. (2003b) 'The War on Terror', in C. M. Dent (ed.) *Asia Pacific Economic and Security Cooperation: New Regional Agendas*, Palgrave Macmillan, pp. 113–35.
Haacke, J. (2006) 'Not Beyond Flexible Engagement', in B. Fort and D. Webber (eds) *Regional Integration in East Asia and Europe: convergence or divergence?* London: Routledge, pp. 150–71.
Hill, C. (2004) 'EU Foreign Policy Since 11 September 2001', *Journal of Common Market Studies*, 42. 1, pp. 143–65.
Hughes, C. (2003) 'Globalisation and Security in East Asia', in C. M. Dent (ed.) *Asia Pacific Economic and Security Cooperation: New Regional Agendas*, Basingstoke: Palgrave Macmillan, pp. 34–53.
Katzenstein, P. J. (2005). *A World of Regions: Asian and Europe in American Imperium*, Ithaca: Cornell University Press.
Koo, N. and M. L. R. Smith (2005) 'China Engages Asia? Caveat Lector', *International Security*, 30. 1, pp. 196–213.
Kurlantzick, J. (2006) 'China's Charm: Implications of Chinese Soft Power', Policy Brief No. 47, June, Carnegie Endowment for International Peace.
Lee, S. (2003) 'Asia-Pacific Economic Regionalism: Global Constraints and Opportunities', in C. M. Dent (ed.) *Asia Pacific Economic and Security Cooperation: New Regional Agendas*, Basingstoke: Palgrave Macmillan, pp. 19–50.
Narine, S. (2002) *Explaining ASEAN: Regionalism in Southeast Asia*, Boulder, CO: Lynne Rienner.
Okawara, N. and Katzenstein, P. J. (2001) 'Japan and Asian Pacific Security Regionalization Entrenched Bilateralism and Incipient Multilateralism', *The Pacific Review*, 14. 2, pp. 165–94.
Putzel, J. (2003) 'Southeast Asia and the US-Philippines Alliance', in M. Buckley and R. Fawn (eds) *Global Responses to Terrorism: 9/11, Afghanistan and Beyond*, London: Routledge, pp. 176–87.
Reiterer, M. (2006) 'Interregionalism as a New Diplomatic Tool: the EU and East Asia', *European Foreign Affairs Review*, 11. 2, pp. 223–44.
Rüland, J. (2005) 'The Nature of Southeast Asian Security Challenges' *Security Dialogue*, 36. 4, pp. 545–63.
Rüland, J. (2006) 'Interregionalism and the Crisis of Multilateralism: How to Keep the Asia–Europe Meeting (ASEM) Relevant', *European Foreign Affairs Review*, 11. 1, pp. 45–62.
Sharpe, S. (2003) 'An ASEAN Way to Security Cooperation in Southeast Asia' *The Pacific Review*, 16. 2, pp. 231–50.
Solana, J. (2003) 'A Secure Europe in a Better World — European Security Strategy', 12 December, Brussels: European Council.
Tay, S. (2005) 'A More Insecure World: Conflicting Perspectives for Asia', *Security Dialogue*, 36. 3, pp. 392–94.

9
Asian (ASEAN Plus Three) Perspectives on European Integration

Toshiro Tanaka

Introduction

The 2006 Summit of the Asia Europe Meeting (ASEM) in Helsinki was a landmark event in many ways. It celebrated the tenth anniversary of the dialogue institution, resulted in two significant declarations and established the groundwork for a significant expansion of its membership. The membership on the Asian side, originally limited to nations belonging to the Association of Southeast Asian Nations (ASEAN) Plus Three (China, Japan and South Korea), would henceforth include India, Pakistan, Mongolia and the ASEAN secretariat. European membership, in turn, also increased to include the two new European Union member states, Romania and Bulgaria, who joined the EU in January 2007. Two months after the Helsinki summit, the Asia-Pacific Economic Cooperation (APEC) forum held its fourteenth annual summit in Ha Noi. This summit's Ha Noi Declaration committed itself to further study the means required in order to promote regional economic integration, including a Free Trade Area of the Asia-Pacific. The proposal for an Asia-Pacific Free Trade Area was a proposal from the United States (US).[1]

It can be argued that, despite these promising developments, both ASEM and APEC seem to have lost their momentum to a significant extent. They have both failed to live up to original expectations. In particular, they have failed to dynamically bring about increased regional cooperation. It can be further argued that increased regional cooperation in East Asia is undermined by a number of factors. For example, there are growing concerns among academics and policy-makers alike regarding the exponential growth in the number of bilateral and regional trade agreements in Asia, and the ensuing Asian 'noodle bowl effect' due to differential rules of origin from different agreements, which in turn present greater challenges for harmonization and broader regional and global integration (Kuroda, 2006a).

Despite the increase in bilateral agreements, new attempts are still being made to promote regional integration in East Asia. This is evident in the establishment of an East Asia Summit (EAS), consisting of ASEAN Plus Six (China, Japan, South Korea, Australia, New Zealand and India). The second EAS was held in January 2007 in Cebu in the Philippines. The Chairperson's Statement reiterated the EAS's 'support for ASEAN's role as the driving force for economic integration in the region', reaffirmed the member states' position that the East Asia Summit is an important component of the emerging regional architecture, and confirmed their view that the EAS complements other existing regional mechanisms, including the ASEAN dialogue process, the ASEAN Plus Three process, the ASEAN Regional Forum (ARF), and APEC in community-building efforts.[2] When such attempts are made, the European experiences in the EU are always cited as a model or reference, putting forward the EU as a possible inspiration for regionalism in East Asia.

In this context, this chapter will concentrate on Asia–Europe relations and attempt to answer the following questions. First, how do the ASEAN Plus Three political, economic and academic elites perceive Europe? Is 'Europe' the European Union, or is it regarded as a conglomerate of individual nation states? Do Asian governments, companies, and academics prefer to deal bilaterally with EU member states or with the EU as a bloc?

Second, do the ASEAN Plus Three political, economic and academic elites regard the EU's achievements in the areas of economic and political integration as a positive development and worthy of emulation in East Asia? What do these elites consider to be the positive and negative aspects of European integration so far?

Third, when these elites look towards the EU, do they perceive it primarily as a market for Asian goods, or as a diplomatic force? Is Europe prominent in the Asian perception of the world order as a global political actor? Is Europe perceived as a balance to US power, or rather a competitor?

The European Union or the Member States?

It is clear that there is no single comprehensive perception of the European Union by East Asian elites. It is equally clear, however, that the relations between ASEAN Plus Three and the EU have intensified in recent years. Quite often these relations have been bilateral between individual states on either side. The creation of ASEM developed the means for interregional dialogue. Given that ASEAN Plus Three consists of a number of disparate countries with often competing national interests and agendas, it is perhaps not surprising that regionalism has not developed among these countries in the way it has within the EU. Nevertheless, interregional dialogue has developed, and this has been particularly manifested in ASEM.

Hadi Soesastro, of the Centre for Strategic and International Studies in Jakarta, has argued that no interregionalism mechanism exists between Asia and Europe. He gives the example of developing relations between Indonesia and a number of European states. Regarding resources, he makes the point that the EU has a limited budget for economic cooperation, and contrasts this with the large funds utilized by individual European member states. The implications of this are that 'European states refuse to use the EU in their economic relations, and thus practices to boost trade are conducted by individual states' (Prasetyono, 2006, p. 30).

A common East Asian perspective, as expressed by the Federation of Thai Industries, is that the EU is a fragmented market. One member of the Federation suggests that it is quite difficult to trade because each country has different demands on imports. Here, the EU is regarded as bureaucratic, obstructionist and hard to handle. This kind of perception still exists despite the existence of the EU's common external tariff and external relations policy.

A similar sentiment was heard from India. One academic, Prof. Jain, explains that 'the Indian elite's perceptions of the European Union continue to be essentially conditioned by the Anglo-American media.... For the most part, the Indian corporate sector continues to perceive the EU not as one entity but as a conglomerate of states, as result of which the business focus continues to be at the member states level' (Jain, 2005, pp. 29–30).

Most East Asian governments however, continue to interact bilaterally with EU countries while simultaneously interacting with the European Union as a bloc. For example, when Premier Wen Jiabao of China went to Helsinki for the ASEM summit and offered to host the Seventh ASEM in October 2008 in Beijing, he also met individually with a large number of European Heads of State. For example, before the summit, he took part in the Ninth EU–China summit meeting with European leaders, the Presidency of European Council, the Finnish Prime Minister Vanhanen and European Commission President Barroso, and on the sidelines of the ASEM summit, he met respectively with President Roh of Korea; Vietnamese Prime Minister Nguyen Tan Dung; Slovenian

Prime Minister Janez Janasa; his Portuguese counterpart Jose Socrates; Prime Minister of Spain Jose Luis Rodriguez Zapatero; and Danish Prime Minister Anders Fogh Rasmussen. Premier Wen also made an official visit to Finland where he met with President Halonen and Prime Minister Vanhanen. He subsequently met British Prime Minister Tony Blair in London and German Chancellor Angela Merkel in Berlin. Finally, he went to Dushanbe, the capital of Tajikistan, to meet Prime Minister Akil Akilov and to participate in the Fifth Meeting of Prime Ministers of the member states of the Shanghai Cooperation Organization, on his way back from Europe.

As these examples illustrate, East Asian interlocutors do not neglect relations with the member states, and other nation states, while concurrently negotiating with the European Union.

Do Asean Plus Three Regard the EU as a Model to Emulate?

Do the ASEAN Plus Three political and academic elites perceive the European Union as a success story and model for their own regional integration? Pengiran Mashor, then Deputy Secretary-General of ASEAN from Brunei, called for an East Asian Economic Community in 2003, due to the challenges of globalization, arguing that the increase in regionalism was a global phenomenon because countries big and small alike have regarded regionalism as a response to global challenges, such as competition for export markets and foreign direct investments. He refers to the powerful regional blocs emerging in Europe and the Americas, and the absence of similar developments in Asia. He starkly states that East Asia has to respond and has to show the world that even in the face of complex regional diversity, there is an avenue for closer cooperation, coordination and integration (Pengiran, 2003).

A Japanese scholar, Motoshige Ito, suggests that the time is now opportune to substantially strengthen regional linkages in the East Asian region (Ito, 2006). Another Japanese scholar, Prof. Fukunari Kimura, recently argued that it is difficult to imagine the realization of integration similar to that in Europe over the next five to ten years in East Asia. He is acutely aware that economic integration in Europe has a long history and has been supported by a strong political will to achieve it. The fact that European economic systems were similar, all belonging to developed countries, has assisted the deepening of integration in these countries. In contrast, East Asia is a group of very diverse countries in terms of their development stages and political systems. He argues that there is no need to develop Asian regionalism along the lines of the European experience, or any particular model. He regards the development of East Asian regionalism as being broad rather than deep, unlike the EU, and characterized by a considerable number of Free Trade Agreements (FTAs) with external interlocutors (Kimura, 2007). There is a trend of referring to the European Union as a point of comparison in debates regarding an East Asian Community and FTAs.

In contrast to those who do not see the EU as a reference point for the development of an East Asian Community, the President of the Asian Development Bank (ADB) and former Japanese Deputy-Minister for International Affairs, Haruhiko Kuroda, has publicly stated that 'as regionalism in Europe has achieved outstanding results well beyond its economic dimension, it is obvious that we can draw possible lessons for East Asia.... The European model has allowed countries to realize the benefits of a common trade and monetary policy, supported by close fiscal and regulatory coordination. Wide and deep integration has dramatically reduced the income gap among EU member countries.... However, rather than duplicating the European experience, Asia must ultimately find an optimum path suited to its own social, political, and economic conditions, and responding to the factors that triggered regional development' (Kuroda, 2006b). Kuroda sees three principles underlying the European approach, which may inspire the evolution of Asian integration: the importance of developing common institutions, the subsidiarity principle and small-country bias. To date, these remain inspirations rather than actual achievements.

Jusuf Wanandi, an influential Indonesian intellectual suggests that East Asia cannot emulate the EU because it is a more diverse region than Europe, but that East Asia can learn from the EU. He correctly asserts that the rationale of the EU was to overcome the calamities and scourge of wars in the nineteenth and twentieth centuries (Wanandi, 2005, p. 323). He goes on to link economic integration and political imperatives regarding peace and stability:

> In that sense, the EU is a modern phenomenon. It was a brilliant political strategy on the part of its founding fathers to establish the coal and steel community as a prelude to the 1957 Treaty of Rome. The sense of being so dependent on each other in vital parts of the economy is seen as a way to prevent wars in the future. This is also the case with the East Asian community idea. It was [a] more political decision to move towards peace, prosperity and progress in the region. While the economic underpinning of the effort provides for the first

rationale for the cooperation, it is also recognized that economic interdependence alone will never be adequate to achieve the goals of regional cooperation' (Wanandi, 2005, p. 330).

A Vietnamese scholar, Luong Dinh, sees East Asian regionalism as characterized by its multi-dimensionality, non-conformity, openness and inclusiveness. This is in considerable contrast with the European experience, which is characterized by institutional build-up. East Asian regionalism exists in various forms, mostly informal and non-binding, involving states and non-state actors. For Dinh, trade and investment flows, and people-to-people contacts across borders for decades have served as a catalyst for regional cooperation in East Asia. The market-driven integration dubbed as 'soft and open integration' or 'soft and open regionalism' has gradually led to growing interest in regional multilateralism and integration among governments in the region, considering them as optimal alternatives for sustainable development (Dinh, 2005, pp. 47–8).

Cae-One Kim, of Seoul National University, has argued that countries in the Asia-Pacific region should work to strengthen mutual cooperation, and in this regard he perceives European economic integration as offering lessons to Asia-Pacific countries in two ways. First, market integration would assist East Asian nations to realize economic benefits and trade opportunities in the rest of the world. Second, in order to overcome obstacles to market integration, these countries should set up a long-term agenda for market integration and strengthen policy coordination accordingly (Kim, 2005, p. 6).

Zhang Yunling, Director of the Institute of Asia Pacific Studies of the Chinese Academy of Social Sciences also sees the EU as a 'successful model, in reconsolidating a divided region through regional cooperation and integration' (Zhang, 2005, p. 61). His emphasis, however, is not simply on the EU's ability to manage regional economic, political and social affairs. Rather, he values the importance of peace, suggesting that the EU illustrates to East Asia that regional integration helps to bring about reconciliation and peace. He regards the key to community-building as being regional institutional building. Like many East Asian analysts, his view is nuanced in recognizing that East Asia does not need to copy the EU model, that, given its great diversity, East Asia should find its own model for political unity, which respects the differences in political systems, social structures and cultural colouring (Zhang, 2005, p. 58).

A distinctive East Asian approach is also evident in discussions regarding state sovereignty, which some scholars regard as a significant obstacle to closer Asian integration. Prof. Alfredo Robles, of De La Salle University in Manila, wrote that 'the conventional wisdom on Southeast Asian regionalism, embedded in ASEAN, holds that it represents a unique construct, which cannot and should not be compared with its (admittedly more advanced) European counterpart. In the early years of ASEAN's history, the European Community appeared to some national leaders as a possible model for Southeast Asia; but as European integration deepened and progressively undermined state sovereignty, the European Community lost its appeal as an exemplar for Southeast Asia' (Robles, 2005, p. 161).

His view is shared by Luong Dinh, who illustrates that sovereignty-sharing and transfer of competences to a supranational body such as the EU still remains taboo for many East Asian governments. She argues that 'In reality, regionalism in East Asia is primarily focused on facilitating intergovernmental and functional cooperation in low politics and less sensitive areas. In this light, companies, business people, academics, NGOs and other civil society actors have bigger roles to play' (Dinh, 2005, p. 48).

Two Korean economists, Hee-Yul Chai and Yeongseop Rhee, argue that the EU's experience of compromise and concession, and the establishment of various institutions for financial and monetary cooperation differ from the East Asian experience. The motivation and rationale for financial and monetary integration are weak and these scholars do not expect Japan and China to establish key bilateral relations to lead financial and monetary cooperation in East Asia. They argue that 'East Asia did not have the opportunities of accumulating experiences through negotiations of trade integration, in solving the issues of contrasting interests, and establishing institutions facilitating collective actions for issues of common interests' (Chai and Ree, 2005, p. 98).

Finally, Cae-One Kim raises the issue of Free Trade Agreements in the East Asia region, which he considers an early but weak form of regional trade agreement. Unlike the European Union, however, he regards these FTAs as a pragmatic approach, in that they minimize the sacrifice of national sovereignty and thus fit different and diverse national interests in the Asia-Pacific region. He gives this as 'the reason why FTAs are preferred in the Asia-Pacific region, where countries remain sensitive to national sovereignty issues in external commercial relations' (Kim, 2004, p. 107).

It is clear that scholars accord differing emphasis to the many aspects of these debates. A Thai academic, Apirat Petchsiri (2005), has categorized Asian academics into three groups. The first group is concerned primarily with economic issues and consists of scholars who seek to explain and analyse the effect of economic integration within and beyond the EU, and who engage in issues related to international trade. They view the EU as a major international economic player similar to the US, Japan and China, and in competition with them as they are with each other.

The second group has an overtly political motivation and regards the EU as the most successful example of modern political integration. Many of these scholars seek to learn from the process of political integration, for example from regionalism and EU enlargements. This group's membership includes international relations scholars, some of whom have shifted their focus to the EU. Members of this group explore relations between the EU and third countries, as well as EU security and defence policies.

The third group focuses on society in the EU in a comparative context. This group examines the strengths and weaknesses of social aspects of integration in a comparative context.

These various points of view form the basis of multidisciplinary lessons that Asia might learn from Europe. Apirat Petchsiri suggests that Asian academics may well develop their own approaches to the multidisciplinary study of the process of EU integration and its consequent impact on the development of Asian integration (2005, pp. 109–110).

Despite the different focuses of these three groups, they share some common foundations. Many scholars emphasize the differences in history, religion, culture, economic development and political systems in East Asia. They consider that there are more cultural distances between East Asians than between Europeans, and so it is not feasible for East Asians to follow the European experiences as a model. The EU's motto of 'Unity in Diversity' is difficult for Asians to understand. It is much easier for Asians to understand pragmatic interests in manufacturing, trade and investments based on international functional cooperation and collaboration.

A Market, a Partner or an Economic Model?

Having discussed Asian perceptions of European integration, and the differing opinions on the extent to which East Asia could, or should, emulate the European model, this chapter now turns to perceptions of Europe, and the EU, among East Asian elites. It explores whether the EU is seen first and foremost as an economic partner or market for Asian goods; whether Europe is prominent in the Asian perception of the world order, and if so, in what way.

Lee Hsien Loong, Prime Minister and Finance Minister of Singapore, perceives Europe as primarily an economic partner. He has said that 'Europe has a long history of engagement in the region, and European companies too are actively looking towards East Asia to tap opportunities in the region. It is in Asia's interest to engage the EU. In areas such as agricultural products, banking sector, aviation and pharmaceuticals, what they offer is as attractive as the US, and gives us more option as consumers' (Lee, 2005, p. 305).

The most important policy area for cooperation among the ASEAN Plus Three members, based on the European experience, is financial and monetary cooperation. With the experience of the Chiang Mai Initiatives, which established a regional framework through 'SWAP arrangements' after the financial crisis of 1997–98, there were numerous calls to promote an Asian Currency Unit (ACU) based on the European experience of European Currency Unit (ECU) under the European Monetary System (EMS). For example, Naoyoshi Kinukawa, Deputy Director of Institute for International Monetary Affairs, proposed an ACU-dominated bond market in East Asia (Kinukawa, 2002).

Recently, the ADB has been actively advocating regional monetary units. The Ninth ASEAN Plus Three Finance Minister's Meeting on 4 May 2006 endorsed the plan entitled 'Towards greater financial stability in the Asian region: Exploring steps to create regional monetary units' as one of the two research topics for 2006–07.[3] Criteria for the creation of an ACU have been given as Gross Domestic Product (GDP), trade volumes and openness of capital dealings of the participating states. Masahiro Kawai from the ADB has envisaged the creation and implementation of an ACU to be a three-stage process. In the first stage, the ACU will be used as an index to observe foreign exchange markets. The second stage consists of issuing bonds in ACUs, and the third stage is to use the ACU to float Asian currencies against the dollar and euro, and to enhance regional exchange cooperation. Kawai estimates that the first stage can be introduced once the appropriate political decisions are made, that the second stage could be completed within ten years, or even a few years, while the third stage will take much longer (*Nihon Keizai Shimbun*, 4 July 2006).

In August 2006, the Network of East Asian Think Tanks (NEAT) issued a series of policy recommendations reflecting the aims of the ADB study. Regarding the future direction of financial cooperation, NEAT reached a broad consensus that the most important long-term objective was to establish a stable exchange rate mechanism in East Asia. NEAT also recommended that a major study be carried out regarding the various options for regional currency units with a view of establishing a common currency basket and avoiding problems arising from pegging national currencies to the US dollar. The recommendation included calls for East Asian countries to study how to compute and use an East Asian currency unit (EACU). NEAT recommends that the initial focus be on including regional currencies and shares in a regional basket, which would allow for the examination of the relationships between component currencies and the EACU. This would be followed by research into ways to use the EACU to coordinate and manage exchange rates. Finally, the Network recommends an in-depth study of policy dialogue and surveillance mechanisms (NEAT, 2006).

Hee-Yul Chai, from Kyonggi University has presented a three-stage roadmap for monetary cooperation in East Asia, aimed at achieving intraregional exchange rate stability and/or exchange rate stability *vis-à-vis* one or several third currencies based on lessons from the European experience. Stage 1 would consist of policy coordination through recommendations by various committees at different levels, the establishment of the post-CMI (Chiang-Mai Initiative) institution and the introduction of the regional currency unit. Stage 2 would include the introduction of the Asian Exchange Rate Mechanism, the establishment of the finance support scheme and the reinforcement of the role of the regional currency unit; and Stage 3 would see the establishment of an Asian Central Bank and a single Asian currency. He concluded that regional integration belongs properly to the domain of politics rather than to economics (Chai, 2006).

Not everyone shares his enthusiasm. Seiya Nakajima, a business economist, opposes the creation of a common currency in Asia along the lines of the euro. He argues that as 'there are huge differences in the stage of economic development among Asian countries, it might distort stable regional economic development if the right to decide monetary policy freely will be deprived of' (*Nihon Keizai Shimbun*, 17 August 2006). Sahoko Kaji, a Japanese economist has put the case that Europe's experience, while relevant, must not be slavishly followed. She explains that, in the aftermath of the 1997–98 currency crisis, many in Asia sought to decide out what sort of currency system would be most conducive to economic stability in East Asia. Many drew on the example of the introduction of the euro for a putative Asian Monetary Union. She is circumspect in suggesting that it is one thing to learn from Europe, and quite another to insist that every step that Europe took must be taken if Asia wants to arrive at the same goal. Rather she suggests that Asians could arrive at monetary union though a sequence of events that does not exactly imitate that of the Europeans. She continues, stating, 'Turning our eyes to East Asia, nations are becoming more and more economically interdependent.... But there is still not the same degree of interdependence in Asia as there is in Europe. More serious is the lack of commitment to integration. If Japan wanted to play an important role in the process of Asian integration, it needs to stabilize its economy and educate its citizens to build consensus for integration. Europe put fifty years to arrive at a single currency. Fifty years from today, Asia may be able to have a single currency, provided we start now' (Kaji, 2005, pp. 68–9).

A leading economic journalist, Naoaki Okabe, has raised the importance of the political will that is necessary in order to establish a currency in Asia, echoing much of the debate in Europe in the 1980s. He regards the idea of an Asian equivalent of the euro as remote dream. Like many scholars, he is acutely aware of the considerable divergences in economic development in Asia and the variety of culture and religions, which differ from the European experience. But, 'there is already a *de facto* economic zone in East Asia. The ratio of interdependence in trade and investment is comparable with the EU. What is necessary now is the turn of "politics" to push from behind to move forward' (*Nihon Keizai Shimbun*, 28 August 2006).

The official statements of the Twelfth Summit Meeting of ASEAN in 2007, affirmed ASEAN's strong commitment to accelerate the establishment of an ASEAN Community by 2015 and to transform ASEAN into a region with free movement of goods, services, investment and skilled labour, and freer flow of capital.[4] This bears an uncanny resemblance to the free-market provisions of the Single European Act of 1986. Many of the methods and instruments tested in European integration have been already taken on board in the ASEAN context. Thus, the European Union is a *de facto* model for ASEAN, at least where an internal market is concerned. Two months later, the Nuremberg Declaration on an EU–ASEAN Enhanced Partnership was adopted at the 16th EU–ASEAN Ministerial Meeting. This Declaration stated that 'the EU and ASEAN hereby cooperate to strengthen ASEAN capacity and institution building processes that will contribute to achieving the goal of the ASEAN Community consisting of ASEAN Security Community, ASEAN Economic Community (AEC), and ASEAN Socio-Cultural Community through, among other steps, exchange of information and experience between the EU and ASEAN on community building.'[5]

As for the failure of the European Constitutional Treaty, it has not greatly affected the way the ASEAN Plus Three elites view Europe's integration project, primarily due to the fact it was already considered too ambitious to follow and too remote an event. In contrast to the European Union, Asians are less inclined towards institutionalization and the rigid application of the rule of law in a regional entity. This is one of basic cultural differences between Europe and Asia.

Competing Hegemons? The European Union and the United States

Analysts of both Asian regionalism and European integration are aware of the need to understand the US stances on these developments over time. How then do American factors influence Asian perspectives towards Europe? Do the ASEAN Plus Three elites look towards Europe as a partner to balance the US power and hegemony or as a competitor in the global balance of power?

The United States has been eager to promote economic cooperation in the Asia-Pacific region through institutions such as APEC. However, the US has also been opposed to any Asian initiatives for economic cooperation which might negatively affect American interests. When Mahathir Mohamad, then the Prime Minister of Malaysia, proposed an East Asian Economic Group (EAEG), Washington was vehemently opposed and many Asian countries, including Japan, were distinctly cool with regard to this initiative. The idea of an EAEG was later reconfigured into an initiative for an East Asian Economic Caucus (EAEC) in 1991. Although the EAEC was approved by ASEAN leaders, it did not work as a motor for intra-trade liberalization. Further, when Japan proposed the establishment of an Asian Monetary Fund (AMF) to stabilize exchange rates among Asian currencies after the financial crisis of 1997–98, Washington put pressure Tokyo to relinquish the idea. Instead, the Chiang Mai Initiative (CMI) was agreed to by ASEAN Plus Three in May 2000, to establish a regional financial arrangement to supplement the existing international facilities. However, the launch of the Asia–Europe Meeting in 1996, the formation of ASEAN Plus Three in 1997 and the launch of East Asia Summit in 2006 did not meet with strong opposition from the United States. These initiatives and meetings were convened with the mute acquiescence of the United States.

The Asian financial crisis of 1997–98 created the impression that the EU's involvement in the region had been less than adequate and that the EU was inward-looking and self-interested. The financial crisis 'looked set to dampen the euphoria and enthusiasm surrounding ASEM. It was feared that the ASEM process might be derailed because of the new triumphalism in Europe, and the loss in attractiveness of Asia as a place for trade and investments. Fortunately, this was not to happen' (Yeo, 2003, p. 36). Nonetheless, a sense of dissatisfaction remained among Asian participants towards the European responses. Although the ASEM Trust Fund was established in order to help the Asian countries in their financial reforms, the Asian leaders had expected European to contribute much more. One diplomat from Southeast Asia resented the fact that 'it had been Europeans who came to us, but with economic crisis they would like to keep distance from us. Europeans were too selfish and inward-looking' (*Nihon Keizai Shimbun*, 5 April 1998).

When the US realized that it would not be invited to Kuala Lumpur for the East Asian Summit, its policy-makers began to question the summit's *raison d'être* referring to it as a 'black box'. For example, Eric John, Assistant Secretary of State in 2005 stated that 'Nobody knows what the East Asian Summit is, other than leaders coming together' (Berkofsky, 2006, p. 101). US policy-makers were concerned about the East Asian Summit, and this may be one of the reasons for the US's recent efforts to revitalize APEC by proposing a Free Trade Area of the Asia-Pacific.

There has been considerable interest among the East Asian elites in the idea of the EU as a counterweight to the United States and even to Japan. Bingran Dai from Fudan University in Shanghai regards the EU as an important international actor, based on its economic growth, the development of its Common Foreign and Security Policy (CFSP) and the expansion of its role. He contrasts the EU's image with that of the United States, while acknowledging that the US presence is stronger. 'The EU has a much better image, though not more pronounced presence, than the US and Japan, which should give it more scope for manoeuvring, and mediating. The EU could, indeed, play a more constructive role in a number of issues Asia is faced with, if it so chooses' (Dai, 2003, p. 32). Indonesian Ambassador Wirjono has suggested that as Europe establishes its power in the international arena, 'Europe is finding its pattern of relations and power in international arena. Europe is looking for more soft-power influence to equalize the United States' hard power' (Prasetyono, 2006, p. 32).

The geopolitical considerations, especially the idea of the EU as a counterbalance to the United States, have been prominent for some East Asian nations. Heung-Hong Kim, of the Korean Institute for International Economic Policy, wrote that 'Europe agreed to launch ASEM in light of the US commitment to economic cooperation with the Asia-Pacific region through APEC. Asian countries have sought to diversify foreign influence that would have been confined to that with the US' (Kim, 2006, p. 36).

Similar arguments were echoed by Prof. Sung-Hoon Park. He concluded that 'as stronger political, economic and cultural cooperation with Europe will provide Asian countries with an excellent balancing weight against their too strong political, economic and cultural dependence on the US and Japan, the ASEM process should be given a high priority in their external strategies' (2005, p. 212).

Interestingly, geopolitical considerations such as these are very rare and have seldom been expressed in Japan. The United States is so dominant in the mind of the Japanese government and even in academia, that the European Union is routinely underestimated and has not been regarded as a card against the United States. This perspective of the Japanese elites is mirrored in the opinion of the Japanese public, which regards the US as the most important overseas country for Japan currently and even in future.[6]

As for the recent American call for a FTA encompassing the APEC zone, Ambassador Ong Keng Yong, Secretary-General of ASEAN from Singapore, has suggested that the United States has finally realized the value of Asia and the possibilities of a single market among the thirteen states of ASEAN Plus Three. He suggested that, at the same time, the US is concerned about a form of regional integration that may not be favourable to US interests: 'ASEAN never thought of economic integration negatively towards the US from its beginning', he said. While ASEAN Plus Three is discussing how to proceed in the path towards economic integration, he regards the US as 'a passenger on the same bus as we are. The US may want to guide its direction. But, we just want the US to sit quietly in the bus.' He concluded: 'In future, however, there is possibility of linkage between East Asian Community and the North American Free Trade Association if the US stands in the middle. The direction is worth studying because it can be a force to counter the enlarging European Union or the Middle East/Africa including oil-producing states' (*Nihon Keizai Shimbun*, 20 November 2006).

As for security cooperation, Koreans often refer to the European experience not with respect to the European Union but to the security dialogue embedded in the pan-European Organization for Security and Cooperation in Europe (OSCE). For example, Ban Ki-moon, then Korean Minister of Foreign Affairs and Trade and now the UN Secretary-General, said in September 2006:

> In the wake of World War Two, Europe, with the collective defence provided by North Atlantic Treaty Organization (NATO) as a firm basis, has consolidated an order of peace and integration. The

comprehensive and cooperative security forged through the OSCE also has been an important element in this process. Countries now unite in their efforts to work together to tackle both traditional and non-traditional security threats. The challenge for Northeast Asia is now how to draw upon the European experience to build a mechanism for multilateral security cooperation. I am convinced that the European experience will serve as a model for multilateral security cooperation in Northeast Asia. However, the backdrop in Northeast Asia differs from that in Europe and the countries in the region will have to exert even more vigorous efforts to this end' (Ban, 2006).

However the CFSP and the European Security and Defence Policy are barely mentioned in Asian statements, except in the writings of academics although there has been successful mission to Aceh, in Indonesia.

Concluding Remarks

It is clear that there is no single East Asian perspective on European integration or on the European Union. There are, however, common approaches and perspectives among East Asian business, political and academic elites. The East Asian political elites tend to perceive European integration favourably, but, despite this, they continue to regard bilateral relations with the member states as more important than links with the EU. East Asian business elites, in particular, think that the EU is still a fragmented market and that they have to deal with the member states rather than the EU as a bloc. In addition, some political elites see European integration only in economic terms and some academic elites see the EU not only as an economic power, but becoming more important in political and social affairs. Many academic elites refer explicitly to European integration or to the European Union, but many still consider that Asia is too different from Europe and that an Asian way of cooperation will be found that does not involve transferring national sovereignty to a largely supranational organization such as the European Union. But there is still no single model of an Asian way. *De facto* economic mutual interdependence in trade in East Asia is now higher than in the North America Free Trade Area and closer to the European Union, although there are still fragmented national markets with different industrial standards and technical regulations.[7]

Toshihiko Kuroda, President of the ADB, said that 'East Asia is on the way to achieving a broader, deeper, and more outward looking regionalism, inspired by Europe, while maintaining its distinctive characteristics of great diversity, high dynamism, flexibility, and adaptability' (2006b). Probably, the most important policy area from which Asians can learn is, and will be, in the area of financial and monetary policy. The initiative for a common Asian currency will be the first to be tested. In East Asia, *de facto* cooperation proceeds at a relatively fast rate, but the institutionalization follows at a slow one.

For this reason, Asian perspectives of the European Union and of European integration will continue to differ from the European experience whilst maintaining their distinctiveness.

Notes

1. The 14th APEC Economic Leaders' Meeting Ha Noi Declaration, 18–19 November 2006. APEC's membership at this time consisted of 21 states and areas, including the countries of ASEAN Plus Three, Hong Kong and Taiwan.
2. Chairman's Statement of the Second East Asia Summit, Cebu, the Philippines, 15 January 2007, paras.12 and 19.
3. The Joint Ministerial Statements of the 9th ASEAN+3 Finance Ministers' Meeting, 4 May 2006, Hyderabad, India, para. 9.
4. Chairperson's Statement of the 12th ASEAN Summit, Cebu, Philippines, 13 January 2007, paras. 13 and 16.
5. 'Nuremberg Declaration on an EU–ASEAN Enhanced Partnership' issued at the 16th EU–ASEAN Ministerial Meeting at Nuremberg, 15 March 2007.
6. In contrast, the populations of Thailand, Hong Kong and Singapore, as indicated in public opinion polls, perceive China as the most important overseas country or region, currently and in future. Koreans perceive the United States to be the most important currently, but that China will be more important in the future. The European Union ranks as between the fourth and fifth most important country or region in the five countries and areas (Holland and Chaban, 2007, Graph 6, p. 13).
7. For details, see Marukawa, 2007.

References

ASEM (2006) *ASEM in its Tenth Year: Looking Back, Looking Forward*, Asian Country Report, co-directed by Yamamoto, T. and Hwee, Y. L., Tokyo: Japan Centre for International Exchange and Helsinki: University of Helsinki, March, available at http://www.mofa.go.jp/policy/economy/asem/tenth/reprt 2.pdf, accessed 9 June 2008.

Ban, Ki-moon (2006) 'Asia-Europe Relations and ASEM', 06-09 at Helsinki, available at http://www.mofat.go.kr/me/me_a002/me_boo6/1210395_980.html, accessed 9 June 2008.

Berkofsky, A. (2006) 'The East Asia Summit (EAS) — Really towards an East Asian Community (EAC)?' *Asia-Pacific Journal of EU Studies* 4. 1, Summer, pp. 95–104.

Chai, H.-Y. (2006) 'A Roadmap of Monetary Cooperation in East Asia: Some Lessons from the European Experience', paper presented at the conference *Europe and Asia: Regions in Flux*, Contemporary Europe Research Centre, University of Melbourne, 6–7 December.

Chai, H.-Y. and Ree, Y. (2005), 'Financial and Monetary Cooperation in East Asia in the Light of the European Experience', *Asia-Pacific Journal of EU Studies*, 3. 1–2, Winter, pp. 81–100.

Dai, B. (2003) 'EU's Role in the Post Cold War Period and Future of Asia-Europe Relations: An Asian Perspective' *Asia-Pacific Journal of EU Studies*, 1. 1, Summer, pp. 83–100.

Dinh, L. T. H. (2005) 'Regional Powers and the Building of an East Asian Community', *Asia-Pacific Journal of EU Studies*, 3. 1–2 Winter, pp. 45–61.

Holland, M. and Chaban, N. (2007) *The EU Through the Eyes of Asia: a Comparative Study of Media Perceptions and public opinion in 2006*, European Studies in Asia, Second Interim Report, Singapore: Asia-Europe Foundation.

Ito, M. (2006) 'Keizai/Shakai no Kaiho wo susumeyo [Open Economy and Society]', Keizai Kyoshitu, *Nihon Keizai Shimbun*, 26 September.

Jain, R. K. (2005) 'India, the European Union and Asian Regionalism', *Asia-Pacific Journal of EU Studies*, 3. 1–2, Winter. pp. 29–44.

Kaji, S. (2005) 'The Euro, the Enlarged EU and Asia', in Z. Mantaha and T. Tanaka (eds) *Enlarging European Union and Asia*, Singapore: The Asia-Europe Foundation and Tokyo: Keio University.

Kim, Cae-One (2004), 'Building a Common Knowledge Society among the Asia–Pacific Region and Europe' *Asia-Pacific Journal of EU Studies* 2. 2, pp. 103–8.

Kim, Cae-One (2005) 'Multilateralism and Regionalism in a Globalizing World, a Perspective from the Asia-Pacific Region', *Asia-Pacific Journal of EU Studies*, 3. 1–2, Winter, pp. 1–6.

Kim, Heung-Hong (2006) 'Korea', Asian Country Report, in ASEM *ASEM in its Tenth Year: Looking Back, Looking Forward* available at http://www.mofa.go.jp/policy/economy/asem/tenth/reprt 2.pdf, accessed 9 June 2008.

Kimura, F. (2007) Seminar 'FTA to Nihon (FTA and Japan)' 18, *Nihon Keizai Shimbun*, 20 March.

Kinukawa, N. (2002) 'A Call to Develop a Regional Bond Market in East Asia', *Newsletter* (Institute for International Monetary Affairs) 7, 15 December, pp. 1–8.

Kuroda, T. (2006a) 'Emerging Asia and the Global Economy', speech given at the International Institute for Asian Studies (IIAS) in Amsterdam on 13 September, available at http://www.adb.org/Documents/Speeches/2006/2006061.asp, accessed 9 June 2008.

Kuroda, T. (2006b) speech at IMF–World Bank Seminar on 'Whither the European Project?', Singapore, 18 September, available at http://www.adb.org/Documents/Speeches/2006/2006065.asp, accessed 9 June 2008.

Lee, H. L. (2005) 'The Future of Asia for Japan', *Asia-Europe Journal*, 3. 3, October, pp. 301–17.

Mantaha, Z. and Tanaka,T. (eds) (2005) *Enlarging European Union and Asia*, Singapore: the Asia–Europe Foundation, and Tokyo: Keio University.

Marukawa, T. (2007) 'Regionalism and Nationalism in Mobile Communications: A Comparison of East Asia and Europe', in T. Nakamura (ed.) *The Dynamics of*

East Asian Regionalism in Comparative Perspective (ISS Research Series 24), Tokyo: Institute of Social Science, University of Tokyo.

NEAT (2006) 'Memorandum of Policy Recommendations for East Asia Co-operation: the Next Ten Years', Fourth Annual Conference of the Network of East Asian Think Tanks, Kuala Lumpur, 22–3 August.

Park, S.-H. (2005), 'ASEM and the Future of Asia–Europe Relations: Backgrounds, Main Characteristics and New Challenges', in Z. Mantaha and T. Tanaka (eds.) (2005) *Enlarging European Union and Asia*, Singapore: the Asia-Europe Foundation, and Tokyo: Keio University.

Pengiran, M. P. A. (2003) 'East Asia Community: Prospects and Implications', keynote speech at 'ASEAN Plus Three — Perspectives of Regional Integration in East Asia and the Lessons from Europe', Seoul, 30 November-1 December, available at http://www.aseansec.org/15655.htm, access 9 June 2008.

Petchsiri, A. (2005) 'How European Integration Is Perceived in Asia: The Academicians' Point of View', in Z. Mantaha and T. Tanaka (eds) (2005) *Enlarging European Union and Asia*, Singapore: the Asia-Europe Foundation and Tokyo: Keio University.

Prasetyono, E. (2006) 'Indonesia' Asian Country Report in ASEM *ASEM in its Tenth Year: Looking Back, Looking Forward*, available at http://www.mofa.go.jp/policy/economy/asem/tenth/reprt 2.pdf, accessed 9 June. 2008.

Robles, A. C. Jr (2005) 'The ASEAN Free Trade Area and the Construction of a Southeast Asian Economic Community in East Asia', in Z. Mantaha and T. Tanaka (eds) (2005) *Enlarging European Union and Asia*, Singapore: the Asia-Europe Foundation and Tokyo: Keio University.

Wanandi, J. (2005) 'Towards an Asian Security-Community', *Asia-Europe Journal* 3. 3, October, pp. 321–32.

Yeo, L. H. (2003) *Asia and Europe: The Developments and Different Dimensions of ASEM*, London: Routledge.

Zhang, Y. (2005) 'Emerging New East Asian Regionalism', *Asia-Pacific Review* 12. 1, pp. 55–63.

10
European Perspectives on Engaging with East Asia

Philomena Murray

Introduction

Despite the recent growth in the breadth and depth of the European Union's relationship with East Asian nations and institutions, the EU's motives for engagement, its attitudes towards the region and the concordance between official EU Asia strategies and their concrete actions in the region remain relatively unexplored, (Wiessala, 2002). Little has been written, for example, on what has shaped European, and especially European Commission (EC) perspectives on East Asia, how the EU conceives of Asia, (as a region or individual countries), the importance of 'Asia' in the European mindset and whether the EU is actively seeking to be a 'normative power' in the East Asian region. This chapter explores these important questions. It focuses in particular on how the EU's strategies regarding Asia and its perceptions of East Asia have changed since the 1994 Asia Strategy.

This chapter argues that EU policy towards East Asia has been essentially reactive, that the 1994 Asia Strategy was driven by EU economic interests in Asia and that its current engagement is characterized by a combination of bilateral and regional arrangements and, in particular, changing conceptions of what constitutes 'Asia'. It argues that while economic interests remain paramount, political and normative elements are also evident. It further suggests that there is no single understanding of the EU's motives for engaging with East Asia. Neither European Commission officials, nor the EU as a whole, possess a single, united EU perspective on East Asia.

Methodology

While this chapter draws on scholarly and documentary analysis, it also addresses a need to analyse the perceptions of EU officials dealing with East Asia. For this reason, interviews were carried out with European Commission officials in September 2006. It is also important to understand how academic analysts in Europe perceive East Asia and the EU–Asia relationship. To this end, a survey questionnaire was designed and sent to 114 analysts in Europe between September and November 2006. The survey examined respondents' assessment of the state and significance of the links between the EU and East Asia. It also dealt with perceptions of East Asia and its place in the world, the EU's relationship with East Asia and the EU's engagement strategies in East Asia. Further questions related to regional integration and interregional relations. A separate section dealt with perspectives on China and a final set focused on conflict between member state perspectives and EU perspectives with regard to East Asian relations. Forty-six surveys were completed and returned, a response rate of 40 per cent. The data were entered into a statistical package for the social sciences file and analysed using descriptive statistical techniques.

EU Motives and Strategies: Reactive to Proactive?

The EU's original motives for engaging with Asia, and its attitudes towards the region as a whole, were primarily economic. Asia is a lucrative market for EU goods. From the outset, however, economic and political aspects have been closely linked. The earliest formal economic agreement between the European Community and the Association of South East Asian Nations (ASEAN) took the form of the 1980 European Community–ASEAN agreement. Although this agreement provided for most favoured nation status, joint trade promotion and investment, and collective research into the reduction of trade barriers (Gilson, 2004, p. 187), it failed to make the relationship significantly more central to either side.

Until the 1990s, European attention was largely focused internally, rather than externally. The Single European Act, the Single Market initiative, the fall of the Berlin Wall and its repercussions in Eastern and Central Europe, and accession negotiations were the primary preoccupations. To a considerable extent, enlargement was the EU's foreign policy tool towards its near abroad and neighbourhood. In terms of external focus, the EU's primary concerns in the 1990s were relations with the United States, development aid to the African–Caribbean and Pacific states, and trade negotiations with individual countries rather than regions. Formal relations between the Community and ASEAN were derivative of the Cold War context, and the relationship between the two regional bodies was primarily strategic, focused on building a united anti-Soviet front.

The EU's first Asia Strategy, released in 1994, reflected a significant shift in EU perceptions and policies.[1] It came at a time when the EU was beginning to engage with other regional units. It was framed in the context of an improved recognition of the East Asian region's transformation, particularly its economic dynamism, and the realization that European links in the region were relatively weak. This was complemented by the recognition of the EU's large trade deficit with the region. The 1994 Strategy focused on trade, political and security cooperation and the need to accord East Asia a higher priority on the EU's agenda. The EU's four main objectives in this document were to strengthen the EU's economic presence; to contribute to stability through expanding economic and political relations; to encourage economic growth, especially in poorer countries; and, finally, to develop and consolidate democracy and respect for human rights (CEC, 1994).

Despite the significance of this document, several of the Commission officials interviewed in Brussels did not know what the 1994 Strategy was, although they were involved in the current engagement. One official saw it as simply 'one of many things that took place... a long time ago' although he stated that the Strategy 'did help to lay down some of the abiding principles'. Another Commission official commented on how EU views of engagement with Asia have altered since the 1994 Asia Strategy: 'when you look at it today, nobody would write a similar thing again.'

So what has changed? The EU's views of Asia? Asia itself? Or both? The answer can, in part, be found in the European Commission's second major policy document, entitled 'Europe and Asia: A Strategic Framework for Enhanced Partnerships', produced in September 2001. This document presented a significantly broader understanding of both the concept of Asia (Asia-Pacific instead of East Asia) and of engagement with Asia (Wiessala, 2002). It sought to establish a 'sound policy framework' as well as to provide for institutional structures for the EU's relations with Asia over the next decade (EC, 2001, pp. 11–12). The new Strategy focused on six key dimensions: strengthening EU engagement with Asia in the political and security fields; strengthening EU–Asia two-way trade and investment relations; contributing effectively to reduce poverty in the region; helping promote the spread of democracy, good governance and the rule of law across the region; in turn building global partnerships with key Asian partners (in combating global challenges as well as in international organizations); and, finally, promoting further awareness between the two regions (EC, 2001).

The New Millennium — Repositioning Understandings of Asia?

The 2001 document is in considerable contrast with the 1994 Asia Strategy. It recognizes that the institutional framework for relations with Asian countries varies, and that only a small number of these Asian countries are in 'fully comprehensive ("third-generation") cooperation agreements' with the EU, in marked comparison with other regions such as Latin America or the Mediterranean. It suggests:

> Upgrading the institutional basis for our relations with key partners in Asia would allow for a more coherent approach to all relevant issues (in the political and security fields as well as on economic and development issues), would create a powerful stimulus for the intensification of our dialogue and cooperation in all areas, and would give a clear public signal of the commitment of both parties to raise our relationship to a new level (EC, 2001, p. 12).

The newer, broader conception of Asia developed by the European officials illustrates deepened understanding of the complexity of Asia and the complexity of the tasks it was undertaking there. For example, it emphasizes the internal diversity of the term 'Asia' as well as covering Australasia for the first time. It also acknowledges the acceleration of internal regionalization in Asia as well as the increase in regional dialogue and cooperation therein. It is at pains to recognize the 'increasing signs of a growing sense of East Asian identity' (EC, 2001, p. 8). This is presented in the context of the realization of mutual ignorance and the sense of distance between the two regions. The document states:

> One element which does not seem to have evolved greatly is the degree of mutual awareness between our two regions, with stereotypes on both sides still casting Europe as introspective and old-fashioned, and Asia as a distant and exotic continent, presenting more challenges than opportunities (EC, 2001, p. 14).

In reviewing and updating the 1994 approach to EU–Asia relations, the Commission took into consideration a number of factors: the acceleration of globalization and emergence of global interdependence and of a global agenda; past and projected internal changes in the EU (such as the development of the European Community into the EU, enlargement, economic and monetary union, and the euro) as well as transformation in Asia (the financial crisis, the acceleration of intra-regional dialogue, and the opening of China).

The desire for a projection of the EU's influence in economic and political terms is evident in the core objective of rethinking its strategy relating to Asia and EU–Asia relations, stated as 'strengthening the EU's political and economic presence across the region, and raising this to a level commensurate with the growing global weight of an enlarged EU' (EC, 2001, 3, p. 28). The six key objectives combine economic interests with political aspects, civil society engagement, the environment and normative agendas. These objectives for the entire region are based on a number of imperatives which reflect the multidimensional aspects of EU policy. The peace imperative aims to contribute to peace and security in the region and globally, and to strengthen the engagement on these issues via bilateral, regional and global forums (such as the UN); to support conflict prevention; and to enhance cooperation on justice and home affairs. The economic imperative sets out to strengthen mutual trade and investment flows; to further develop bilateral economic relations with Asian partners; to support private-sector cooperation between Europe and Asia; to strengthen policy dialogue; to enhance market access for the poorest countries; and to recognize the link between environmental issues, transport and the energy sector. Its commitment to development, as the world's largest aid donor, is evident in the objective to promote development in Asia; to reduce poverty via measures in health and education as well as better economic and social governance; to strengthen the dialogue on social policy issues; and to reform the management of the Commission's external assistance portfolio.

Normative elements are evident in the desire to spread democracy, good governance and the rule of law and to strengthen the respect of human rights via regional, bilateral as well as global forums; and to encourage civil society dialogue (see chapter one for a discussion of normative and soft power). There is a desire to build global partnerships and alliances with Asian countries and to strengthen cooperation within the United Nations; strengthen the open international trading system via the World Trade Organization (WTO); strengthen dialogue and cooperation on global challenges (the environment); and reinforce inter-regional scientific and technological cooperation. Finally, there is a commitment to increase awareness of the EU in Asia, to be achieved by strengthening and upgrading European Commission delegations in the region, strengthening educational and cultural exchanges and enhancing civil society dialogue. By 2003, Pascal Lamy, then Trade Commissioner, suggested that the opening of new EU offices in the Asian region was a physical expression of enhanced relations between the EU and Asia (Lamy, 2003, p. 3).

Finally, the new Strategy recognized the vastness and diversity of Asia, as evidenced by its regionally targeted action points: South Asia (strengthen dialogue on security, reduce poverty, improve human rights and prevent conflict); Southeast Asia: (deepen cooperation via EU–ASEAN, enhance global partnership via WTO, reduce poverty, promote social policy reform); Northeast Asia (deepen bilateral relationship with China, encourage China's engagement in the international community and multilateral fora, promote democratic reforms in China, ensure the autonomy of the Special Administrative Regions, enhance global and regional partnerships with Japan, deepen the partnership with South Korea and support the inter-Korean reconciliation process) and, finally, Australasia (expand economic and commercial relations beyond agriculture; strengthen cooperation on global environmental issues).

In terms of common concerns between the two regions, then Commissioner Pascal Lamy (2003, p. 4) focused on diversity; common views of globalization and its opportunities and challenges and the common challenge of 'reconciling the way they manage their societies with the need to modernize and integrate into the global economy'. This included striking a balance between market forces and the role of the state. One official, when referring to the EU's changing perceptions of Asia suggested that the relationship is getting stronger and stronger. Twenty or thirty years ago, there were the 'tigers', a black wall in India (due to its closed economy), China was nowhere, and South East Asia was still in the middle of civil conflict. There was no European geo-strategic vision at the time. He sees contemporary Asia as totally different, due to the opening up of India and China, greater political stability and increased complementarity in the region. He suggests that there is a need for the EU to have a global vision of the region.

Understanding the EU's New Approach to Asia

Just as conceptions of Asia are complex and multifaceted, so too are the reasons the EU sought deeper engagement with East Asia, as evidenced by the Commission interviews and the surveys administered in late 2006.

When asked the open-ended question, 'What do you think was the main reason that led the Commission to rethink and revise the EU's approach to East Asia?', survey respondents referred to economic, political, and strategic factors, although the most commonly cited reasons were those relating to trade and economic relations. Economic factors included the EU's lack of economic visibility in East Asia; East Asia's rapid economic growth; trade with the lucrative and growing Asian markets; the desire to be on a level playing field with the US; and the rise of China. Political and strategic factors included the end of the Cold War; the fact that the EU was not perceived as a global actor in Asia; the recognition that the EU could not rely solely on multilateral fora such as the WTO; the need to improve relations with ASEAN; the evolving strategic situation, geopolitical shifts and alliances; the perceived gap in the predominance of the US in this ever-growing region and the personal commitment of Chris Patten, former European Commissioner for External Relations. Importantly, respondents noted that separating out the political considerations was not feasible with regard to Asia, and suggested that economic relationships could be utilized in order to cultivate political relationships.

Survey respondents also acknowledged the recent need for an EU-level institutional framework to govern relations and the necessity to meet the European Parliament's expectations of adding a stronger political dimension to the relationship. The desire to enhance the EU's soft power and the promotion of the EU's development model, as well as the desire for positive global governance based on multilateralism and rule of law also featured as possible incentives for the EU to engage further in Asia. An element of competitiveness was evident in the comment that the EU wished to have 'a piece of the cake' rather than allowing the US to reap all the trade benefits of East Asia.

European analysts were asked in the survey how they rated the overall importance to the EU of its relations with East Asia. None regarded it as

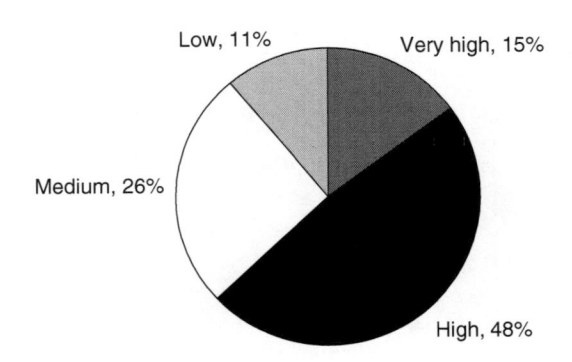

Figure 10.1 Assessment of the importance to the EU of its relationship with East Asia.

very low. As Figure 10.1 illustrates, it is regarded as high or very high by the majority of respondents.

Changing European Conceptions of Asia

Given that the EU has broadened its conception of Asia since 1994, what does 'Asia' mean to Europeans? Interviews with European Commission officials illustrate that there is no monolithic or shared image of Asia in the EU's official 'mindset'. When asked what came to mind when they heard the term 'Asia', respondents often referred to it as multifaceted, a heterogenous concept, as artificial, and as a 'very European concept'.

> their very, very different histories, with their very, very different economic systems, with their very, very different political systems, with incredible differences in terms of population and GDP and everything else. Far, far more different to any differences that we've had in our own region, where we've had a common, or largely common, history, largely common culture, largely common religious background.
>
> It's more than half the world's populations, it's all the world's great religions, it's the majority of the world's ethnicities... it is the one great continent of the world which is by far the hardest to define ... so there is no simple response to that question.

Respondents regarded Asia as far more complex than stereotypes might suggest, particularly on the political side. One stated that 'often the economic issues dominate, but when you look deeper, there is so much history influencing political stability'. It was emphasized that there was no EU 'one size fits all' approach to Asian countries and that this was emphasized internally within the Commission, with recognition of countries and subregions' specific needs. Other ideas that came to mind with regard to Asia were a sense of hierarchy, respect for authority and an orderly society.

While there was a general consensus among the Commission officials interviewed as to the geographic boundaries of Asia, extending from 'the Eastern shore of the Bosphorus to the Pacific Ocean, most points north, most points south and the eastern part of that spectrum', no such consensus exists in functional and negotiating terms. For example, the Commission has traditionally dealt with Korea and Japan as part of the group of industrialized nations while other nations were primarily recipients of development aid[2] and others again were simply in a category of their own, such as China. This is reflected in the fact that the Commission Directorate General (DG) responsible for external relations

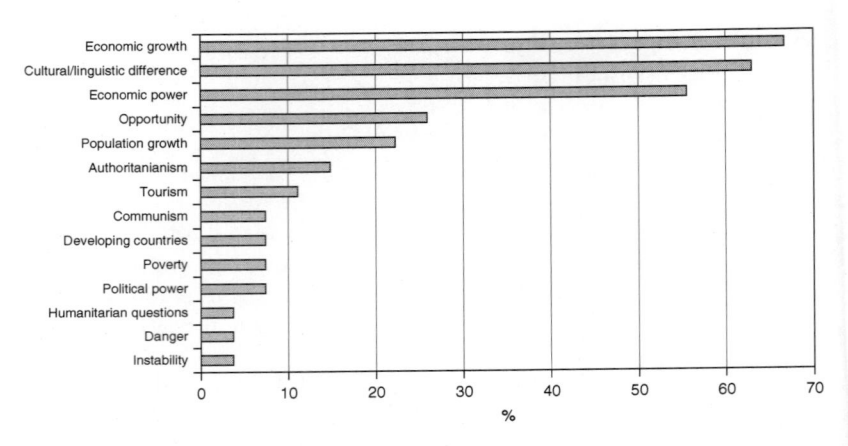

Figure 10.2 Asia: What comes to mind? (analysts' responses).

(DG RELEX) in the Commission has a section entitled 'Asia, except Japan and Korea'. Further, a Commission official referred to the allocation of portfolios in DG RELEX as being 'a segregation of North and South, developing versus developed'. Another spoke of a bureaucratic split between different directorates and DGs, with discussions taking place in-house about regionalising the EU's approach.

When analysts based at European universities were asked in the survey what comes to mind when they think of Asia, similar responses to those of the officials were given.[3] As seen in Figure 10.2, economic power and growth are considered to be very important, along with cultural/linguistic difference. Opportunity came as a fourth choice, while instability, humanitarian questions and danger were considered to be least relevant.

New European Perceptions of Asia?

The responses given by analysts, particularly the overwhelming conception of Asia as a dynamic economic power, suggests that the EU's new strategic approach has done little to change the way in which the EU perceives Asia.

This is reinforced by responses given to another survey question, 'have the EU's New Strategies changed how the EU perceives Asia', to which 81 per cent of respondents answered 'not at all' or 'very little'.

A further optional open question asked 'If yes, in what way?'.[4] Those who responded referred to the EU's intention to engage more in East Asia through Free Trade Agreements and other agreements and to a 'slowly evolving realization that the economic strategy must be underpinned

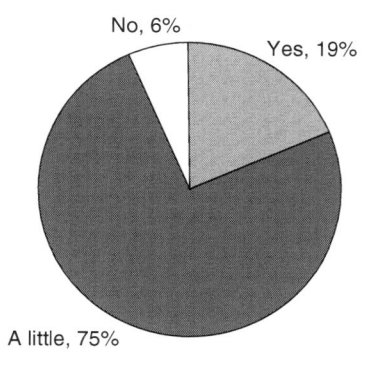

Figure 10.3 Have the EU's New Strategies changed how the EU perceives Asia?

with a political relationship and that the political relationship is more complex than ever imagined'. There were suggestions that East Asia has a higher priority today than previously and that the EU seemed to have commenced a more coordinated strategy towards the region. The EU was regarded as having become more proactive and more aware of the heterogeneity of Asia and of the need to differentiate between a number of foreign policy options.

An assessment from one survey respondent was that the EU's 1994 Strategy marked an increase in cooperation as a response to Asia's growing economic power, while subsequent strategies appeared to show a withdrawal from the multilateral process as a response to the 1997 Economic Crisis. These strategies are 'easier to pursue because they are more highly based on material interests and are less impacted by more complicated, and less likely to be negotiable, ideational interests. It is also more likely that the EU might be able to add conditionality clauses into relationships it perceives as less beneficial.'

Despite a perception that the EU's perception of Asia had not significantly changed since the 1994 Asia strategy, both officials interviewed and analysts who participated in the survey regarded the EU as being increasingly involved in the region. In response to a question asking what was the greatest change in the EU's relations with Asia since the mid-1990s, there was a noticeable concurrence of views on the increased importance of strong economic ties. Some thought that the EU privileged the relationship with China, perhaps at the expense of other countries in the region and was beginning to accord more attention to India. There was a sense of a developing political dialogue among equals, with strong efforts to solve trade disputes, partly through the WTO.

Respondents remarked on the increased EU understanding of Asian cultural diversity, resulting in 'less lecturing to Asians on how they should govern their countries'. There was the improved institutionalization of the relationship and greater awareness by the EU of the need to have a co-ordinated external relations policy. There is the factor of globalization and absence of effective global governance. Further, some respondents regarded the last decade as characterized by positive developments such as increased contact, the launch of the Asia–Europe Meeting (ASEM), enhanced coordination among the member states and the development of programs for stronger business and cultural exchanges. The EU approach since the mid-1990s is perceived by some respondents as both more comprehensive and more proactive.

Contemporary Assessments of the EU–Asia Relationship

It has long been argued that the EU is not fully cognizant of the complexities of the Asian context. As recently as 2005, the European Institute of Asian Studies (EIAS, 2005, p. 4) argued that, if the EU wished to take part in East Asian integration processes, it must further familiarize itself with the region's complexities. It suggested that the EU did not seem to pay sufficient attention to the region's rapid changes. The Institute proposed the establishment of an EU-level programme involving member states and the Commission, to 'act as a catalyst to develop interdisciplinary competences on Asia' (ibid., p. 11). There is certainly some disparity of views among officials in national and Commission bureaucracies and increased coordination can only be beneficial.

The concern about the relative lack of EU attention to East Asia is not confined to think tanks. Gilson (2005, p. 318) has commented on the fact that the EU has less interest in East Asia than the region's growing economic and political weight might merit. She ascribes this to the EU's commitment to its internal integration processes, a lack of contentious issues related to the region — with the exception of human rights issues in Myanmar and, to a limited extent, in China — and the existence of multiple fora for addressing these issues, which, she suggests, 'provide the EU with a growing set of relations with East Asia and serve quite different and complementary purposes'. The analyst respondents in the survey also referred to a lack of contentious issues on the agenda.

We have seen that the fact that Asia did not prominently feature on the EU radar screen until the roar of the Asian Tigers was heard by Europeans and the realization of the growing trade deficit with Asia led to a change of EU policy. Meanwhile, the US remained the external hegemon for many governments in Asia, backed up by its military presence in the region. While individual member states of the EU have engaged fruitfully with individual Asian countries over a number of years, there had been neither a united European response to Asian events, nor a great deal of interaction and mutual understanding between the regions until the 1990s. Dent (2001) goes so far as to argue there was persistent under-socialization between Europe and East Asia. Even today, although there has been useful cooperation in the educational and cultural spheres, there is a perception that this dimension is not very developed, evident in the survey responses. This is not to state that this relatively low EU presence in many areas will continue. Indeed, one EU official interviewed predicted increased cooperation on education, culture and understanding between civilizations, and collaboration regarding the way that cultures in Asia live peacefully with each other, and suggested that the EU could learn from this.

For its part, the EU's focus has not been on East Asia, as we have seen. The EU–Asia relationship is considered by Commission officials as less important than EU engagement with the US and with the European neighbourhood. It is, however, regarded as increasingly significant. For example a Commission official stated:

> The distance of course is a problem; the fact that the visibility is low and people don't know Asia, they don't know what it means and what it is going to mean in the world of the future. . . . [W]e don't have the kind of visceral relationship that we have with our near abroad. We don't have the kind of relationship like the transatlantic relationship, of course we don't. But I think slowly but surely . . . we are beginning to realize just how important it is that we build up this relationship for our own future, because we are totally interdependent and more interdependent with Asia than with any other part of the world, in real terms, because of trade.

Commission officials regard EU engagement with Asia as politically active through ASEM: 'increasingly we are trying to engage with Asia through civil society, through links between academia and parliaments'. Another official referred to the EU as slowly beginning to realize its interdependence with Asia and how much it needs to focus on the relationship. One official attributed the low visibility of aspects of the EU–Asia relationship as due to a lack of a special relationship: 'no countries of the EU are really fighting strongly to put Asian countries at the centre of EU policy (unlike with Latin America)'.

Approaching Asia

Not surprisingly, there is no single or coherent assessment of EU–Asia relations in interviews and the survey, in part because the EU does not have one single comprehensive engagement with East Asia. This chapter has shown that the perception of Asia by Commission officials is multifaceted. This is because the relationship encompasses economic and political dimensions, development aid and human rights issues, and is pursued in at least four complementary approaches.

In addition to political engagement through civil society and parliaments, the relationships are also conducted in traditional bilateral contexts, such as member state to individual Asian country; in New Regional Bilateralism (NRB), such as EU–Japan or EU–China relations; in New Inter-Regional Bilateralism (NIRB) through region to region engagement, such as in ASEM, and, finally, in a multilateral global regionalism where the EU negotiates and even, on occasion, caucuses with ASEAN or ASEAN Plus Three (China, South Korea, Japan) in the WTO or other multilateral fora. Indeed, many officials who were interviewed said that the EU needs the political support of Asia in order to push its global agenda on issues such as climate change and trade reform. Each of these approaches and dimensions to the Europe–East Asia relationship possesses significant policy and sectoral (political, economic and societal) differences. For example, the Commission works on political issues with North and South Korea, Japan and Pakistan. In addition, the Commission deals with business issues with Japan and Korea in regulatory reform dialogue, for example. The Commission is regarded as working hard on the relationship with China, 'although along a different vector', implying that a it adopts a different approach to China than it does towards other parts of Asia. A broadening of political relationships, while not on a par with economic engagement, is attributed to factors such as Japan's and Korea's greater interest in international relations — they are regarded as belonging to 'the same cohort of international politics as the EU' — and a similar mindset on governance issues.

There is an assumption in many interviews that the more the EU is proactive, the more the EU–Asia relationship flourishes. For example, the EU is regarded as having been very proactive with ASEAN, while with ASEAN Plus Three, the Commission has been much less so, preferring to expend its energy on EU–China and EU–Japan relations. The EU is primarily an economic interlocutor with East Asia, and secondly a political interlocutor. Several officials commented that inter-regionalism is limited because of a lack of internal coherence in Asia, so there is not a bloc-to-bloc relationship.

Many officials suggested in the interviews that the EU–Asia relationship is accorded insufficient political attention by the EU, despite the burgeoning trade and investment links. The changing nature of the relationship is due to the current Commission's approach of according increased — though still inadequate — attention to Asia compared with the previous Commission. Multiple factors have been regarded as responsible for this increased attention. Globalization and the emergence of Southeast Asia, Japan, China and India have been significant. The expansion of the EU's political agenda and international role cannot be underestimated, as it has led to increased EU involvement in Asia's political sphere, due to concern over conflicts in Asia. Many of the issues contributing to the lack of sustained interest in Asia in the 1990s, such as enlargement, have been resolved or are less pressing. There has been a promotion by some countries (such as Australia) of the need to be aware of security risks in East Asia. Difficulties between Japan, China and Korea, the 2004 tsunami and the situation in Aceh have all drawn additional international attention and EU involvement to the region. There was a view among many officials that the EU should be more proactive in its Asia policies and strategies. This applies in particular to the political relationship.

With regard to the security dimension, the EU works on issues such as poverty and natural disasters that threaten security. One Commission official referred to a need to stabilize the region and the fact that the EU is attempting to become a security partner, as in Aceh. The EU is engaging in further cooperative work with Asian partners, both in their regions and in other neighbouring regions, such as Afghanistan. The development of the Common Foreign and Security Policy (CFSP) and the European Security and Defence Policy (ESDP), has presented the EU with the opportunity to explore what it can deliver. There is a perception that the EU could 'be used in a neutral fashion' on issues such as human rights and governance standards. One official also stated that he felt the EU possessed a sense of duty toward the region, particularly in terms of development assistance and crisis management.

The EU's Current Approaches: Combining Bilateral and Regional Arrangements

As discussed earlier, the EU pursues a variety of approaches to its engagement with Asia. Often it chooses to pursue new inter-regionalist dialogue

(NIRB). In other cases, it pursues a largely NRB approach with one country, as evidenced in its relations with China. The importance of China as the central focus of EU thinking is evident in the fact that in 2005 alone, some 370 trips were made by Commission officials to China, considerably more than to Japan or other regional powers. This shift in EU interest, from EU–ASEAN relations to China and Japan was raised by more than one EU official.

With regard to assessments of the state of EU–East Asia relations, some respondents commented on the need to distinguish between the EU and its member states, stating that, with regard to China, bilateral relations with major European countries are more important than EU-wide relations. Individual member states often pursue their own agendas with East Asia, in a type of traditional bilateralism. Bilateral links between some individual EU states and individual East Asian countries are influenced by a colonial legacy, such as the Netherlands's economic and political links in Indonesia or Britain's links with Malaysia, Singapore and Myanmar (Forster, 2000, pp. 790–1).

When asked 'Which (if any) EU member states do you think try to unilaterally build up bilateral relations that favour national rather than European interests?', survey responses were in agreement that the largest member states work the most on individual bilateral links. France, the UK, and Germany were named most often, while several respondents suggested this was a strategy employed by most member states and particularly those with a colonial link.

The EU and Asia both utilize traditional bilateral as well as interregional relations, as seen in chapter six of this volume. Gilson (2004, p. 188) regards ASEM as an interregional forum that has been use to enhance, rather than replace, bilateral linkages. Due to its format, it also provides a less controversial framework to deal with issues such as human rights and pollution as they relate to trade. Gilson has referred to what she calls 'minilateral encounters' that are held in advance of larger meetings, to reduce potential arguments, and this practice has been noted by interviewed Commission officials. In multilateral contexts, the EU Commission has suggested that ASEM partners should consult regularly before key international meetings (such as UN gatherings) and try to find common positions in international trade bodies such as the WTO (Gilson, 2004, p. 191). Further, the Commission is advancing the idea of 'issue-based leadership', whereby countries and groups of countries within the ASEM family declare their political commitment to a particular issue such as climate change, in order to raise the quality and dynamism of international dialogue.

While the EU has always sought to advance its agendas of globalization, its norms and values, the approaches it pursues are pragmatically shaped by the particular issue at hand. Where feasible, the EU has utilized NRB, in recognition of the considerable differences among Asian states and because, in certain cases, region-to-region approaches are not practicable. This may be because sectoral agreements are most appropriate or it may be because it is easier to deal with some countries, such as China, as a single state rather than through regional fora such as ASEAN Plus Three. Region-to-region agreements may also not be possible because the pace of regionalization in Asia has differed from that of the EU. For example, there is no comparable regional approach in sectors or in functional cooperation to those that may exist in the EU, as noted by one Commission official:

> Our Asia strategy has been a bit a [sic] function of the integration pace in Asia, which is quite slow and so once again that explains why we go for bilateral relations. We individualize the countries and we deal with them individually.

The EU seeks to complement its commitment to multilateral fora and inter-regionalism with bilateral agreements and summits with countries in Asia.[5] These complement recent initiatives such as TREATI, the Trans-Regional EU-ASEAN Trade Initiative and READI, the Regional EU-ASEAN Dialogue Instrument.[6] Trade Commissioner Peter Mandelson (2005) considers the key issues in relations with Asia to be the need for the EU to build a stronger, more dynamic relationship with Asian countries individually and as a region. He is aware that, on the European side, a partnership 'that moves beyond good will and warm words, will present a formidable political challenge to the EU member states', requiring the EU to be welcoming of economic change, innovative and open, and to adjust to changing world economic balances brought about by Asia's rise. Further, Europe and Asia need to work together to create new economic and trade opportunities within a rules-based economic system — through the WTO and bilateral and interregional trade agreements. This combination of traditional bilateralism and regional responses (NRB) would complement multilateralism.

An example of how the EU is developing its regional and bilateral agendas in tandem, in both economic and political domains, is seen in the comments that the Commission regards ASEM as the prime point of convergence between Europe and Asia at the multilateral level. It is attempting to develop thematically and politically consistent relations at the bilateral level, with regards especially to developments in the major players in the region, China, Japan and India. This combination of bilateral and regional approaches by the EU is regarded by an official as being mutually reinforcing and conveying a clear message to Asia that the EU is serious about engaging on topics of international importance, which featured on the agendas of the 2006 ASEM Summit and the EU's bilateral summits with India, Korea and China held the same week.[7] An official referred to the EU's attempts to demonstrate that ASEM is the prime point of EU–Asia convergence, signalling the need for 'thematic and political consistency between multilateral and bilateral relationships with the countries in the Asian region'.

Normative Elements in the EU's Strategy

Youngs (2004) has argued that 'analysis of EU external policies can benefit from a more precise exploration of how strategic calculation invests a broadly normative agenda with notable characteristics.' He suggests that we need to understand the ways in which security concerns and normative values inform each other.

Many of the Commission officials interviewed in Brussels saw a normative element in EU policies towards the region. For example:

> It [the EU] has a predilection for encouraging people doing similar things to what the EU has done, such as ASEAN.
>
> Normative power? Yes, to a certain extent, but we know our limits. We have no comprehensive security guarantees for any of these countries. Put the normative agenda out there and see how much is acceptable. We offer our own set of norms and see how much we can push.

This view was not shared by all interviewed Commission officials. One official emphatically stated that 'the EU is not a normative power, it does not want to impose rules' and has been in Asia primarily as an economic and political interlocutor. In contrast, survey respondents overwhelmingly agree that the EU is trying to export its norms, as seen in Figure 10.4.

The EU has expanded it role, reach and scope over a number of decades. It is now an influential international actor in a number of forums, ranging from the WTO to UN agencies, in political and economic domains. There is an interest in conflict transformation and assistance to conflict-torn areas of the world that previously did not feature prominently on the EU's radar screen. One Commission official suggested that the growth of European integration and the current level of the EU's involvement in

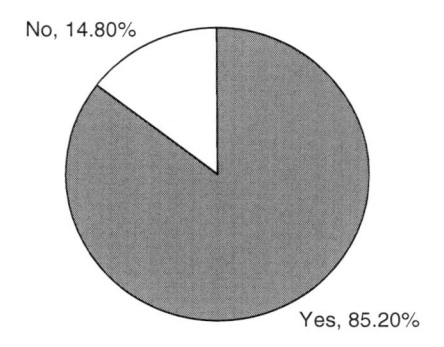

Figure 10.4 Is the EU promoting norms?

the international political sphere would have been 'inconceivable' some fifteen years earlier. Not only does he see the EU as much more aware and concerned about conflict situations around the world, such as East Timor, Sri Lanka, Afghanistan, Aceh and Nepal, but he sees the EU's recent engagement in Asia on security as completely new, particularly with regard to the operation in Aceh, where the EU played one of the leading roles.

EU–Asia relations, Multilateralism and Regional Integration

EU documents, speeches and interviews with Commission officials all indicate that the EU regards East Asia as sharing goals in the international area. Foremost among these is multilateralism. There is a strong belief that if East Asia and the EU can work together in fora such as UN and the WTO, then they are in a strong position to effectively shape global agendas. There are also other shared policy goals of the two regions such as trade liberalization, cultural diversity and sustainable development. According to one official, defending and promoting these objectives is 'central to [the EU's] philosophy of engaging the region, irrespective of the geographical contours, essentially the heartlands of Asia, East, Southeast, South.'

There is also a perception of a natural affinity:

> they are *demandeurs*, they come to us because they see us as the natural counterpart to them in the world, to a large extent because of our values, because of the commonalities that they see. We don't agree on everything... but to a degree it is quite impressive the extent to which Europe and Asia gel with each other and we need to probably,

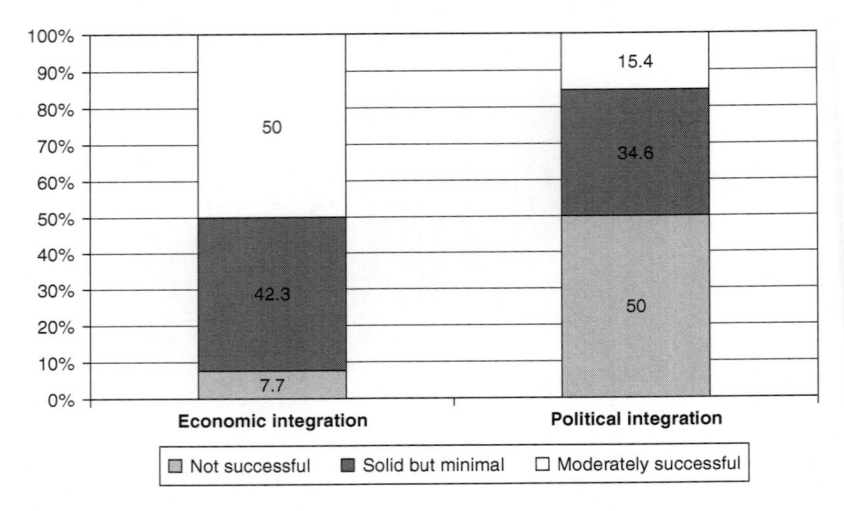

Figure 10.5 Assessment of East Asian economic and political integration.

Economic integration: Not successful 7.7, Solid but minimal 42.3, Moderately successful 50.
Political integration: Solid but minimal 15.4, Moderately successful 34.6, Not successful 50.

in the overall scheme of our relations, give even more importance to relations with Asia.

Many interviewees and survey respondents referred to the lack of advanced regional integration in Asia. The survey results, for example, illustrate that while there is some positive assessment of economic regional integration, there is more negative assessment of political integration, as seen in Figure 10.5.

Survey respondents referred to a number of factors that provide a context for their lukewarm assessment of regionalism in East Asia. They referred, on the political aspects, for example, to the lack of regional leader(s) with a mandate to generate sustainable regionalization and to the fact that the EU's 'top-down approach, political incentives, core countries' could not be replicated in Asia. There is an assessment that the nations of ASEAN recognize the need to integrate, but will proceed at their pace, and that for this reason, a common currency and other initiatives may well follow later, while 'cohesion' policies and a single market might come at an earlier stage.

Conclusions

This chapter has argued that EU policy towards East Asia has been essentially reactive. While in the early years, the EU's Asia Strategy was motivated by economic interests, its current engagement is characterized by a combination of bilateral and regional arrangements and, in particular, changing conceptions of what constitutes 'Asia' and 'East Asia'.

The EU is less reactive than in the past in response to the political, economic and other events taking place in Asia, but it still appears to be playing 'catch-up'. While there is some evidence that the EU is trying to encourage or even accelerate further changes, particularly in human rights dialogues, the results are patchy at best. In terms of the broader implications of these developments, there is a keen interest in engaging Asia in multilateral fora, and in confronting globalization with shared agendas across a range of policy approaches. It is not inconceivable that both sets of partners will work more closely together in international fora. Much depends on developments in China and India and the development of Japan–China–Korea relations.

EU engagement in Asia is increasingly multidimensional and pursued via a variety of approaches. While economic interests remain paramount, political and normative elements are also in evidence, although it is difficult to assess their impact. The EU is advancing normative values in Asia, but discreetly, and in a way that places them on the discussion table as a potential soft power. It is not clear at this stage if we are witnessing normative means by the EU to achieve economic ends in Asia.

Interregionalism will be a key characteristic of the relationship, and there is certainly a form of mutual attraction in the EU–ASEAN engagement. Economic and political considerations will continue to overlap and this enmeshing will become stronger over time. There will also be a meshing of the traditional bilateral relationships, particularly those pursued by the UK, France and Germany, with the EU approach to both bilateral relations and to interregionalism. The EU and its member states will continue to advance their interests in the region, based on considerations of economic power and of normative power. Both Asian and European regionalism will continue to be market-driven, but with differing leadership structures.

It is difficult to predict what the next major challenges for Europe and Asia will be, and there is always a risk that the EU will once again place Asia further down its own agenda. If the EU continues to invest resources in the relationship with East Asia, engagement will remain vibrant and more than reactive. Security concerns will possibly become prominent. One official suggested that Europe came late to Asia. Perhaps it will stay, and continue to advance its interests there.

Notes

1. Current figures illustrate that the EU still has a considerable trade deficit with Asia — 174.6 billion euro in 2005 (merchandise trade with ASEAN, China, Japan and S.Korea). Asia receives 21% of the EU's external exports and is its 3rd largest regional trading partner (after Europe outside the EU, 31% and NAFTA, 28%).
2. Some 80% of EU aid flow goes to the lowest-income countries in Asia. From 1998–2000, the EU provided an average of 77 million euro in humanitarian assistance to Asia, following natural or man-made disasters, see http://ec.europa.eu/comm/echo/index_en.htm, accessed 23 November 2006.
3. The question was: 'When you think of "Asia", what comes to mind? Please mark the three most relevant choices for you.'
4. 'In your opinion, have the EU's newly-designed strategies (such as those listed above) changed the way that the EU perceives or interacts with East Asia?' => 'If yes, in what way?'
5. These include, for example, cooperation agreement between the European Community and the Lao People's Democratic Republic; agreement between the EC and Vietnam on market access; cooperation agreement between the EU and Cambodia; agreement on trade and economic cooperation between China and the EEC and a communication on developing closer ties between the EU and Indonesia; Communication from the Commission EU–China: Closer Partners, Growing Responsibilities COM(2006) 631 final, Brussels, 24 October 2006, http://ec.europa.eu/comm/external_relations/china/docs/06-10-24_final_com.pdf, accessed 17 November 2006; Commission Working Document accompanying COM (2006) 631 final: Closer Partners, Growing Responsibilities. A policy paper on EU-China trade and Investment: Competition and Partnership COM(2006) 632 final Brussels, 24 October 2006, http://trade.ec.europa.eu/doclib/docs/2006/october/tradoc_130791.pdf accessed 17 November 2006; Commission Working Document Country Strategy Paper 2002–2006: China, http://ec.europa.eu/comm/external_relations/china/csp/index.htm accessed 17 November 2006; and 15th Japan-EU Summit Tokyo, 24 April 2006., Joint Press Statement, http://ec.europa.eu/comm/external_relations/japan/sum04_06/jps.pdf, accessed 17 November 2006. See also 7th EU-India Summit Helsinki, 13 October 2006, Joint Statement, http://ec.europa.eu/comm/external_relations/india/summit_10_06/eu_india_joint_statement.pdf accessed 17 November 2006.
6. TREATI is a framework for dialogue and regulatory cooperation developed to enhance EU trade relations with ASEAN. It is a key component of the Commission's Communication on 'A New Partnership with South East Asia' in July 2003. The priority areas for cooperation under TREATI are closely linked to ASEAN's own drive for economic integration and comprise sanitary and phytosanitary standards in agro-food and fisheries products, industrial product standards and technical barriers to trade, and forestry and wood-based products. Trade facilitation and co-operation on investment will be tackled as cross-cutting issues. The Commission regards work under TREATI as being based upon a gradual deepening of co-operation starting

with exchange of experience and moving on to develop more substantial regulatory commitments between the two regions over time.
7. The following summits took place in Helsinki: EU–Korea (9 September 2006); EU–China (9 September 2006); ASEM 6 (10–11 September 2006); EU–India (13 October 2006).

References

CEC (Commission of the European Community) (1994) *Towards a New Asia Strategy*, Communication of the Commission to the Council, Com (94) 314 final, Brussels, 13 July.

Dent, C. M. (2001) 'ASEM and the "Cinderella complex" of EU–East Asia economic relations', *Pacific Affairs*, 74. 1, Spring, pp. 25–52.

EC (European Commission) (2001) *Europe and Asia: A Strategic Framework for Enhanced Partnerships*, Communication from the Commission, Brussels, 4. September 2001, COM (2001) 469 Final, available at http://ec.europa.eu/comm/external_relations/asia/doc/com01_469_en.pdf, accessed 17 November 2006.

EIAS (European Institute for Asian Studies) (2005) *The EU's Strategic interests in East Asia, Volume I: Main report and synthesis*, 22 August, Consortium of European Institutes for Asian Studies and Nomisma.

Forster, A. (2000) 'Evaluating the EU–ASEM relationship: a negotiated order approach', *Journal of European Public Policy*, 7. 5, pp. 787–804.

Gilson, J. (2004) 'Trade relations between Europe and East Asia', *Asia Europe Journal*, 2. 2, July, pp. 185–200.

Gilson, J. (2005) 'New Interregionalism? The EU and East Asia', *Journal of European Integration*, 27. 3, September, pp. 307–26.

Lamy, P. (2003) 'Asia-Europe Relations: A Joint Partnership', *Asia Europe Journal*, 1. 1, pp. 3–8.

Mandelson, P. (2005) 'Tilting the Global Balance: Asia's New Trade Growth', Keynote Address, WEF Asia Forum, Singapore, 29 April.

Wiessala, G. (2002) *The European Union and Asian countries*, London / New York: Sheffield Academic Press.

Youngs, R. (2004) 'Normative Dynamics and Strategic Interests in the EU's External Identity', *Journal of Common Market Studies*, 42. 2, pp. 415–35.

Index

APEC (Asia-Pacific Economic Cooperation) 3, 9, 15, 16–17, 23–4, 28–30, 32–7, 42, 44, 49, 50–3, 57, 62–4, 102, 106, 107, 108, 152, 170–1, 181, 182, 183
ASEAN (Association of Southeast Asian Nations) 1, 2, 3, 4, 6, 7, 8, 9–10, 12, 13, 16, 17, 18, 19, 20, 23, 24, 27, 28, 29, 30, 32, 33, 34, 35, 36, 37, 38, 42–9, 52, 54, 55–8, 61, 62–7, 70, 72, 73, 80, 84, 87, 90–101, 102, 104, 105, 106, 107–9, 111, 114, 115, 116, 117, 118, 122, 136, 149, 151–5, 159, 161–7, 170, 171, 172, 176, 180, 181, 183, 189, 193–4, 200, 202, 203, 204, 206, 207
ASEAN Charter 3, 4, 63, 97, 98, 99, 100
ASEAN Plus Three (APT) 3, 6, 9, 10, 17, 18, 19, 20, 29, 32, 42, 54, 61, 62, 63, 67, 87, 151, 152, 162, 163, 165, 166, 170, 171–3, 178, 180, 181, 183, 200, 203
ASEAN Regional Forum (ARF) 9, 17, 29, 32, 36, 42, 44, 49, 50, 52, 57, 108, 152, 162, 163, 164, 165, 171
ASEM Asia-Europe Meeting 1, 10, 16, 18, 63, 102–20, 163, 164, 165, 166, 170, 172, 181, 182, 183, 198, 199, 200, 202, 203, 204
Asia Pacific 2, 3, 9, 10, 17, 23, 35, 42, 44, 46, 49–3, 56–7, 61–80, 106–8, 161, 167, 170, 175, 176, 181, 182, 190
Asia-Pacific regionalism 44, 49, 52, 57
Asia Strategy 20, 104, 105, 106, 116, 188, 190, 191, 197, 203, 206
Asian Currency Unit (ACU) 178–9
Asian Development Bank (ADB) 9, 136, 174

Asian economic crisis/Asian financial crisis 10, 12, 13, 17, 32–5, 37, 42, 53, 54, 57, 63, 65, 111, 114, 154, 156, 162, 178, 179, 181, 182, 191, 197
Asian identity 3, 35, 42, 191
Asian values 3, 35, 93
Asia-Pacific Economic Cooperation (APEC) 3, 9, 15, 16, 17, 23–5, 28–3, 35–7, 42, 44, 49, 50–3, 57, 62, 63, 64, 102, 106, 107, 108, 151, 152, 170, 171, 181–3
Association of Southeast Asian Nations (ASEAN) *see* ASEAN

bilateralism 4, 55, 57, 107, 118, 158, 202, 203
Bridges, Brian 8, 9
Burma (Myanmar) 2, 25, 47, 48, 74, 79, 93, 96, 97, 98, 105, 111, 116, 163
business networks 134, 142

Cambodia 2, 32, 35, 45, 47, 68, 69, 75, 77, 79, 93, 96, 97, 98, 105, 107, 111, 129, 136, 142, 161
Central and Eastern Europe 29, 34, 111, 129, 130, 131, 140
China 2, 11, 12, 13–14, 15, 17, 18, 20, 29, 30, 35, 36, 37, 42, 45, 47, 50, 52, 54, 55, 56, 57, 58, 61, 63, 65, 67, 68, 70, 71, 72, 73, 86, 94, 102, 103–6, 108, 109, 114, 116, 118, 125, 133, 136, 137, 140, 142, 143, 151, 152, 162, 164, 166, 167, 170, 171, 172, 176, 177, 189, 191, 193, 194, 195, 197, 198, 200, 201, 202, 203, 204, 207
climate change 200, 202
comparative regionalization 24, 26, 27
conceptual framework 17, 23, 24, 26, 37

Index 211

conditionality 12, 34, 35, 38, 98, 197
cross-border regions 135, 138–41, 144
currency 24, 54, 100, 123, 128, 130, 145, 178, 179, 180, 185, 206

development 2, 5, 9, 16, 18, 30, 32, 33, 35, 37, 47, 50, 63, 91, 93, 94, 98, 103, 117, 122–3, 124, 129, 130, 132, 136, 142, 151, 152, 173, 174, 177, 179, 180, 189, 191, 192, 194, 195, 200
development corridors 122, 134, 141–145
dialogue and cooperation 105, 113, 191, 192

East Asia Summit (EAS) 17, 171, 181
East Asian regionalism 1, 2, 14, 16, 19, 20, 43, 44, 53–7, 174, 175
economic integration 9, 17, 18, 36, 61–80, 84, 85, 86, 89, 91, 99, 100, 117, 134, 170, 171, 173, 174, 177, 183, 206
enlargement 2, 29, 31, 32, 33, 34, 35, 64, 71, 88, 111, 118, 119, 129, 130, 145, 150, 177, 189, 191, 201
EU (European Union) 1, 4, 18, 23, 43, 61, 64, 74, 84, 88, 102, 104, 105, 111, 122, 149, 150, 152, 155, 156, 166, 171, 172, 173, 174, 176, 180, 181, 183, 184, 185, 188
EU governance 25
European Commission 2, 4, 14, 16, 102, 103, 105, 113, 116, 138, 141, 163, 172, 188, 189, 190, 192, 195
European Community 12, 66, 89, 103, 104, 105, 129, 176, 189, 191
European integration 7, 16, 18, 19, 86, 87, 89, 171, 176, 177, 180, 181, 184, 185, 204
European Union *see* EU
Europeanization 32, 36

France 14, 31, 45, 105, 108, 124, 129, 140, 141, 156, 157, 202, 207
free trade area 19, 32, 49, 61, 64, 66, 70, 108, 122, 170, 182, 184

free trade agreements (FTAs) 12, 51, 55, 56, 61, 65, 66, 67, 118, 174, 176, 183, 190, 196

Germany 14, 31, 74, 92, 123, 124, 131, 133, 134, 138, 140, 141, 142, 156, 157, 173, 202, 207
globalization 7, 9, 11, 12, 23, 27, 30, 38, 44, 48, 57, 64, 107, 124, 128, 145, 154, 173, 191, 193, 198, 201, 203, 207
Gilson, Julie 11, 12, 13, 163, 189, 198, 202
growth polygons 122, 135–41, 144

Haas, E. B. 24, 85, 85, 89, 99
hard power 14, 15, 182
heterogeneity 3, 5, 90, 129, 197
homogeneity 5, 6, 18, 90

identity 3, 4, 14, 15, 19, 23, 27, 28, 29, 30, 34, 35, 36, 38, 85, 88, 107, 119, 121, 165, 191
Indonesia 2, 29, 30, 35, 46, 47, 48, 52, 52, 66, 70, 90, 92, 95, 98, 99, 109, 125, 136, 143, 151, 154, 159, 160, 161, 162, 164, 172, 174, 182, 184
industrial districts 122, 124, 126, 132–5, 141, 144
Institutionalization 63, 75, 89
institutions 1, 5, 6, 7, 8, 18, 25, 30, 31, 34, 44, 52, 62, 84–6, 91, 100, 107, 119, 134, 145, 165, 166, 174, 176, 181, 188
integration *see* European integration, Asia-Pacific regionalism, economic integration, East Asian regionalism, political integration
international production networks 19, 122, 124, 125, 128, 137, 144
intra-industry trade 62, 74, 76, 77, 80
investment 7, 9, 10, 12, 14, 16, 18, 62, 63, 65, 66–73, 100, 101, 107m, 108, 109, 112, 114, 117, 122, 123, 125, 128, 130, 133, 136, 173, 175, 177, 180, 182, 189, 190, 192, 201

Index

Japan 3, 13, 14, 15, 17, 18, 30, 32, 33, 35, 36, 37, 42, 47, 50–8, 61, 63, 65, 66, 67, 70–4, 80, 102, 103, 104, 105, 106, 107, 109, 112, 118, 123, 125, 128, 129, 130, 131, 133, 134, 136, 142, 143, 151, 152, 164, 166, 167, 170, 171, 173, 174, 176, 177, 180, 181, 182, 183, 193, 195, 196, 200, 201, 202, 204, 207

Katzenstein, Peter 3, 9, 10, 43, 50, 151, 152
kûdôka 63
Korea (Republic of/South) 3, 14, 16, 17, 18, 35, 42, 50, 53, 54, 55, 56, 58, 61, 65, 66, 67, 72, 100, 102, 104, 105, 109, 113, 114, 115, 118, 125, 128, 129, 131, 133, 134, 136, 142, 143, 152, 170, 171, 172, 183, 193, 195, 196, 200, 201, 204, 207
Korea (North) 20, 42, 52, 58, 157

Lamy, Pascal 7, 192, 193

Malaysia 2, 45, 46, 47, 48, 53, 56, 65, 66, 70, 71, 72, 98, 105, 109, 136, 143, 154, 159, 161, 162, 181, 202
Mandelson, Peter 203
Manners, Ian 15
market access 104, 109, 192
model 2, 6, 8, 14, 19, 20, 24, 33, 64, 84, 86, 89–100, 107, 171, 173, 174, 175, 176, 177, 180, 184, 194
multilateralism 11, 12, 13, 14, 32, 57, 107, 112, 114, 115, 119, 165, 175, 194, 203, 205

New Asia Strategy (1994) *see* Asia Strategy
New Inter-Regional Bilateralism 200
New Regional Bilateralism 200
new regionalism 2, 9, 10, 17, 23, 24–7
norms 4, 11, 15, 23, 25, 31, 32, 34–8, 46, 52, 56, 57, 94, 108, 203, 204–5

old regionalism 9

peace 29, 45, 46, 48, 54, 85, 108, 109, 150, 152, 153, 164, 174, 175, 183, 192
political integration 2, 4, 18, 19, 84–101

READI 117, 153, 203
regionalism *see* East Asian regionalism, new regionalism, old regionalism,
regionalization 8–9, 12, 17, 18, 20, 23, 24, 26, 27, 28, 30, 37, 38, 43, 122–8, 134, 135, 127, 138, 140, 141, 142–5, 191, 203, 206
regional trade agreements 63, 170, 176, 203

security 1, 2, 14, 15, 16, 19, 27, 29, 30, 31, 32, 34, 36, 38, 46, 48, 50, 56, 57, 84, 85, 86, 87, 88, 106, 108, 149–67, 177, 180, 182, 183, 184, 190, 191, 192, 193, 201, 204, 205, 207
Singapore 2, 45, 47, 48, 55, 56, 65, 66, 67, 70, 71, 72, 73, 93, 94, 97, 98, 100, 105, 106, 108, 128, 129, 133, 134, 136, 137, 142, 143, 159, 161, 162, 178, 183, 202
Sri Lanka 205
soft power 11, 13, 14, 15, 30, 182, 192, 194, 207
South Korea *see* Korea
Southeast Asian regionalism *see* also ASEAN 44–9, 176
sovereignty 5, 6, 8, 31, 36, 43, 48, 62, 64, 91, 92, 100, 151, 152, 165, 175, 176, 184
structural similarity 18, 62, 74–6

Thailand 2, 35, 45, 46, 47, 48, 50, 53, 56, 66, 70, 93, 97, 98, 105, 136, 143, 154, 159, 160, 161, 162
trade 7, 8, 9, 10, 11, 12, 13, 16, 18, 19, 20, 30, 32, 33, 36, 49, 51, 55, 61–80, 94, 97, 98, 103, 107, 108, 109, 112, 114, 117, 118, 122–5, 130–6, 163, 165, 170, 172, 174, 175, 176, 177, 178, 180–4, 189, 190, 192, 193, 194, 196, 197, 198, 199, 200, 201, 202–3, 205

trade complementarity 62, 71, 78–80
traditional bilateralism 4, 107, 202, 203
TREATI 117, 203

United Kingdom 14, 31, 45, 103, 156, 157, 202, 207
United Nations 47, 96, 155, 192
United States 2, 10, 14, 15, 29, 42, 66, 88, 103, 150, 155, 170, 181–3, 189

Vietnam 2, 32, 45, 46, 47, 66, 96, 97, 98, 104, 105, 128, 129, 136, 143, 159, 172

World Trade Organisation (WTO) 11, 20, 30, 33, 37, 63, 66, 109, 114, 165, 192, 193, 194, 197, 200, 202, 203, 204, 205